FIVE YEARS, ELEVEN MONTHS
*and a lifetime
of unexpected love*

Also by Visakha:

*Harmony and the Bhagavad-gita:
Lessons from a Life-Changing Move to the Wilderness*

Bhagavad-gita: A Photographic Essay
(2011 Independent Publisher Book Award winner)

Our Most Dear Friend, Bhagavad-gita for Children

Photomacrography, Art and Techniques (as Jean Papert)

FIVE YEARS, ELEVEN MONTHS
*and a lifetime
of unexpected love*

a memoir
VISAKHA DASI

Our Spiritual Journey Press
our-spiritual-journey.com

© 2017 Jean Griesser (Visakha Dasi)
Photographs © 1965–1985 Jean and John Griesser
(Visakha Dasi and Yadubara Das)
The photographs on pages 194, 198, and 254
are by unknown photographers.

ISBN-13: 978-1522838449
ISBN-10: 1522838449

Cover design: Raghu Consbruck and Govinda Cordua
Cover photos: Vrindavan, India 1972

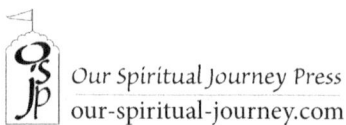

Our Spiritual Journey Press
our-spiritual-journey.com

To Srila Prabhupada

Contents

Prologue: April 1971   i
ONE   Boots and a Kodak Brownie   1
TWO   The Pinkie   13
THREE   Earthquake   27
FOUR   Meditations   41
FIVE   Immersion   49
SIX   Atlas's Burden   59
SEVEN   An Aristocratic Lady   85
EIGHT   Honeymoon   95
NINE   Under a Bombay Mosquito Net   119
TEN   Relativity On Pause   131
ELEVEN   On Tour with Dichotomy   149
TWELVE   Homecoming Heretic   173
THIRTEEN   A Brown Bottle   195
FOURTEEN   Hobbled Holy Times   197
FIFTEEN   Platonic Love and (In)Equality   209
SIXTEEN   Bedrock and Evil   227
SEVENTEEN   Krishna's Cuisine and a Calamitous Cloud   249
EIGHTEEN   Five Years, Eleven Months, Sixteen Days   261
Epilogue   271

The Photographs   273
Glossary   274
Acknowledgments   278
About the Author   279

Prologue: April 1971

The elderly Indian guru considered our question with what seemed to be equal parts gravity and amusement. "You do not speak the language," he said. "Wherever you go, they will simply cheat you and steal your cameras." His unique candor, far from what I'd expected or wanted, set the stage for a skeptical heart to stumble upon unexpected love.

My friend John and I were standing in the spotless master bedroom of an apartment on the seventh floor of the Akash Ganga Building, one of Bombay's many high-rises. Outside, the sun blazed on morning traffic plying and honking along city thoroughfares while seagulls cruised overhead, calling. Inside, the walls, ceiling, and curtains were a creamy white; white sheets covered wall-to-wall cotton floor mats. The room's two large windows, one overlooking the Arabian Sea to the west, the other facing a long stretch of beachfront high-rises to the south, were open, and a sea breeze billowed their gossamer curtains. The room's quiet ambience, infused with the airy freshness and exaltation of the ocean, was full of expectancy and possibilities.

The only furniture was a rectangular coffee table. The guru, Bhaktivedanta Swami Prabhupada, sat behind it, cross-legged, on a mattress covered with a white cotton sheet. He relaxed against two large white bolsters stacked on top of each other next to the wall. On either side of him were similar bolsters, together making a u-shaped seat. Due to the heat, besides his wraparound dhoti, Prabhupada wore only a saffron cloth knotted over his right shoulder and falling under his left arm, leaving his left shoulder and part of his chest bare—a traditional style for a renunciant. I was wearing my customary thin blouse and slacks.

John and I were photography students at Rochester Institute of Technology in Rochester, New York—he a graduate, I an undergraduate. We'd set our hearts on creating a *National Geographic*-style photographic essay of a quaint Indian village, showing how villagers live without the complexity and stress typical of Western life. We envisioned lithe and healthy farmers guiding oxen that strained to pull crude wooden plows through fertile fields, lovely women weaving colorful cotton cloth on looms, organic stone-ground flour, pure well water, live dramatic performances under starlit skies and in general, an aesthetic, happy, technology-free life.

The difficulty was that we were new to India—John had been here five months and I five weeks—and we didn't know which of the thousands of Indian villages would be most suited for our purpose. So we'd come to ask someone who'd lived and traveled extensively in India, the resident of this master bedroom, Prabhupada.

As we placed our query before him, Prabhupada (pronounced Prabhoo'-paad) looked at us squarely and listened attentively. The time, the place, the circumstances under which the three of us were face to face in that room's buoyant light—the immediate prosperous career prospects that hung suspended on the words that would pass from him to us—the sense that our immediate and long-term future could be determined by the knowledgeable, cheerful gentleman who sat comfortably before us—whirled my thoughts.

For some moments Prabhupada considered our question—Which is India's most photogenic village?—and then replied with such a pin of realism that it instantly popped my bubble of idealism. Only a couple of weeks before on one of the jammed Indian third-class trains, John had been pickpocketed. What was I doing in this overpopulated, overheated, desperately poor, mismanaged, theft-riddled, very foreign country, anyway? Angst churned in me as Prabhupada continued.

"Best that you go to Vrindavan and do your story there."

Vrindavan—an unusual sounding name I'd never heard before. Little did I envision this modest, historic town as a Waterloo for all my youthful schemes, a town that would change my life—create its whole purpose afresh, its hopes and fears, its struggles, its interests, and its sacrifices all turned forever to a new direction—this unseen possibility would later become as clear as the dazzling sun beyond those large windows.

CHAPTER ONE

Boots and a Kodak Brownie

Great Neck—A two-mile-wide, four-mile-long peninsula that juts north into the placid Long Island Sound, a backdrop for F. Scott Fitzgerald's famed The Great Gatsby, the residence of magnate giants like Walter P. Chrysler, renowned entertainers like the Marx Brothers, and well-to-do Jewish families escaping New York City congestion—was home for my parents, brother and me.

We lived in 'The Windsor,' an expansive, tall, drab, rent-controlled brick apartment building that had the architectural flair of a cement block. When I was small, my Dad's fur business was flourishing: our Pontiac was new, Mom had new mink and sable coats and valuable jewelry, and Beatrice was our full-time nanny. I used to watch as Mom prepared for the posh shows and dinners she and Dad went to. She'd sit before her three-sided mirror and apply a little makeup, especially her fire-engine red lipstick, with a cultured woman's innate sense of how to make men's eyes turn in respect rather than covetousness. Dad was proud of her.

My parents could have bought an upscale Great Neck house with its own yard and a German shepherd, but Mom (sensing coming troubles?) wanted us to stay put. Our apartment, she said, was centrally located, easy to heat and clean, saved money and, best of all for me, was directly across the street from Grace Avenue Park.

To a passerby, Grace Avenue Park was hardly noteworthy. A fenced-in, open, grassy square taking up half a suburban block, it boasted a slight hill leading up to its east fence, two separate playgrounds—on the north side for toddlers and the west side for youth—some wood-planked park benches scattered here and there, a paved walkway running through it diagonally, and toward its center, a shallow cement kiddie pool small enough to be confused for an oversized birdbath.

But *my* beloved Grace Avenue Park—the most unutterably fine and enchantingly graced place the world had ever known—boasted acres of open meadows, vales and hills for romping; magnificent sand, slides, swings, and seesaws to share and fight over with friends; colossal trees to climb; bugs, birds, and bushes to investigate; ever so many adults to wonder at; and a stern park custodian to tease. This glorious park encompassed my delightfully complete universe.

The park pool was my swamp and I was its alligator, quickly dashing at and encircling unsuspecting victims, stopping at nothing and for no one until a piercing whistle obliged all waders and an alligator to stand aside for five horribly long, dripping, goose-bumpy minutes while an attendant added chlorine to the water. Then we dashed in again, but now I was a deep sea explorer with full scuba regalia, searching for treasures at unfathomable depths.

In the fall, the fat-limbed oaks that arched over the playground were drenched in crimson-gold leaves that gusts sent spinning to the ground, falling in free-flowing flocks like exhausted ballerinas. The air had a tang; the cold of the stainless steel slide (fourteen steps up—it was like mountain climbing!) pierced my pants, and the coolness of the sand under the swings pressed through my sneakers. As I pumped the swing upward, my eyes smarting from bracing gusts, a crimson canopy danced around me.

At the end of one typically long park-filled day, Mom kissed me goodnight and was about to leave my room, when I asked, "What will happen to me after I die?" I'd never asked such a question before, but after seeing a stirring, black-and-white photograph of an immense, rolling graveyard vanishing into the somber Manhattan skyline, it popped out.

Mom was surprised. Then a look that said, "Why don't you ask me the color of vanilla ice cream?" swept her angular face.

"Nothing happens. You're buried or cremated. That's it," she said.

That was not an adequate answer.

"There has to be more to it than that," I said, upset with Mom for being un-understandable, and from under the covers kicked a box of tissues that was at the foot of the bed, sending it sailing to Mom's feet. Mom glanced at the box, gave her insolent ten-year-old a "What's your problem?" look, turned out the light and left the room, closing the door behind her and leaving her daughter securely tucked into wrinkle-free, floral-patterned polyester sheets along with her unanswered, pivotal question. At that moment life seemed flimsy and imperiled by emptiness. But by morning my question no longer seemed relevant, and over the ensuing years, death's aftermath seemed more and more ungraspable, like the vanishing point of railway tracks.

As I was growing up, each year before the first day of school Mom and I would drive to personable, inviting downtown Great Neck. She'd park our olive green Pontiac in front of Abe's Bakery; I'd get out and inhale the luscious smells of freshly baked bread as Mom came around from the driver's side and joined me, enclosing my hand firmly yet kindly in hers. We'd cross the two-lane Middleneck Road, squeeze between parked cars on the opposite side, walk past the pungent smells of Homer's Deli, past fashionable Betsy's Boutique, popular Liz's Hair Salon, dependable Irving's Hardware and on to Brown's Shoes. Shelves of children's and youths' footwear lined glass display windows at the store entrance. Inside, Stuart Brown, an affable man with anxious eyes, greeted us by name. It always seemed he'd been waiting for us. Mr. Brown knew our footwear preferences—practical, comfortable, hardy, earth-colored. His white shirt gleamed under the lights, and in moments he'd measured my small feet—length and width—pressing them firmly against his specialized foot-measuring device and remarking on their growth. Mr. Brown would disappear into the back and then emerge with an assortment of boxes of shoes for me to try. Opening a likely box, he'd remove the new shoe from its tissue wrapping and in one smooth motion whip out a shiny steel shoehorn from his back pocket, place it in the heel of the shoe and ease my foot effortlessly into it, casually returning the shoehorn to his back pocket as, with his other hand, he assuredly squeezed the sides of the shoe, checking its width against my foot, and then pressing the tip to see where my toes came. Once the second shoe was on, I'd caper around his small store feeling special, unable to take my eyes off those spanking, ever-so-fine shoes. Their feel, their look, their sheer smell of newness made me euphoric. My mother, hardly speaking, would watch this procedure closely. When she was satisfied with the choice, she'd pay, exchange pleasantries with Mr. Brown, and we were on the street again, my year-old, outgrown battered shoes in a bag swinging from my wrist, destined for the Thrift Store where Mom volunteered every Thursday, the profits going to the local hospital. Mom strode along, head held high, not looking down at me but exchanging courtesies with acquaintances as we went. If she stopped to chat, I could wait patiently, gazing with contented joy at my new acquisitions, basking in their secure embrace, in the palpable satisfaction of having them, in being sheltered by my mother's care. I was ready to play hopscotch on the clouds.

Before my first day of high school, Mom and I went to Brown's Shoe Store as usual, where I got ankle-high, soft leather hiking boots with rounded toes, sturdy soles, thick stitching, and wide brown laces. Rugged and practical, they were meant for tramping out miles, for romping and roving, for protecting and supporting young, adventurous feet.

In school, under long fluorescent tubes in the morose, tunnel-like hallways lined with gray metal lockers that were always being banged shut or open, I noticed other girls wearing fairylike summer flip-flops with dainty golden straps and thin soles. Some had flimsy ballerina-type silver booties, stylish smoky wisps that hardly existed. The girls' condemnation of me started with my clumsy boots and went up—my frowzy clothes, my plain hair, my lack of makeup, my expressions, my interests. Clearly, I wasn't one of them. Swift scornful glances at me were promptly followed by superior young heads with Marilyn Monroe hairdos brusquely tossing away as if to say no one should see such a dreadful sight. I was in a blizzard of contempt, outclassed and outcast.

From day one I stopped liking my new shoes. I began scrutinizing my clothes and pondering their unsuitableness. Within a short time I'd realized that—shoes, clothes, and hair aside—the very words I spoke weren't right (how was it that everyone but me said smart things?). A dark cloud of poisonous gas gathered over my high school epoch. On the family front, Dad's business was starting to founder. To help pay the bills Mom stopped volunteering at the Thrift Store and became a secretary in a dental office. My brother Tony, independent and rebellious, would get into arguments with Dad about his late nights out with his friends, sometimes resulting in Dad chasing him around the dining room table, Tony laughing.

If, from who I am now, I could have spoken to myself—a floundering and scorned girl—I'd have said, "You're miserable now, but don't worry."

Brewing with a struggling need to protect myself, in school I adopted a stoic shell as thick and impervious as I could fake it. Bearing my classmates semi-secret snide remarks, sometimes said just loud enough to hurt, with a stony silence, I became passive, letting the situation determine events by adapting and subordinating myself to others and saying what I thought they wanted to hear—most often lies that corroded my self-respect. The situation was sometimes unbearable but I knew it couldn't be changed. Any program of self-betterment was doomed—I was not about to become stylish and socially adept. Was it worth trying if I wouldn't succeed? And when I tried and failed, then what would become of whatever remnants remained of my self-esteem?

Unforgiving doors of conformity had slammed shut; the drawbridge was up. I was a banished, lone figure beyond the moat, looking up at impervious stone walls that blocked the sky, listening as gleeful party sounds drifted out. Later, I understood the social struggle that dominated my classmates' lives. A preoccupation with being accepted caused a meanness that flowed not only to me but between them as well. They'd abandon friendships unhelpful to their social progress, fawn before those higher in the scale, and have secret motives in almost every action. Competitiveness, selfishness, and class-consciousness made them as sad and confused as I was.

Fortunately, bitterness and resentment weren't part of my family heritage. My proper British mother harbored occasional disdain for the uncultured ways of Americans, and my work-forever-but-try-to-be-cheerful father was disappointed in his business; but neither was rancorous.

I accustomed myself to sitting in the back of the classroom and observing. The school building had only recently been carved out of acres of forest, and through large classroom windows I'd often see, beneath immense drifting clouds, a lone rabbit munching the short grass on the slope leading from the forest edge to the building. The rabbit was speckled brown, with a white belly and pricked ears and long, black, twitching whiskers. "This building has displaced you and me both," I thought. "You're vulnerable to predators, me to being left out." Yet the rabbit had advantages over me: it had ready-made and unconditionally acceptable footwear and clothes, and surely, whatever sounds it made were all right with its fellows. Surely it didn't live with endlessly critical peers.

As the rabbit could retreat to a tangle of wild forest, so I also needed a sanctuary. Gradually, one emerged: photography. Aunt Ethel had given me a Kodak Brownie box camera when I was seven, and I began using it regularly. I became an avid recorder of tree roots, ducks, soccer games, buildings, boats, bicycle riders, my parents, the Great Neck population—developing and printing photographs in my bedroom-cum-darkroom. My fingers stank of photographic chemicals.

The saga of the following year was interrupted by John F. Kennedy's assassination. A dumbfounded thirteen year-old, I sat on my parent's bed staring at our black-and-white television: Lyndon Johnson sworn in as president; the accused, Lee Harvey Oswald, shot dead as I watched—so beyond belief it was surreal; slender Jacqueline in her black dress, her black veil hardly hiding her face, puffy with shock and grief; the solemn, leaden

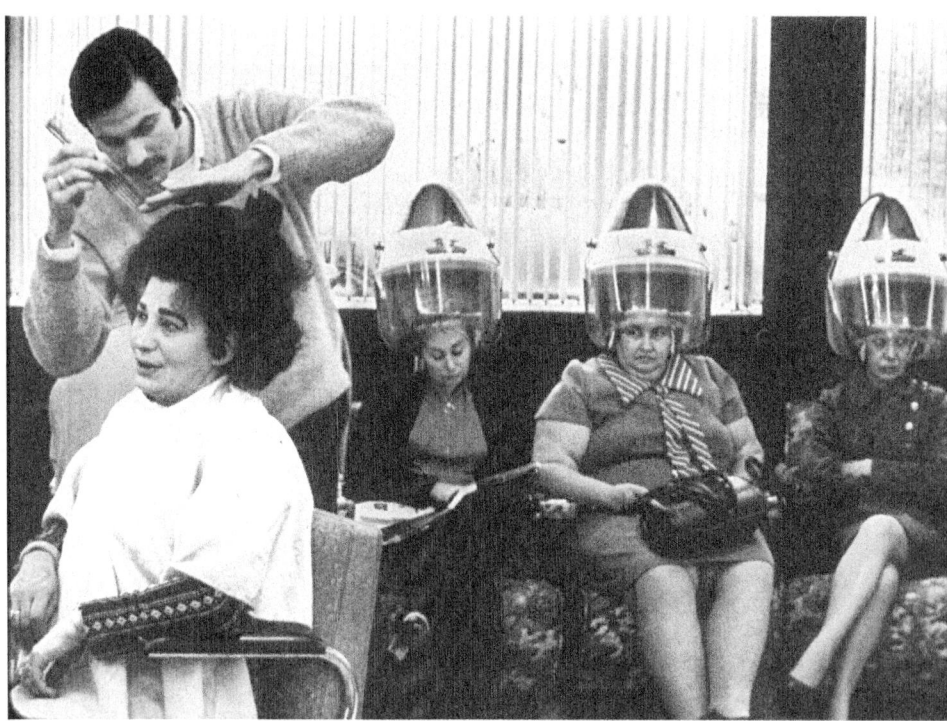

procession through Washington, D.C., with Charles de Gaulle towering over the ninety other world leaders who accompanied the flag-draped coffin. America was traumatized. And so was I.

I was picketing for equal rights (*"We shall overcome someday …"*) and protesting the Vietnam War (*"Give peace a chance …"*). Our family dinners were quiet now; the talker, Tony, had gone to Princeton. Even our Christmas get-togethers had a pall over them: Uncle Steven had divorced Aunt Ruth. Half the family had sided with her, the other half with him, and both sides stopped speaking to each other.

The future seemed horribly bleak. And dangerous.

In later years I'd sometimes skip a day of school to catch the Long Island Railroad's 7:27 with Dad. I'd be the youngest person on the packed train, surrounded by shoulder-to-shoulder suited businesspeople, their heads swaying with the train's motion, absorbed in their precisely folded newspapers, hardly looking up during the twenty-four-minute ride past suburbs and dusty trees.

What did these people live for, I wondered. Around Great Neck on the weekends, I'd see them watching televised football, mowing their lawns, sipping drinks under their awnings, walking their poodles, driving with their families. They were coping and doing the needful, lost in a rational world. Did they ever consider shutting off the demands of normalcy to access their incomprehensible, momentous aliveness? What captured their hearts and made them insanely happy to exist? Would a deadening abyss of comfort and security also engulf me? Somehow, the cultural values and norms I'd grown up immersed in were not serving me well.

Before 8 o'clock, after much thumping and rocking and clacking, Dad and I, along with thousands of other passengers, would be streaming out of Manhattan's Penn Station like sawdust spewing from a spinning blade. In a gray stone building three blocks away, Dad unlocked his tired two-room office—Papert & Co. Soon, Sandra, Dad's indispensable secretary, would sit at her desk in the large outer room; a little later, Murray and Sydney, Dad's two problematic salesmen, would be at desks near hers. Dad's private adjoining office overlooked grimy 32nd Street. I'd sit and wait with the worn tedium those rooms seemed built of, until gigantic Willoughby's camera store, half a block away, opened. Then I'd shop for a new camera or camera accessories with my saved-up babysitting money.

In tenth grade, the first year of senior high, Lucy Rodriguez joined our class. Newly moved from Bogotá, Lucy spoke only broken English. She was tiny—her head two inches below my chin—with straight auburn hair that fell below her waist, steady hazel eyes, an aquiline nose, and a buck-tooth smile. Lucy and I were both outcasts, and we became inseparable. Together we bought a small, inexpensive, Styrofoam sailboat for long excursions in the Long Island Sound. Lucy had never met an atheist before, and as we skimmed over the rippling water, I explained what Lucretius had said centuries before:

Had God designed the world, it would not be
A World so frail and faulty as we see

"The black people in America are fervently religious, yet they've been suffering slavery, brutality and discrimination for hundreds of years—and they're still suffering! Besides that, Catholics themselves—Bible followers—can be evil. Just look at the suffering the Crusades and Inquisition caused."

"The Biblical stories are not facts," I told her. "God is a myth. Otherwise, why doesn't he answer your prayers?" Lucy's mother was suffering chronic leg pain, and Lucy sought relief through prayer.

"Do you think God doesn't care or he's impotent? No, it's not that. It's that he's imaginary. Everything there is, everything we see and experience is due to natural forces." Although my thoughts were neither well informed nor systematic, they gave Lucy pause.

With my long-in-coming bosom friend Lucy I was not alone in the world but could share my most secret delights. There was nothing to be overcome; we joined like pieces of a puzzle. She was such a joy that I wanted her for myself. When she befriended Ziona, my neighbor in the Windsor apartment building, I was overcome with envy. Although Ziona and I spent time together in school and at home when her mother wasn't around, now I stopped speaking to her, thinking Lucy would do the same. Naturally, Ziona was hurt, and kind-hearted Lucy spent more time than ever with her. I was too proud to apologize and explain myself. What wanton wicked tyranny made me shun Ziona, a person I liked? Why was I giving Ziona the same pain of exclusion that had devastated me? I was no better than my snotty torturers. I'd betrayed myself. For the first time in my life I felt the full force of regret, and sent a private wail of shame and guilt to the sky: "My god, how could I?"

Two months before I graduated, Martin Luther King, Jr. was assassinated. The month I graduated, Robert Kennedy was assassinated. The image of him lying on his back, neck tense, head raised, arms stretched above his head, fists clenched, remained chiseled in my mind.

My existence in a placid, well-placed suburb was punctuated by the staccato of upheaval and pain—my own mortified feelings, life's hollowness, looming sudden death. Every one of us, it seemed, was constantly undercut by our physicality and life's fickleness. We were all subject to an unpredictable jumble of circumstance, choice and fate.

Not knowing what else to do, in September I was off to college.

I'd decided to major in photography. The greats in that field—Ansel Adams, Margaret Bourke-White, Alfred Stieglitz—had vision and values that inspired me. I'd applied to the photojournalism department at Rochester Institute of Technology in Rochester—the home of Kodak—and was admitted with a generous scholarship.

Mom and Dad drove me to the campus in upstate New York. When the three of us walked into my dorm room, I noticed both my roommates—tender and talented Tina Spruce and quick-witted Stacy Bryant—had ankle-high, soft leather hiking boots with rounded toes, sturdy soles, thick stitching and wide brown laces. Incredible. After six years of sneers due, at least in part, to that same footwear, I thought, "I can be myself here."

Beaming, I hugged my parents goodbye and said, "Don't worry about me. I'll be fine."

But I wasn't. Within a week I was crying at my desk over monstrous technical tomes on filters, focal length and light waves, refraction and diffusion, apertures, shutter speeds, and chemicals' sensitivity to light. I'd sit before onerous charts and diagrams while mentally reviewing the steps that had brought me to this place. Where had I gone wrong? At what point should I have made a different decision? Each time I plodded through the various choices I'd made over the past months and years, I wound up in that room in front of those books. I was meant to be doing just what I was doing. I loved photography, and this was the place to learn it. I'd sigh deeply and go on studying.

In a mandatory writing course I had a chance to vent:

> To endure the gross, inflexible monotony of high school life, most students enter and maintain a state of limbo that may carry them through their entire school career ... their mental juices of novelty have been carefully stowed away in some hidden cerebral crevice that may one day be coaxed to the surface when the trauma of high school has become a memory ...

Professor Neff gave me an A. I imagined he had also lived under the cold drizzle of disapproval in high school.

The following summer I took a close-up photography term project from "Photo Illustration I," to Amphoto, a publisher of photographic books in New York City. The CEO, Ron Ingle, a rangy 38-year-old trying to act older than his years, was interested. Thinking he may have discovered the next shining star in the sky of famous photographers, he decided to take a risk. I went to his office a couple more times and—glory be!—signed a contract. I was going to be a published author—*at nineteen!*

With a sense of urgency and importance, I returned to RIT for my second year, and started the serious work of turning a term project into a book. Not wanting the distractions of dorm living, I moved into a furnished ground floor apartment in an old, three-story colonial five miles from campus and there, seated at a scruffy dining room table, absorbed myself in creating a fully illustrated how-to photography book.

CHAPTER TWO

The Pinkie

A few weeks passed. One Saturday morning in late September '69, I was battling the boredom that crept over me like a fog as I retyped my manuscript for the third time, when a solitary and eccentric professor, Owen Butler, who lived on the top floor of the same house, invited me to help hang a show of photographs at RIT's Student Union. A wiry, hunched fellow with rounded jowls, dark, languid eyes and a youthful face, Butler asked for my help in a reserved way—he was ready to take no for an answer. The day was dreary. I was determined to progress on my book. I definitely did not want to go to the college on a weekend.

And yet I said, "I'd be happy to."

The Student Union was modern architecture at its oddest—a sweeping, well-lit irregularly-shaped, concrete-glass-brick monolith. I followed Butler through its revolving doors. The moment I was inside, my attention swiveled to one person. Suddenly, all that existed for me in that spacious, bustling area was a hardy, mustached young man casually leaning against the far wall. His bushy, tawny hair was swept back; he had a wide brow and Roman features. He stood with one knee up and his foot resting on the wall behind him while he nonchalantly spoke with someone. I was more than attracted; I felt a bond with this complete stranger. A small but distinct inner voice told me, "That's him."

Odd. I'd had boyfriends before, but never a crush. I was not the type to have crushes. And I was certainly not the type to hear inner voices, what to speak of listening to them.

From the moment I saw him that gray Saturday morning in the fall of 1969, I was attracted to John not only physically, but by something deeper. I felt he filled an emptiness in my life that I wasn't fully aware of before. It was as if I was meant to be with him, and he with me, although he didn't know it. How or why this was so I couldn't say—and perhaps never would be able to say—as there were thousands of other young men that I'd seen in my nineteen years and felt no attraction for. Whatever the emotion was, it was powerful and inescapable.

"Are you a freshman?" were the first words I spoke to him as he and I and a few others started hanging photographs together, following Professor Butler's directives. Although I asked the question, I was sure he was a freshman because I hadn't seen him the previous year (my freshman year) and I was prepared to be dismayed when he said, "Yes," as it would mean he was younger than me and probably not interested in a relationship.

"No," John said. "I'm a graduate student in the photojournalism department," and with that he entered the inviting light of eligibility. He had a degree in American history from the University of Berkeley, had spent two years in the Peace Corps in Malaysia, one year as an Outward Bound instructor there, and now was at RIT for a master's in photography. Within days John and his stereo system were sharing my apartment.

We did our assignments, played *Here Comes the Sun*, partied, and I kept extra busy writing my photography book. On sunny weekends we'd plop ourselves into the front seats of John's VW bus.

He'd look over at me and ask, "Where shall we go?"

"Doesn't matter. Anywhere you'd like," I'd say, relieved to be doing anything besides my book. John would contentedly drive off, sometimes to some beautiful hilly place where we'd roll down leafy hills while hugging, or we'd wander hand in hand in a historic place, like the house where the American social reformer, Susan B. Anthony, was arrested for attempting to vote in a presidential election. I loved John for his adventuresome spirit, his taste in photography and music that was so similar to mine, his nonchalance, and especially his keen desire to help others and do some good in the world.

When summer came, we stayed at my Great Neck home where my parents reservedly welcomed John. To me, they seemed to be wondering, "Is this guy right for Jean? Is he good enough?" Thankfully, John didn't notice he was being assessed but happily took his photography portfolio to art directors and magazine editors in Manhattan. Some days later he got a call from the editor of *Asia Magazine* asking for a photo article on the Hare Krishna devotees. Not long after that, *Earth Magazine* also commissioned John for an article on the same subject.

I thought the Hare Krishna devotees were a bizarre, irrelevant and unnecessary social fluke, although their daily singing parades did add color and rhythm to the otherwise cheerless and cacophonous city streets. Out of curiosity and possibly to write an article to accompany John's photographs, I went with him into the Brooklyn Hare Krishna ashram at 439 Henry Street. The devotees' organization was officially called ISKCON, the International Society for Krishna Consciousness, and the Brooklyn temple/ashram was one of many such centers throughout the world where devotees lived together and practiced bhakti—devotional service to Krishna, their name for God.

When we arrived, four exuberant, cherubic devotees about our age welcomed us. They wore buttercup-yellow, thick polyester robes—wrapped into dhotis for the men, whose heads were clean-shaven except for a tuft of hair in the back, and saris for the women, who used them to cover their heads as well as their bodies. After introductions, the devotees, practically skipping with joy, led us down a hall and into a long narrow room where a dozen other devotees were swaying and chanting. On entering, the four devotees with us fell flat on the ground, their faces to the floor, their arms stretched over their heads and their toes pointed straight out behind them.

"How excessive!" I thought. *"What is wrong with these people?"*

In the noisy ashram hallway I interviewed Mrs. Cohen, the mother of one of the resident devotees. A nervous version of my lovable Aunt Ethel, Mrs. Cohen had a pronounced Brooklyn accent, heavy makeup, and hair dyed the color of straw and then frozen into a bulging permanent that swelled and roiled around her head.

"Do you think people here have disappointments, frustrations, anger?" I asked.

"Yes," she said.

"Do you see that?"

"I know that. My son is one of them. They cannot take the pressure on the outside. He went to City College for two and a half years. He got good marks. I noticed he was going downward. He had no interest anymore. He couldn't cope with the outside. He saw corruption. Let's face it—it's all corrupt. Religions, faiths, beliefs—they're all about the same. That's why I can't see why they should go away from the outside. Cope with it, whatever it is."

"Some cope with it and some try to change it and some run away," I offered.

"And some run away. My son was always confused somehow with life. He always went too deep into life. He was analyzing and thinking and writing."

I hadn't met Mrs. Cohen's son, but I suddenly respected him. He was a seeker trying to avoid the abyss of world-weariness that so readily afflicted people.

"He never really knew what he wanted," Mrs. Cohen continued. "He went through everything, I want you to know. He was a marijuana kid. Went up to LSD. Mescaline. Everything. He went places. The material things he had: beautiful clothes, the best of everything, stereo sets. He had a disappointing love affair, too. She was oversexed, oversexed."

"Wow," I thought. A young fellow tries everything, comes up empty-handed and turns to exotic spirituality. "How long has he been in the ashram?"

"He's very much involved. And they're very happy to get one with a brain. He's got a good head on him. This is exactly what they need."

I wondered who "they" were in Mrs. Cohen's mind. Did she have information on some authoritarian cult leaders among the Hare Krishnas who were controlling devotees' lives?

Mrs. Cohen went on. "He gives lectures. He's learned in the scriptures. They're not all smart here. Some are running away and haven't got a brain to learn, so it's not so aggravating, but when you see a boy who's an intellectual, who's always been fighting for the colored people—and then at the end he throws it all away. …"

"I went through that too, fighting for civil rights, but it was frustrating because nothing was done," I said.

"Nothing was done. My son started going to all these spiritual places and he found this. And he came and brought the news to me. He says, 'You always said if I'm happy, you'll be happy, Mother.' And I said, 'How far do you go?' He says, 'This is what I'm doing. I'm happy with it.' And he seems to be."

"What would you like him to do?"

"I would like him to be on the outside, get his degree. He has a very good vocabulary, if you ever speak to him. He talks nice. He was going in for teaching."

I considered that for a moment. Of all the occupations, teaching seemed a gratifying one. Why give up a teaching career to live in an ashram to wear robes and recite mantras?

"Was your son raised religiously?"

"Yeah, I gave him four and a half years of Hebrew school. But the rabbi always said he'd never be a rabbi. I pushed my son, you see. He really didn't believe in anything. He didn't believe that there was such a thing as God. My brother says to him, 'If you're not a believer, become an atheist. Why pick up something else?' But you see the chanting and everything, it does something to them."

It sounded as if she thought the chanting put devotees under a hypnotic spell. "Have you tried chanting?" I asked Mrs. Cohen.

"Me? No. I can't go into it. I don't think it could do anything for me. And I'm not ready for it, let's face it. I was raised my way and I've coped with a lot of things in my lifetime, I've had a lot of problems, which we all have, and I went through it all. I may not be the happiest person, I wouldn't say, but who's to say who's happy? How do I know they're happy here? Is there such a thing where they're all happy? It can't be. I don't believe it. That's why I come every week to look at him."

Like Mrs. Cohen, I also questioned the devotees' happiness—what it was based on and how long it could last. Yet I was glad *I* wasn't being regularly observed to see if my happiness level was decreasing.

In his office, the Brooklyn ashram president "preached" to John and me with the delicacy of a charging rhinoceros. "People are frustrated," he said. "They're in anxiety—all the time they're in anxiety—yet they refuse to accept a logic that can simply absolve all their anxiety and make them happy. Simply because they're so conditioned and because they think they are the lords of material nature. We're all suffering from the fact that we want to be god. That's why we're here. We're in this material world due to our desire to lord it over material nature. But we can't do it. We can't control the wind. We can't even control our own bowels. We can't control the sun coming up and setting every day and night. Never. But we want to lord it over material nature. But actually material nature has got us."

I agreed that lots of people were frustrated and anxious. But I didn't know anyone who wanted to stop the wind or prevent the sun from setting.

"Do you ever think about going back to your other life? Would you like to?" I asked.

"Well, of course, in Krishna consciousness one should be spending his time thinking of Krishna. But honestly, sometimes I think of going back.

I left once for a month to go back. Everyone was so happy to see me. I thought, 'I escaped. I was about to lose my old self.'

"When the concocted barriers we use to protect our ego start getting taken away by Krishna consciousness, you can get a little panic-stricken. And then you worry about getting hurt again—'What if it's not real, what if it isn't true? Oh no!' I think there isn't any devotee who doesn't go through that."

The term "Krishna consciousness," he explained, was Prabhupada's translation of the Sanskrit phrase, *krishna-bhakti-rasa-bhavita,* which means "absorbed in the mellows of executing devotional service to Krishna, God." Old-fashioned and unfortunate, I thought, to try to become absorbed in and serve *(with devotion no less!)* someone who doesn't exist. I decided that devotees had opted for a personal delusion—they had a psychological need to believe in Krishna consciousness. It seemed harmless enough, if a delusion can ever be harmless. It also seemed like a waste of time.

As journalists, John and I stayed in the ashram for a week, he in the men's ashram, me in the women's, which was on the top floor above a large all-purpose room. The women's ashram leader was a soulful, pale, skinny woman with a flickering smile. In a singsong voice—like she was telling a story to a child—punctuated by her vanishing smile, she explained philosophical points to me that I couldn't grasp. Whatever she said vaporized before I could even formulate a question. My lack of understanding didn't deter her; she didn't seem to notice.

Like the devotees, I slept on a mat on the floor, rose at 4 a.m., attended the temple program and then sat cross-legged in a line, knee to knee, on the linoleum basement floor to face breakfast: a gooey mass of cereal served with a plop into the center of a 12-inch square of wax paper placed in front of each of us. As soon as it was served, we'd each try to corner the hot sweet cereal before it oozed beyond the edges of the paper, alternately scalding and then blowing on our fingers in the process—there were no spoons. The urgency of our task—to keep the cereal off the floor—depended on the consistency of the cereal, of course, which varied from molasses-like (very urgent) to gloppy (less urgent) from day to day.

Lunch—moist vegetables, rice, legume soup and semi-digestible deep fried breadsticks—and dinner—popcorn and tepid, too-sweet milk—

were served the same way but with paper cups for the soup and milk. The "Sunday Free Love Feast" for the public was the devotees' weekly gastric highlight. After the program in the temple room, each guest and devotee received an opulent vegetarian meal on a paper plate. Unlike the guests' modest portions, devotees' heaped their plates, making a pyramid of food they'd eat from the tip down. When they'd finished and after the guests had left, they'd eat the guests' leftovers, too.

Daily I thought, "Why don't these people go where they can eat properly?" I lost seven pounds that week. (Years later, the ashram president's wife told me that she used to hide stashes of delectable milk sweets to tide her over between Sundays.)

After one Sunday feast, John and I were talking in the tiny garden behind the temple when a grim, pallid, saffron-robed celibate student asked us not to speak together.

"Men and women," he said, "remain apart in the temple to avoid sexually attracting each other and arousing lusty ideas in the minds of the devotees." I was sure that he was joking. He wasn't.

Alan Niederman wrote the article that accompanied John's photographs in *Earth Magazine*. I brought Niederman's manuscript to the photojournalist W. Eugene Smith, who had a studio/home on the Avenue of the Americas in Manhattan. When Smith was a guest speaker at RIT, he'd seen my close-up work and kindly written a foreword for my book. Besides being known as one of the world's top ten photojournalists, Smith was also famous for being intolerant of yellow journalism. In that mood, Smith anointed the margins of Niederman's article with cryptic comments. Where Niederman referred to devotees as "sexless," Smith wrote, "Remarkably intuitive research." Where Niederman wrote that the devotees were draped in "sheet-like attire," Smith commented: "Typical blindness of a writer on a nonperceptive ego trip." Where, toward the end of the article, Niederman quoted a devotee saying, "Giving up illicit sex is not so hard," Smith wrote, "Since they are 'sexless.'"

Niederman also wrote about the devotees' celebrating "the time when Krishna lifted an entire mountain with his pinkie finger to shield his people." Considering the quality of Niederman's research, Smith thought this statement might be false and advised me to confirm it. So, late one night, in Smith's brooding, cluttered studio, while standing in one of several narrow paths that wended through tables, chairs, desks, and stools, each piled high with photographic prints, papers, books, magazines, and files that fell like sediment at the mouth of a riverbed—I called the Brooklyn Hare Krishna ashram. The phone rang for some minutes before a drowsy devotee picked up the receiver with a tentative "Hello?"

"Did your God lift a hill with the finger of one hand?" I asked.

There was a pensive pause, and finally, "Yes, he did. That hill is called Govardhan. You can still see it in India, not far from Delhi." I hung up the receiver and told Smith. Together we laughed, shrugged, and shook our heads in pity and wonder. Niederman had gotten that one right.

John's color photograph of a demure young devotee of Krishna in a pink patterned sari was on the cover of the December 20, 1970 issue of *Asia Magazine*. Her head was covered; chanting beads hung straight down her neck as she gracefully held an issue of *Back to Godhead* magazine, removed from and nonplussed by the city bustle that blurred behind her. Inside, John's photos showed robed devotees chanting fervently on the streets and devotees riding horses and tilling in New Vrindavan, their West Virginia farm. (When John was in New Vrindavan he wrote me, "The devotees have strange beliefs, but they are alive and happy. Maybe it's just the result that counts?")

On the first page of that issue, the publisher of *Asia Magazine,* R. V. Pandit, wrote:

> The Hare Krishna people featured in this issue are the result of a coincidence. A few weeks ago, while coming out of our New York office at 122 East 42nd Street, I was greeted by very familiar sounds—the brassy clang of cymbals, the resonance of Indian drums and the chant of Hindu hymns. On the pavement, encircled by a curious crowd, was a bizarre group of men and women, the men with heads clean shaven, the women graceful in saris, all clad in saffron.
>
> Within days we had the American freelancer, John Griesser, on their trail—joining them in their street corner conclaves, visiting their temple in New York and their commune in West Virginia.
>
> Days later, I encountered a similar group—the same chant, the same clang, the same saffron robes—opposite the Sony Building on the Ginza in Tokyo. That put our Tokyo-based photographer, Takeshi Takehara, on their Japanese trail … Judging by the progress of these pilgrims, it will not be long before you hear the Hare Krishna sounds and see the sights in your streets.

In the fall of 1970—some 14 months after John and I had first met—my photography book was released: *Photomacrography: Art and Techniques*. An out-of-the-way gallery in Manhattan held a one-person show of my original illustrations, and I impatiently waited for permission from Cuban government officials for John and me to photograph in Cuba—the next project I'd dreamed up. John, meanwhile, flew to Bombay in December 1970 to begin his master's thesis on the Hare Krishna devotees—a small group of them had accompanied their elderly leader, A. C. Bhaktivedanta Swami Prabhupada, to India. (John had considered doing his thesis on Zen Buddhism, but practitioners in Buffalo, New York, were observing a day of silence when he arrived and couldn't discuss the idea with him; the devotees though, were immediately enthusiastic about his project and loved his photographs.)

Left behind in the States, that old emptiness in me got louder, those lingering questions of: "What exactly is my purpose? How would my doings help me or anyone else? And for that matter, what did it mean to help myself and others? What is life all about, anyway?" In the deepest part of me there was something hollow, something that decidedly needed filling. But the questions were a whisper and I had no idea of who could give me answers. Anyway, everyone around me was astonished by my early success. Why ask existential questions?

John's letters from India started coming, one after another. In the first he wrote,

> I spoke with Prabhupada this morning. He asked me if I was enjoying being with them and what I had learned … He said that some of his devotees who wear the robes and seem like devotees are not, actually, because they have not given up attachments. I have seen that too much in living with the devotees. They hardly measure up to the way a true devotee should act in some cases.

This resonated with me. From what I'd occasionally heard from my mother, who was consistently suspicious of people's motives, and from what I'd read from time to time, it was considerably easier to wear religious clothes and speak pious words than to focus one's thoughts and heart on divinity. History and the daily newspaper was replete with "pious" people who had acted impiously, who used religion as a tool to exploit others, who did harm in the name of God.

John's letter continued,

> Prabhupada recognizes this. He really is compassionate and understanding. His only idea is that people, no matter how they fumble, should find Krishna. He doesn't let petty things bother him. I went with him on his walk yesterday and had trouble keeping up. He is 74!

Let's see how Prabhupada's actions stand up over time—the great revealer—I thought. More than likely he's another silky swami who extorts money and has affairs with young followers.

On December 27, 1970, John wrote from Gujarat,

> About twenty devotees and Prabhupada and I are staying in the home of a wealthy man in Surat. We are given great care. The people show great respect for the devotees and stand a bit in awe of them. Sankirtana is really amazing. The devotees walked up and down the street today and hundreds of people followed them chanting, giving them wreaths of flowers, and touching them. The difference between here and America is unbelievable.

Reading this I laughed. When the devotees went on sankirtana around New York City, people would ridicule and scorn them, often yelling, "Hey, get a job!" or "You guys are nuts!"

John went on,

> I met Prabhupada the morning after I arrived. He was nice to me and asked me what I was doing and if I studied their philosophy. I showed him a copy of *Asia Magazine*, and he liked the pictures—all the Indians in town have seen it by now.

A few days later,

> I am still in Surat and am still rushing around with the devotees to speaking, eating and chanting engagements—there's no end to it. Today we went to an industrial site and the people there had a large carpet covered with soft mats spread out on the grass under trees. The devotees and Prabhupada sat there and chanted, as did the hundred or so Indian people. I took a few rolls of Prabhupada as he was lecturing to them. He really is an amazing old man. Indians question his ideas, and he beats them every time. His logic and reasoning is unbeatable, it seems. He uses analogies and draws on what people know to explain what they don't know. …
>
> The devotees are a strange bunch. I have seen that some of them have lost a sense of their selves and have become almost like puppets following

Prabhupada around. They are not pleasant to be around. It seems that there must be a self for the teachings to act on. In this way there is discovery. It is against the philosophy to deny one's individual self, and it seems that this is what some of the devotees are doing. It is sad to see and Prabhupada recognizes it but he continues to lecture and tries to explain as fully as he can what he has discovered.

During my week in the Brooklyn ashram I had had similar feelings. In the process of following their beliefs it seemed that some devotees had lost touch with themselves and become mouthpieces for the Krishna creed. Like a pat of cold butter on cold bread, it was as if they'd adopted a philosophy and lifestyle that was unconnected to them as persons. Their lack of integration between head and heart was disconcerting.

A few days later John wrote,

> Traveling with the group is like going on a road show. There are big crowds wherever they go and it has begun to be the same thing … Traveling alone is not for me and it would be great if you were here. I would like you to come, if you want to … I think it would be nice to hike through the valleys of Nepal in springtime and get lost in the tall grass. Then live on an island in Malaysia and sail around in boats of different kinds.

Yes! This was for me.

From the Kumbha Mela in Allahabad John wrote,

> There are thousands of people here, and in a few days there will be millions. It was very eerie when I arrived at 2 in the morning and saw thousands of people camped on both sides of the Ganges River. It looked like two opposing armies on either bank and reminded me of something out of Roman times. There are about 30 devotees, myself and Prabhupada here camped in several large tents.

I tried to imagine the scene John described. A temporary city was quickly forming around a sacred place in celebration of a sacred time. It reminded me distantly of Americans avidly lining city streets to see the Fourth of July parade, or going in droves to baseball or football stadiums. Except that the Kumbha Mela was not for a few hours but was a month-long event, that it drew not thousands of people but *30 million(!)* of them, and that those pilgrims underwent hardships in the hope of making spiritual progress. I couldn't grasp their mentality or how many of them there were—almost four times the population of New York City!

A week later, on January 20, '71:

> I've been wondering how much I have changed since I left. Being constantly with the devotees is trying mentally at times because they are different and very serious and deep-thinking—more deep than I feel I want to get, but then again they have answered questions that most of us have asked at one time but given up on trying to find the answer to because we cannot perceive the answer with our senses and no one else can give a satisfactory answer. Why are we here? What are we doing? Is there a higher power? So at times, I feel like a split person—taking photographs and doing a thesis and trying to understand their philosophy ... What a hardship and what drudgery it is to wander around trying to find the truth and die not having found anything. That is the way most people end up. Much better to believe and be free ... Do you want to be with me even if I do talk philosophy a lot and tell you THE TRUTH every once in a while? Because I do believe there's an answer for us both. We have to be open enough to let it in and to share together.

I hoped John wasn't getting religious on me, for if that was the case I'd have to move on without him. Yet I couldn't deny that I had long submerged questions about life and death, about why people did what they did, about powerful forces like ambition that I felt driving me and those around me.

After my second year at Rochester Institute of Technology, I'd received an Associate of Applied Science degree with honors and needed a break from college. I'd waited for months but had heard nothing from the Cuban government. So I bought a $350 one-way New York-to-London, Brussels-to-Bombay ticket on Basco Airlines. The rest of my savings—$300—I cashed and took with me for my first overseas trip.

In February 1971, my mother, looking willowy and uncertain, waved goodbye as I boarded the plane. Once seated, I looked out the window at her and felt a surge of gratitude for the steady love she and my father had given me for all my twenty years. They both had encouraged me to find my own calling and pursue it wholeheartedly. They genuinely wanted me to be happy and had given me a solid foundation for happiness: security, self-confidence, good habits, an ongoing desire to learn, their unconditional good will.

Why I was leaving now and what I was going to do were utterly vague to me. But perhaps at least in part it was my parents' trust in me, that I would find my calling and make my life a good one, that was pushing me.

CHAPTER THREE

Earthquake

Our Basco Airlines plane reminded me of Charles Lindberg's *Spirit of St. Louis*. Not that it was a single-engine, as Lindberg's was, but it was propeller-driven and petite—40 passengers filled all the available seats. Since it was my first flight, I didn't know the thunderous engine roar and the whooshing and rumbling, whirring and thumping, were unusual. I also didn't know that on other planes, the bathroom door wasn't a large piece of frayed burlap tacked to the top of the doorframe or that it was unusual to see a taut rope running along the length of the plane near the ceiling (much like the exit cord one pulls on a bus), or for the pilot to use a foot pedal to control the rudder and a compass to navigate.

My fellow passengers remarked uneasily about these oddities and antiquities, but I was scared only about what I would find once I arrived.

For the one-night London layover, I made my way to the Hare Krishna ashram, where I hoped I could stay for free, at 7 Bury Place, near the British Museum, and knocked on the door. A lanky devotee, dressed in a polyester dhoti and several layers of sweaters, let me in out of the cold. When he'd heard I'd lived in the Brooklyn temple and was on my way to India to photograph, he agreed I could spend the night. The women's ashram was a smallish room on the top floor, empty except for an old-fashioned, knee-high portable electric heater near a wall. That night, the six women who lived in the ashram slept on mats in semicircles close to the heater, four women, who were invited guests, formed the next ring, and I, an uninvited newcomer, was at the farthest reaches of the room where the heater's warmth was more of an idea than an experience.

The next morning I shopped on Oxford Street, and before I rejoined my fellow Basco passengers to ferry over the Channel en route to Brussels, I had an ultralight, royal blue, pure down sleeping bag fit for subfreezing weather strapped to the bottom of my backpack.

In Brussels, we learned that the plane scheduled to take us to Bombay was under repair. Basco provided us hotel rooms and, as the days passed and our wait continued, airline hosts offered repeated assurances and consolations. Meanwhile, I ate something I shouldn't have and got sicker with diarrhea than I thought possible. Outside my bathroom window an icy overcast sky poured down a discouraging light on Brussels, a dreary mass of gray buildings, gray streets, gray sidewalks and gray-bundled people. Once, with trepidation at being far from my toilet, I ventured out for a walk and saw a life-size statue of a naked boy perpetually peeing. If someone made a statue of me, I'd be doing only a slightly different function.

After five days, both the plane and I were better. We were airborne before I remembered that I hadn't told John of our departure. He didn't know when I was arriving.

"Twenty years old and adrift in Bombay," I thought, "with not one address or phone number or contact except John—and I have no idea where he's staying or even if he's still in Bombay." I didn't have a return ticket or enough cash to buy one. Potential calamities surfaced in my mind as I sipped tea and watched a desolate Sahara slowly pass below. The two Muslim passengers next to me started a conversation. On hearing what I was doing—I had to yell over the deafening engine—they yelled back, explaining that the sacred text, Bhagavad-gita, was immorally supportive of violence. "It was spoken on a battlefield in favor of war," the younger of the two said. "And it was spoken by Krishna, who had many, many affairs with other people's wives," said the older.

"What *am* I doing," I wondered.

The moment I looked out the window at Bombay's international airport, the term "third-world" shed its mystery. The entire terminal—the tarmac, the personnel and the buildings—begged for a thorough hosing, soaping, brushing and hosing again. All the airport vehicles—baggage trucks, passenger buses, maintenance and catering vans—looked grimy and battered from decades of neglect. Except for their size, they could have been children's toys, fought over and abused for generations. The airport's construction team was a few sinewy men in loincloths, who continually shoveled earth into straw baskets, hoisted the baskets onto the head of one of many lean, sari-clad women, who then took the earth to a distant area, dumped it and returned for another load. For this purpose, a long train of women was going back and forth single file.

As we stepped out of the plane door, the other passengers and I were enveloped in a sauna-burst of heat and humidity (what was I doing with a state-of-the-art subzero sleeping bag that I couldn't afford?). At the baggage claim area, we sweated and bumped into innumerable other passengers, and sweated some more until finally our luggage was deposited in a massive mound on the floor. The conveyor belt was out of order. Passengers who recognized their suitcases on the surface of the mound wrestled and slid them down the pile, revealing other suitcases below, and so it went.

Backpack in place, at the immigration check I stared in disbelief at the immigration official's once-white shirt collar—clearly adorned with a thick dark brown line of sweat and dirt—and at his teeth and lips—stained bright red.

Finally, I walked to the waiting area and straight toward John (who knew of the arrival from the Basco Airlines information center), thinner than before, his mustache hiding his upper lip and smile. A sense of lightness and strength entered my heart. I was no longer a lone dinghy adrift in an alien night sea. Now two dinghies were adrift together.

The first time I sat down in India, next to John on a bus going to our hotel, I looked around at the wilderness of dark-eyed somber Indian faces unabashedly fixated on me in incredulity, and had the distinct but spooky sense that I'd experienced all this before.

Mr. Chhabria, a supporter of the Hare Krishna Society, owned the Sea Palace Hotel in south Bombay. Since John was the devotees' friend, Chhabria gave John a small, dingy, back room at a reduced rate. That evening John and I strolled along the waterfront and bought snacks—bananas, guavas and unshelled peanuts that had been roasted in hot sand. The Gateway of India loomed in the distance, a colossal and cumbersome colonial relic of arched concrete that, in 1911, had commemorated the arrival of England's King George V and Queen Mary to Indian shores.

After Brussels, I was cautious about what I ate, so the next day John and I went to the Hare Krishna ashram for prasad, a holy vegetarian meal. The devotees had rented a spacious, three-bedroom, three-balconied apartment on the seventh floor of the Akash Ganga Building overlooking the sea. Bombay was such a rickety amalgam of disintegration that an everyday machine like an elevator made me nervous, but the Akash Ganga elevator proved fairly clean and, though punctuated by pronounced groaning and creaking, worked. Malati, a spry devotee a little older than me, with a carefree manner and a quick smile, greeted us at the door. She seemed to know something I didn't but should.

"What brings you here?" Malati asked.

"I want to photograph the essence of India," I said, wondering at my grandiosity.

"Well, you've come to the right place," she said.

John and I left our shoes just inside the door, quietly passed through a small foyer redolent of too-sweet incense, and then entered a spacious, well-windowed living room that served as the temple. Bombay's mayhem of ceaseless jostling, clamor, and pitiful corruption (we were overcharged buying bananas) made me feel lost and rootless, like a runner from a strawberry plant that had somehow meandered into a field of Jerusalem artichokes. My mind was scrambled. The tranquil temple room and companionable devotee calmed me.

Before my arrival, John, with extra time on his hands, had been rolling puris in the ashram kitchen, and that morning he continued. I stood to the side near a large window, watching him and a tall, formidable, middle-aged Indian man in impeccable saffron robes, who was deep-frying the puris in a large wok. As they cooked, each puri puffed up into a ball, and the saffron-clothed gentleman scooped it up with a slotted spoon and set it aside to cool. After a short time the kitchen door swung open and a short Indian gentleman strode in, also saffron-robed. He had an unpretentious dignity and a grave yet curiously sprightly countenance. Within a moment, he seemed to take in everything in the kitchen, including John and me, with a simple, charged alertness. He walked over to the Indian cook, briefly discussed something, and left. That, I was told, was Prabhupada, the founder of the Hare Krishna movement.

Before lunch, Malati directed me to the women's quarters (one of the three bedrooms) to wash my hands. I opened the indicated door and a piercing, primordial scream began. It continued, reverberating in my eardrums for interminable moments. And then more interminable moments. What was going on? Inside the room, Yamuna Devi, a stocky woman dressed in her underwear, was sitting cross-legged on the floor before a low table a few yards in front of me. When she had seen me from the corner of her eye, she had thought a man off the street had barged into the women's quarters and so had fully used her unusually powerful vocal cords.

"No women wear pants in Bombay," she explained.

Shaken, I offered to knock first next time. Yamuna laughed.

Unlike the New York and London ashrams, the Bombay ashram food was satisfying, novel, varied, and tasty. John and I went regularly, supplementing our ashram meals with kulfi—a thick, solid, rectangular block of naturally-flavored, ice-cold cream—and other dessert delicacies from restaurants. In Bombay, the Western-style cooking I tried was generally pap-like and the meat I saw people eating seemed as chewy as worn leather.

I spent hours wandering and photographing the traffic, trash, animals, people, construction, disintegration, and destruction snarl that was Bombay—a city that could comfortably accommodate only a fraction of its actual population. The congestion and chaos seemed normal for everyone but me—in fact, I was the abnormal one. My Caucasian skin ever announced my foreignness, and a multitude of eyes, distracted from their work or idleness, followed my every move.

As I explored the city, I saw billboards and banners: "Hare Krishna Festival at Cross Maidan, March 25th to April 4th, His Divine Grace A. C. Bhaktivedanta Swami Prabhupada and His American and European Disciples, All Are Welcome," with a larger than life photograph of Prabhupada. After successful programs in Surat, Indore, Gorakhpur and other towns, the small band of devotees who had arrived in India with Prabhupada in the fall of 1970 were staging their first grand program in a major Indian city.

A few days later, John wanted to introduce me to Prabhupada. After breakfast and with permission from Prabhupada's secretary, we knocked on Prabhupada's door, heard "Come in," and entered. The room was spacious and simple without being austere. It had a cheering depth to it I couldn't name.

Behind a small coffee table, Prabhupada sat cross-legged on a small cushion on the floor. He looked up at us from the book he'd been reading. Bobbing on waves of suspicion and skepticism, I looked back at this small, thin-limbed holy person. John introduced us.

"This is Jean. She's just come from America."

"Yes, welcome. It's nice to meet you." His accent was heavily Bengali-British, but I understood him.

I attempted a smile while John took the book I'd written and illustrated from under my arm and presented it to Prabhupada.

"This is what she's done."

With interest, Prabhupada took my book—*Photomacrography: Art and Techniques*—from John and unhurriedly turned its pages, handling it with his fine, long fingers as if it were something to savor. There was a singular grace about his hands. He paused at the color illustrations, took in the binding and paper quality, scanned the writing style and content and, when he was satisfied, closed it and handed it back to John, his thin arm stretching so John could reach it easily.

"We do not know much about these things," he said.

Although I was proud of my book, I hadn't been enthusiastic to show it to Prabhupada. "What interest would a guru have in a how-to photography book?" I thought. Yet I was now glad he'd seen it, glad I had had the chance to watch him touch and look at it. Our meeting was brief and ordinary without, I was relieved to note, any intimation of spiritual dimensions. It contained no holiness.

Later, at the Sea Palace, John said, "What did you think of Prabhupada?"

"I don't know what to think," I said. I was surprised at myself for not being negative about him, but in fact there was nothing in my exchange with him for me to be negative about. At the same time I could not be positive. I lacked a context for Prabhupada.

I soon discovered that Bombay was a potpourri of beliefs from fervent to fallow. I saw men worshiped like gods: bearded Ramakrishna and Guru Nanak, solemn Swaminarayan, stocky Satya Sai Baba, and even a whippersnapper of a boy, Guru Maharaj Ji. Bombay was also home to a melee of deities: the goddess of fortune Laksmi, with coins flowing from her hand, loitered over millions of cash registers; the elephant-god Ganesh sitting atop his mouse hung above almost every door and dangled from the rearview mirrors of taxis and rickshaws; crude, orange-colored Hanuman monkeys were set in bas relief on walls; angry Durga rode her lion on posters around the city; Shiva danced with snakes; half-man half-beast mixtures displayed ferocious canine teeth; sacred cows strolled the streets—all these deities, man-gods and sacred animals occasionally received reverence but mostly were ignored.

In the melange of these idols and the legends that accompanied them, I found similarities to Greek mythology, which I'd been reading with fascination for years. How had similar gods, goddesses, and stories wandered so far from home? Or was their home India and they'd wandered to Greece? Either way, I was in a cauldron alive with impossibly muddled convictions.

―∞∞―

When I had arrived in Bombay, I had given John the remainder of my life savings, which he'd carefully put in his worn, already plump leather wallet, forever kept in the front pocket of his jeans. One day, John and I decided to go to a horse race on the outskirts of Bombay. John paid for our train tickets—third class to save our much-needed money—and we crushed into the train in the typical Indian fashion. People hung out of the doors, sat on the train car roofs and even stood between the cars, taking up every possible inch of space. At the racetrack, although he didn't place any bets, John astonished me by picking the winning horses in each of three races. On our return trip, when John reached into his pocket I was surprised to see his eyes became wide with disbelief and dismay. He quickly searched in all his pockets with increasing dismay. They were all empty.

"I've been pick-pocketed!" he said.

"What? Oh, my God!" I didn't want to believe him.

Thinking back, we realized that when he'd paid for our tickets, two men had seen the flash of U.S. dollars and boarded the car with us, crushed themselves against him and lifted his wallet. I felt violated. I wanted to yell at John for his carelessness, but he was so disturbed and disheartened by the theft that I swallowed my outrage. We despaired together. We were penniless. We didn't even have a way to get back to the States!

John wired his dad in Orange County, California. Fortunately, Robert Griesser, Sr. was a generous and supportive father. He sent us more than we'd lost (over $3,000 U.S. in today's currency).

The devotees could not have picked a better location for their festival than Cross Maidan, a huge, easily accessible area in the center of Bombay enclosed for the occasion by a colossal rented pandal—a red-and-blue-striped rectangular tent that accommodated 20,000 people. Within, tables stretched along the left side, where guests received free *halavah* and puris each evening. On the right side, the devotees set up a question-and-answer booth and book tables with Prabhupada's books, ancient yogic texts that he'd translated and commented on. At the far end stood a stage where forty Western devotees sang, danced and worshiped brass deities of Radha and Krishna on a central altar. To the left of the altar was a slightly raised seat with a throne-like back for Prabhupada.

The expansive area in front of the stage and extending to the back of the pandal was for guests, and each evening for eleven days, beginning on March 25th, 1971, 15,000 people poured in to sit on one of the many chairs (for VIPs and the handicapped) or, more likely, on one of dozens of immense, thick, red-and-blue-patterned cotton dhurries that covered the ground.

The crowd's attention was riveted on the young, zealous Americans and Europeans who had brazenly adopted their culture and were playing two-headed drums and small hand cymbals and boisterously singing in Sanskrit while dancing to the beat.

There was hardly a Westerner in the audience. I sat on the stage with my fellow Caucasians, feeling awkward and hypocritical. I was not a believer, not a follower, not even a supporter of the devotees. But the devotees didn't mind my presence, and the stage gave me a good view of the audience. As the Western devotees mesmerized the multitudes in front of them, the multitudes mesmerized me. This ocean of people was as spellbound by the devotees as children are while watching a deft magician. And they sat for hours, utterly enchanted. Their reverence had an honesty and innocence and power I'd never before experienced. I didn't know what to make of it.

The eccentricities of the devotees in the Brooklyn ashram, the cold and austere London ashram, the airy Akash Ganga ashram and my brief unbelieving dip into the Krishna doctrine had in no way prepared me for this event. The personalities and backgrounds of the Western Hare Krishna devotees in India made them an odd group, but whatever they didn't have in common with one another—which was a lot—they made up for with their audacious, total endorsement of Prabhupada and his mission. Their enthusiasm exuded on the pandal stage, springing forth in song and vivacity, and making what seemed to me like an indelible impression on the droves who sat before them.

After some time, Prabhupada arrived, climbed the six steps onto the stage, came before the deities of Radha and Krishna, and offered his prostrated obeisance. He then rose, folded his hands in reverence before the deities, walked a few steps to the raised dais to the left of the deities that was meant for him, set aside his cane, and climbed onto the dais to sit cross-legged before the huge crowd. He was the only Indian on stage. One of his disciples led a song-prayer, and Prabhupada and the other devotees sang responsively while a priest performed an evening deity ceremony. When the blowing of the conch signaled the ceremony's end, the devotees bowed down, their foreheads touching the stage floor. Prabhupada recited lengthy Sanskrit prayers, his voice sonorous over the many loudspeakers stationed throughout the pandal. Then he began to play his small, shiny, brass hand cymbals in a steady one-two-*three* beat—ching, ching, sizzle. He closed his eyes and sang:

jaya radha madhava kunja bihari

I could not place his voice. It was neither Western nor Eastern nor anything in between. Its refined baritone strains were resonant with emotion. The devotees around me, two of them playing drums in time to the singing, and several more playing small hand cymbals like Prabhupada's, responded by singing the same words. Prabhupada listened to their singing and then sang the next line:

gopi jana vallabha giri vara-dhari

Again the devotees responded. The vast audience was still and silent.

jasoda-nandana, braja jana ranjana

Prabhupada's voice had a penetrating sincerity, and the devotees offered his words back to him.

jamuna-tira-vana-chari

Once the devotees had responded, Prabhupada began the lines over, picking up the beat. I vaguely remembered that I had heard this short song in the Brooklyn temple, but it hadn't impacted me then. Now it sounded Elysian.

Prabhupada deepened his concentration and increased the tempo as he sang the same lines a third, fourth, and fifth time. He suddenly stopped, opened his eyes, put his cymbals aside and leaned into the microphone, his brow wrinkled with earnestness. Again he recited prayers while the devotees bowed in supplication.

The devotees sat attentively as Prabhupada cleared his throat and began to speak.[*] "Ladies and gentlemen, thank you very much for taking so much trouble to participate with us in this great movement of Krishna consciousness. As I am repeatedly placing before you with all humbleness that this movement is very, very much essential, not only at the present moment, but also all the time."

My skepticism bristled. "Of course he's going to say the movement he started is essential," I thought. "Don't all leaders think what they're doing is essential?"

Prabhupada continued, explaining that this is the age of disagreements and quarrel. Everyone has their own opinion and is prepared to fight with others. So putting forth different theories can't solve the world's problems, he said, because there have always been different philosophers and different scriptures.

---

[*] Prabhupada's talks were recorded. so these quotes are verbatim.

He said, "So simply by argument and reasoning you cannot make spiritual advancement. You may be a very good logician, putting forward nice arguments, but somebody may come who is better than you. He will spoil all your logic and he will establish his own logic. Therefore you cannot understand the Absolute Truth by argument, by material dealings."

As he spoke, my mind drifted to the exotic circumstances in which I now found myself—sitting on a raised platform in the hub of India's most cosmopolitan city before thousands who were eagerly hearing from a slight, well-spoken guru. I missed what he said next, but perked up when he spoke of Malati's three-year old daughter Saraswati, who had charmed the audience earlier with her dancing and singing.

"You'll be surprised," Prabhupada continued, "this little girl, the other day we were walking in Hanging Gardens, and this little girl, as soon as she saw some flower, immediately she expressed her opinion that these flowers should be taken and made into a garland for Krishna. This is Krishna consciousness. She is being taught from the very beginning of her life how to become Krishna conscious. So it is not difficult. It depends only on training. Even in this old age, and *especially* in this age, this method is very simple. Simply we have to agree to accept it. That's all. Krishna consciousness is the simplest form of self-realization and advancement in spiritual life."

Saraswati was a sweet girl who usually seemed happy, despite living in such a foreign place. "But," I thought, "was she being trained or indoctrinated? When she came of age, would she continue to think that flowers were meant to be used for God's garland? Or would that idea, and so many others that Prabhupada promoted, become irrelevant to her and forgotten?" I felt alienated from the devotees, who themselves were aliens.

As Prabhupada left at the close of the program, a swarm of admirers from the audience engulfed him, scrambling to touch his feet. Devotees encircled Prabhupada, trying to hold back the crowd's swell. The fervid pushing, jockeying, and tussling was reminiscent of Beatlemania. Prabhupada had spoken with urgency and intensity, but in a measured and logical way, yet he'd evoked frenzy. I stood to the side, watching and wondering and distanced. India was so often a soup of showy reverence, I didn't take this display too seriously.

Every morning and evening the curious came en masse to Cross Maidan to drink in the music, dance and ceremonies and listen closely to Prabhupada. At one point toward the end of the eleven-day program, in his lecture Prabhupada spoke disparagingly of nationalism. Nationalism, he explained, is based on the bodily concept of life and we are not these bodies but are the soul within the body. The soul does not belong to any particular nation. Then a bit later Prabhupada said,

> Now people are hankering after this culture, Krishna culture. You should prepare yourself to present Bhagavad-gita as it is. Then India will conquer all over the world. Rest assured. Our government men simply beg help from others: "Please give us wheat. Please give us money. Please give us soldiers." Begging does not glorify your country. Try to give something to the others, to other countries. Here is a thing you can give them.

The audience responded with a cheering ovation. "Wait a minute," I thought, "After condemning nationalistic pride, Prabhupada just aroused it. How odd."

On Sunday evening the crowd mushroomed to twenty thousand. The gargantuan pandal was as packed with people as an Indian rush hour train. Prabhupada oversaw a marriage ceremony between Jorgen, who was Swedish, and Marian, an Australian. She wore a glamorous, ornate, red sari and Indian jewelry, complete with nose ring; he was in a starched hospital-white dhoti and kurta. They looked impressionable and inexperienced, but the audience, awed and enthralled, burst into uproarious applause when Prabhupada said of their union, "This is the real United Nations."

On the final night of the festival, devotees carried the deities, splendidly dressed and decorated with jewels and garlands, in a regal palanquin to the seaside. Again the devotees sang before a huge crowd and Prabhupada spoke. I inwardly groaned with disbelief—the same mood I'd had when, eight months earlier, I'd heard that God lifted a hill with his pinkie. Now Prabhupada was talking about a saint who'd received spiritual instructions while in his mother's womb. Strangely, no one else seemed fazed by the idea of a fetus attaining enlightenment.

In early April the festival ended, the pandal was dismantled and Prabhupada was leaving for Malaysia. Leaving the disordered city far behind, John and I planned to photograph India's glorious essence: elegant village life as it had been lived through millennia, life imbued with the wisdom of the ages, life made healthy and prosperous from nature's bounty, life filled with the freshness and joy of vibrant tradition, simple and pure life as it was meant to be lived.

When we asked Prabhupada which village we should photograph, he summarily demolished our plan by pointing out that wherever we went, villagers would rob us of all we had. We were crestfallen. We stood silent and still. We'd already experienced the painful reality of his words.

My relationship with Prabhupada could have begun and ended with that passing conversation. But during my stay in Bombay, Prabhupada had created a vortex that had started to pull me, not so much willingly as curiously, to its center—to him. At the Cross Maidan pandal Prabhupada was a sage, a savant, a simple devotee worshiping his God, pulling at the hearts of his followers and awakening his fellow citizens through his followers' remarkable dancing transformation. At Akash Ganga, he was a warm and personable and encouraging grandfather.

"How does he have such power over his followers, how does he influence them so deeply?" I wondered. When someone praised him during a conversation in his room, I heard his reply to my question.

"What have I done?" he said. "I've not done a miracle. I've simply followed my Guru Maharaja's instructions to give this message of Krishna in English. I've tried to do that. That's all."

It was somehow an endearing answer.

Now standing before him in his airy room, he off-handedly concluded, "Best that you go to Vrindavan and do your story there." We excused ourselves and left.

The heat and humidity had become unbearable for John and me. Before going to Vrindavan—the village where Krishna had grown up five thousand years before—we would trek the Himalayas in Nepal.

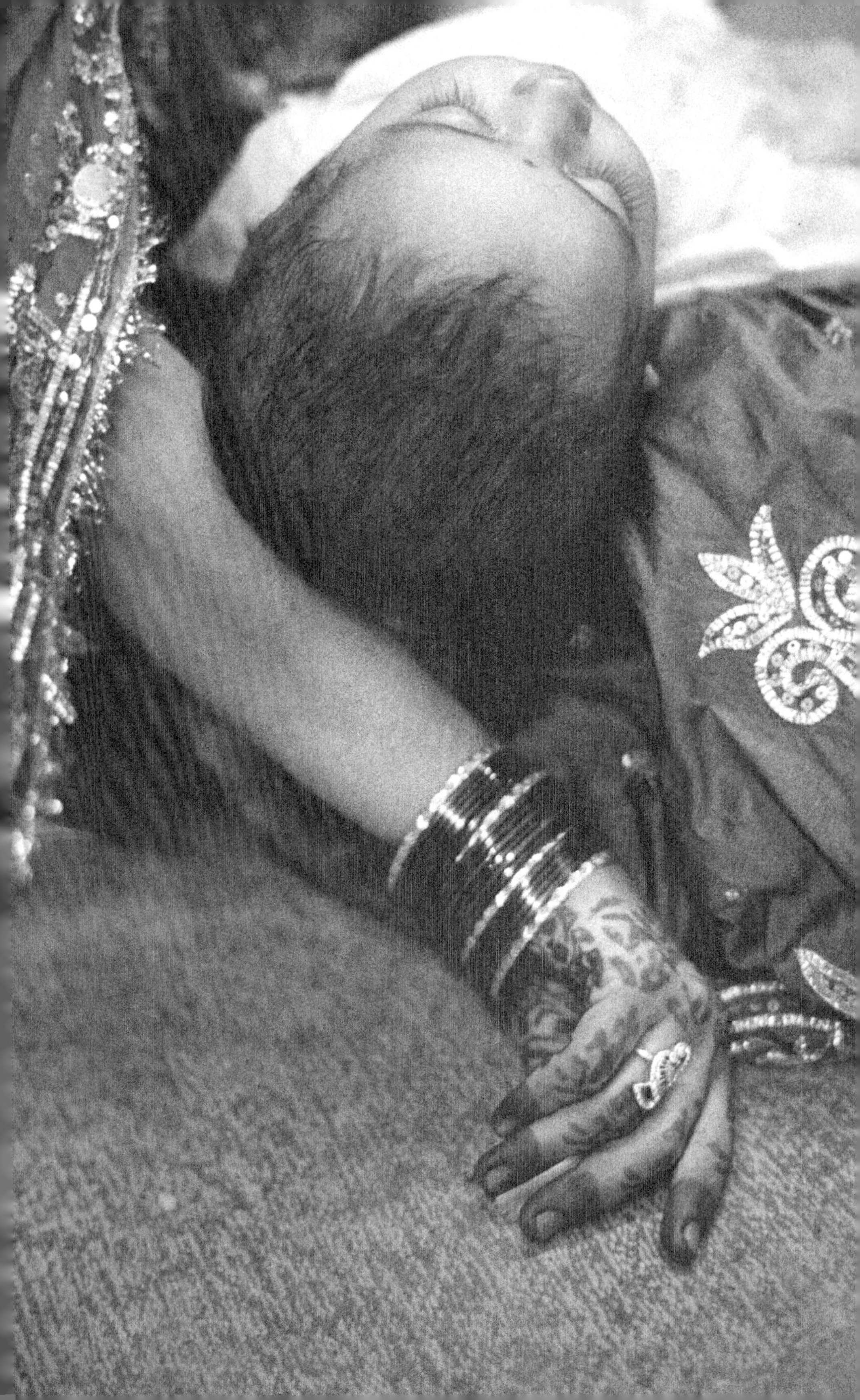

CHAPTER FOUR

Meditations

We took a sleeper train to Gorakhpur and then a thirteen-hour bus ride to Kathmandu. The bus was designed for people shorter than John and me, and our knees jammed against the seats in front of us. The roads were etched with potholes, and the wooden seats had no padding—our bottoms became bruised from the bumps. For as long as we possibly could, we braced and raised ourselves above the seats. The bus driver had only a casual interest in driving and often turned to look at us or speak with passengers who'd ambled to the front. When I wasn't harrowed by the bus's lurching along narrow, curved, ill-maintained, wet roads inches from sheer, hundred-yard drops, I was captivated by the Himalayas' ponderous bulk. Its foothills were a series of plateaus, some just yards wide, following the land's contours like a map showing elevation patterns. Each plateau was sowed; not a square yard lay fallow. Everywhere, the verdant earth exploded with life.

John and I briefly shared tiny tables with some bedraggled hippies in Kathmandu restaurants, and then bussed a further 130 miles northwest to Pokhara to begin our trek. John's backpack weighed fifty-five pounds; mine was slightly lighter and had my London down sleeping bag strapped to its frame. We carried a bright blue Indian kerosene stove, kerosene, a pot, powdered milk, rice, beans, oatmeal, cashews, raisins, water, a water filter, plates, spoons, cups, warm clothes, maps, Band-Aids, antiseptic cream, cameras, lenses, film, hats, and a hope that everything would be okay.

On two-foot-wide trails that went uphill through evergreen forests, the earth had a homey scent and the soft, springy duff beneath my feet softened the sounds of snapping twigs and branches. We passed locals who, from their facial features and stature, seemed part Chinese, each carrying on his or her back a heavy large woven basket supported by a strong, thick, flat rope across their forehead. Leaning forward to counterbalance the basket's weight, they walked quickly, looking at the ground before them. In Nepal, we seemed less foreign than we did in India—people focused on their own activities instead of ours.

Ever going up, we passed from one tiny village to another. From his years in Malaysia as a Peace Corps volunteer and later as an Outward Bound instructor, John was relaxed and friendly with the villagers and they readily warmed up to us. Night after night we were welcomed, fed, and housed in the simple cottages of kind farming families whose doors had no locks. By the time we got to the snow line at 10,000 feet, the villages were behind and below us. All around, white jagged peaks cut into the circle of the brilliant sky. We camped in an abandoned cowshed and took short hikes without our backpacks, feeling like we were levitating once relieved of the weight. Below, rivers curled through undulating hills spotted with villages, and placid golden sunlight stretched unhindered into kale-colored valleys and meadows of wildflowers. I was seized by the joy and naturalness of the scene and felt as if I were holding communion with something greater than myself that reached out from the sweeping pellucid expanse to touch me.

From the bottom of his backpack, John pulled out a blue paperback with a line drawing of a regal-looking person on the cover. During this cowshed stay, I sat for hours on a rock in the silent crystal-clear air with no humans other than the two of us for miles around, trying to read this early edition of Prabhupada's *Bhagavad-gita As It Is*. I understood little. Yet my entrenched skepticism abated slightly: I was intrigued. The idea of tolerating dualities and remaining equipoised in their midst enticed me, as did the concept of an eternal presence within all living beings and the thought of improving my character as well as the quality of my life through knowledge.

Three days later we started down and within minutes came on a group of Buddhist monks walking in rows of two to their monastery. We hadn't known about these quiet neighbors. They wore simple robes and home-made shoes and were unencumbered by baskets or backpacks and, it seemed, from the weight of material wants and meaningless work. Compared to me, they seemed unearthly, as if they were embodying the Gita verses I'd just been reading and so were removed from the dualities of happiness and unhappiness, loss and gain. They simply were. The fullness of their simplicity, the paucity of their needs, the satisfaction of their being, moved me. Freed of the unnecessary, they appeared to have a natural and full sense of the necessary. I watched them, confounded by how deeply the mere sight of them impressed me.

Suddenly, I felt I'd never paused in my life. I'd been continuously running—excited and breathless in my childhood games, unable to catch up with my high school classmates, pounded by some ambition that sent me bounding into college and book publication, and now to exotic places. Seeing monks on a remote Nepalese mountain, who were so unlike any people I'd ever seen, I stopped.

"What did these people live for?" I thought. "What secret thoughts did they harbor that I'd never considered? And how could they be happy in their isolated, unnoticed lives? Were they deprived and a little crazy? Or had they found something better than fame and a big bank balance?"

Since I'd arrived in India and especially now in the Himalayas, I'd felt a growing need to rid myself of the pedantries and pettiness, the unbearable banalities that decayed my thoughts and left me confused and depressed. Yet before this glimpse, I hadn't thought about people who devoted themselves to life's questions, who harmonized their lives with a higher purpose, who chose to control their minds, who were not at the mercy of passion, who were striving for something pure and great.

After this glimpse, the long Himalayan descent became a misty epiphany. I admitted to feelings that had before only nibbled at me: What did I want? Fame? W. Eugene Smith, my photojournalist mentor, was an internationally famous photojournalist, but during the two summer months I'd gotten to know him, he was never more than an arm's reach from a glass of straight Scotch, he'd been rejected by his long-time wife, he was cohabiting with a Japanese woman half his age and he was daily tormented by the upkeep of his image. My hero, the renowned photojournalist, humanitarian, and idealist W. Eugene Smith was an alcoholic and, his girlfriend confided, was becoming increasingly disappointed and bitter as he aged. Fame and altruism did not assure contentment or fulfillment.

The previous summer, just a month or two before I'd met John, I'd worked on Park Avenue in Manhattan for Peter Oliver, a commercial photographer. In his studio, I met the women who decorate the covers of fashion magazines, the advertising tycoons who orchestrated those women's careers, and the swell of talent drawn to that glamorous, moneyed arena. That glitter quickly acquired a stench. Peter Oliver was divorced and his two young children, who lived in England, required psychiatric help. His girlfriend, a model, got jealous whenever Peter hired other models, yet Peter had to—otherwise ad agents would see him as biased. So we did many secret shoots, diverting his girlfriend if she happened to come to the studio. Peter all but twitched with nervous energy, and the models he worked with were obsessed with their appearance and the impression they made. Once, while I was high on a stepladder (to be out of the picture frame) under huge lights daubing a viscous clear gel (a substitute for water, which evaporates too quickly) on a model wrapped in a luxurious towel, I realized the idiocy of the situation. I could no longer see fashion as an art form; for me it became an empty, insipid goal and a crass business.

While I was working for Peter I was living with my brilliant brother, Tony, who'd transferred to Columbia University in uptown Manhattan. I rode my bicycle five miles from 125th to 25th Street and back each day. Tony and a band of similarly minded students were socialists, daily absorbed in complex historical-political-economic-sociological analyses. Preoccupied, Tony consistently neglected Susan, his sweet and simple wife, who was a talented dancer and who loved him dearly. Tony missed her recitals and other small daily reciprocations, until after years of trying Susan finally left him. His two other marriages would have similar conclusions. Although his absorption tripped up his relationships, doleful Tony never seemed to stop scheming. I couldn't envision living his life, a life where concepts overshadowed people.

In Great Neck, my father was working longer hours yet making less and less money. Cold War embargoes cut into his business; an animal rights movement that encouraged consumers to buy artificial furs cut into his business. My dad's largest buyers hired their own full-time fur brokers. That cut into his business severely. Dad had graduated from law school but had accepted his uncle's offer to take over the then-prosperous fur brokerage business. At home, his dusty college law books lined the top of our bookshelves, and as his business ebbed, he'd occasionally gaze at them and

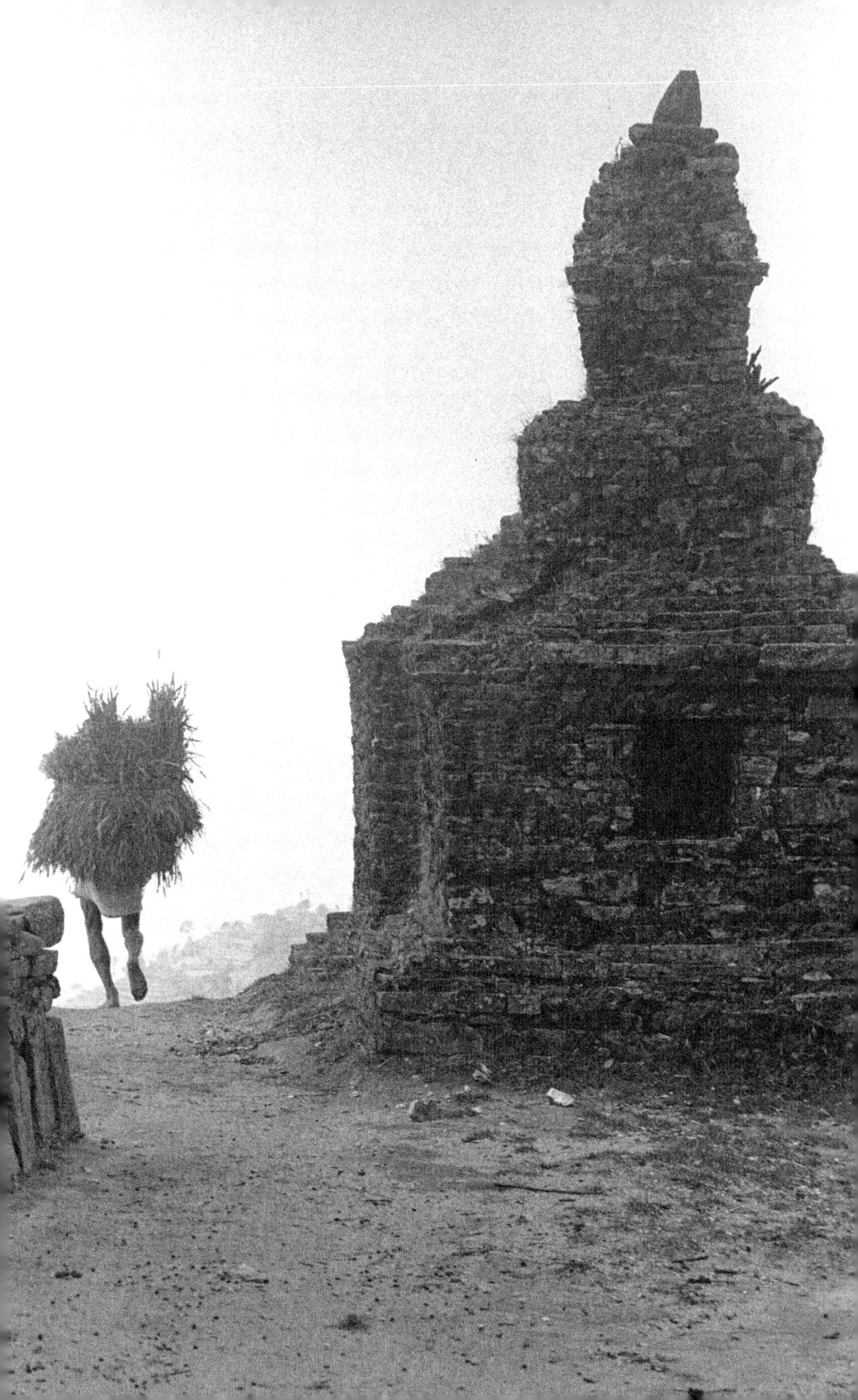

regret not having become a lawyer. But it was too late. He laid off a few employees and worked 14-hour days. On the weekends, sitting at a desk in the corner of our living room, he made long business calls, his loud, intense, almost desperate voice filling our apartment. Although he was paying his employees more than he himself earned, my father somehow kept alive a hope that he would revive his flagging business. Weekdays I'd see him with a heavy head and bent back returning home with feeble steps and all life's troubles in his gentle eyes. My heart cried to see him so drained and disheartened.

Smith was famous, Oliver was wealthy, yet their lives were in ruins. Tony's intelligence hadn't helped him; Dad worked harder than anyone I knew and was comforted by neither success nor happiness.

"What should I do with my life?" I descended the world's tallest mountains in the midst of a premature midlife crisis.

With those monks, an enticing realm beyond the little world I knew had wafted past—a tiny realm that mysteriously included everything, like a fisheye lens. But I knew a life of renunciation wasn't for me. It was too difficult. I wasn't ready for such a radically austere lifestyle.

The promise of my future—for happiness, fame, wealth, adventure—had been pitilessly sabotaged by my ruminations. I felt trapped and hollow; my goals were as substantial as a vapor trail. Scythed and husked, my life lay naked before me, generating a despair that choked any positive thought.

I'd been lost once walking back to summer camp through a birch forest, and I now had the same grim feeling that no amount of hope would help me find my path, no amount of assuaging could hide the abomination of desolation within me. The feeling of bleakness was intolerable. I was sick with longing.

> *How weary, stale, flat and unprofitable*
> *Seem to me the uses of this world!*
> — William Shakespeare

As my mood plummeted, I was desperate for relief. Wild longings for a different life hammered away in my heart. But all I could do was to descend both the psychological and physical mountain.

Therefore I loathed life, since for me the work that is done under the sun is evil: for all is vanity and a chase after the wind. And I detested all the fruits of my labor under the sun ...
— Ecclesiastes

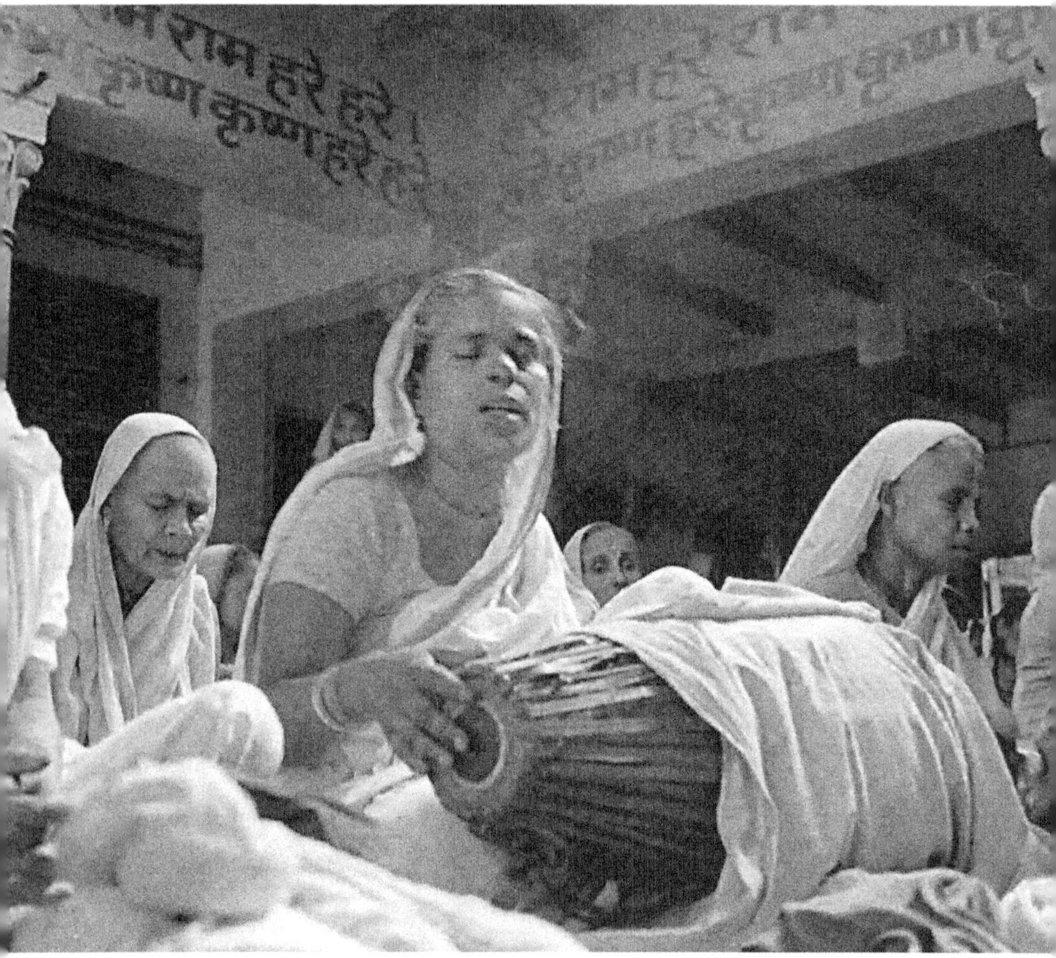
राम हरे हरे
कृष्ण कृष्ण हरे हरे

CHAPTER FIVE

Immersion

Two days and two nights on a dirty train and a bumpy, cramped ride on an antediluvian bus brought John and me to Vrindavan. It was past midnight, July 17, 1971. I was twenty-one.

Ashrams were locked, streets were deserted, and the only noises were the occasional soft grunts and shuffles of dozing animals. We slept on a sandstone ledge outside an ashram and woke the next morning to a symphony of birds and the common bustle of Indian village life. A woman bent low to sweep the unpaved road with a short, stiff, straw broom, raising billows of dust; a man washed his clothes by pounding them against a large flat rock; a girl coaxed flames from a small cow-dung fire, preparing to cook breakfast for her family; a salesman pushing a cartful of fruits meandered by, shouting about his goods; a boy on a clunky farmer's bullock cart lumbered past; men balancing milk jugs on both ends of a long stick that straddled their shoulders struggled by, looking down and bouncing the weight as they walked; school children in dark blue uniforms gleefully ran to their classes along sunlit roads.

Yet there was something different about Vrindavan. The air, sweet and caressing, carried song—the washerman's lilting tenor, the sweeper woman's warbling soprano. The moment I stepped into the street, the chant "Jaya Radhe!" was directed toward me from a smiling, elderly woman. She walked past in a white sari, her right hand in a small white cotton bag. I didn't know what either "Jaya" or "Radhe" meant, or how to return this friendly greeting.

Using sign language and broken Hindi, John and I found an elderly resident who spoke English.

"We'd like to rent a place to stay in Vrindavan," John told him.

"Yes, yes, I can arrange, I can arrange," he said with a wiry grin.

A couple of hours later, with our loaded backpacks on our backs, John and I walked with him along the dusty, cobbled streets to a rental.

"I have traveled all over India," he told us as we went. "And I see Vrindavan is the best place. Best place."

I glanced at John, who was listening politely.

"In other places," the old man continued, "in the cities, in the ordinary towns, the people's hearts are heavy. So many responsibilities they have, so much worry, pressures. They cannot escape. Prisoners—all the men, women—they're life's prisoners. Here, in this place, you will find the people are more free. Not so burdened by family, job, endless duties." He looked from John to me, smiling, "You will see."

After turning enough corners to make me lose my sense of direction we finally stopped walking. "Here it is," he said. "This is a good location—just a couple of minutes from the river," and he pointed down the street to our left, "and only a few steps from the Radha Raman temple!" and he pointed to our right, where I could see a sign announcing the entrance to the famous Radha Raman temple.

By that afternoon we'd rented it, a fine, three-story house for fifty rupees (about seven U.S. dollars) monthly. The house's one drawback was its pitch-dark bathroom and the bat family that lived in it. I thought bats avoided crashing into things by using ultrasonic echolocation, but these Vrindavan bats didn't. After a couple of them had flown into my face, I noticed their flying altitude was four feet and higher, so I began crawling into the bathroom, remaining crouched while in there, and crawling out. If I accidentally stood up, a bat would inevitably dash into my head. To feel those furry, bony, muscled lumps hit, be momentarily stunned, recoup and then fly off was absolutely spooky.

The top floor of our new home was hotter than the average outdoor temperature of 110 degrees Fahrenheit, but since any hint of a breeze only reached the top floor, John and I stayed there. The day after we moved in, we both got pinkeye from the soot that had poured into the train windows during our trip. Our elderly friend got us some medicated eye drops.

"I'm going to bathe in the Yamuna and wash my eyes in it too," John, ever the experimenter, said. The Yamuna, a holy river that flowed around Vrindavan, was supposed to be purifying.

"I'll keep up with the eye drops," I said, and put a couple more drops in each eye. As fate would have it, John's eyes cleared up before mine.

Pinkeye made my eyes tear continuously, acute hay fever made me sneeze often, my nose ran continuously, and the heat made me sweat profusely. For three days, between sneezes, I lay motionless on my back under a mosquito net—which stopped swarms of flies from reaching me but also stopped any vestige of a breeze.

An incapacitated mess, I wondered, "Why is garbage and rubble strewn throughout this crooked and crumbling town? Who would ever think with longing of this place with its fetid stench from the open sewers that line the streets and the dust so thick it catches in your throat? Who would want to cohabit with bats, mice and rats, or dwell in the dismal, stale rooms with their chipped plaster and tyrannical heat or bathe in the filthy brackish water of the river? Who could be inspired by the scores of sullen, sneering young men lolling in the streets? Who would even want to *visit* this place?"

When I was mobile again, though, in the relative cool of the mornings and evenings, camera in hand, I took to the streets and alleys of Vrindavan, a Mecca for Vaishnavs—followers of Vishnu. Our elderly Vrindavan friend had explained that I should return the oft heard "Jaya Radhe!" with a "Jaya Radhe!" of my own, which I did with caution at first, like dipping a tentative toe in a swimming pool. One morning while John was shopping for our fruits, vegetables, and yogurt, I tagged behind a few "Jaya Radhe!" women to a temple where 150 widows in white saris sat for three hours chanting Hare Krishna, Hare Krishna, Krishna Krishna, Hare Hare/ Hare Rama, Hare Rama, Rama Rama, Hare Hare. Half the women listened as the other half chanted, and then the roles reversed. Their feeling for the song more than made up for any lack in melody or harmony. They sang like this,

I learned, every morning throughout the year. I wondered at the softness and satisfaction in their faces, at their concentration.

In the afternoons, I saw these same women scattered throughout the town, giving water to pilgrims, cooking rice, begging from shopkeepers, cleaning with those absurdly short brooms, offering prayers in temples, talking with friends, drying or gathering dry cow-dung patties. They seemed secure in their apparently impoverished lives. Decades later, I learned that estranged families sent their widowed, childless women to Vrindavan; even "modern" families abandoned these burdensome women on God's doorstep. But the widows I observed in those early years seemed grateful to be in Vrindavan. At least some of them appeared to have declared their independence from the rigid caste hierarchy and petty family squabbles that often pervade Indian society, and from ambition and its complexities. It was clear to me, even with my nascent spiritual senses, that some had even reached a rare point of satiation with material things and had moved into a more transcendent world. As I saw them serving their sister widows, they seemed angelic to me. None of the grasping neediness often seen in the poor was visible; they really seemed selfless. I even saw some of these widows giving portions of their rations to hungry dogs and cows. And they seemed spontaneously joyful, having embraced the humility of their circumstances. I was inspired as I watched them, these few evolved human beings, and I was not alone; other Vrindavan residents seemed exceptionally fond of them.

Like the monks in Nepal, these widows opened me up to an alien paradigm. Perhaps social status—through academic accomplishment or a prestigious position (or a position gained through one's husband)—wasn't necessary. Perhaps things weren't what mattered. Instead, perhaps like these widows, I could learn to have the strength to live in a place of "enough"—a place no one in my world knew existed let alone desired. It was a place I wanted to explore. If I felt complete within myself, greed and envy would have no place in me, and ambition would become meaningful only when I strove to better myself in the moment, doing whatever I did in the best possible way each time I did it, conscious and focused on making it of value. Fame would become irrelevant, I wouldn't use knowledge to prove myself, and power would be used solely to help others.

In that place of enough, I would know that I mattered, just as, it seemed, these widows knew they mattered. They mattered not from gathering attention of any kind but by living and mining a rich tradition. Perhaps, freed of smugness and self-approval, I too could be at ease with life and perhaps even my death one day. I could learn to be amiable, mellow, disciplined, restrained, honest, tolerant. I could put my being in order. Such rumination, sparked by the Vrindavan widows, challenged me: perhaps they had something I was unaware I lacked. Perhaps I was missing something.

The Vrindavan residents' sincere devotion and the atmosphere of service and worship that permeated their town affected me deeply. I had come as a removed photographer to observe and document, as one might observe and document dolphins in the wild, but inside I was lurching about in an ocean of uncertainty searching for landmarks. Some faraway dike in my consciousness had cracked, and a new openness to alternative notions was starting to trickle through.

Who was the elegant, graceful woman who danced carefree through the streets and alleys of Vrindavan, who peeked at me from among the fervent, singing widows or the sincere supplication of pilgrims or from the children playing in temple courtyards or who sat among the mystical and alluring rites? She was a stranger my mind distrusted but my heart yearned to know—a sublime confidence who vanished before skepticism, suspicion, and disbelief.

In Vrindavan, that elusive person—faith—was nearly palpable. She was present in the services in the temples (there were five thousand temples, from five to five hundred years old, from vest-pocket to palatial, from simple to ornate). She was present in the evening worship on the banks of the sacred Yamuna, in the shops selling devotional paraphernalia, and especially in the reverence of the town's residents. These people, as a community, had set their hearts on divinity. I saw that, although they were at the mercy of the sweltering heat, or the pains of aging or poverty, they could tolerate these because their faith gave them the hope of being united in spirit with a supernatural presence.

I still denied that presence. My denial, I was realizing, was my armor; it allowed me to deflect a barrage of difficult questions. But it didn't answer those questions. It protected me from charlatans, yes, but it didn't fill my emptiness or give me direction. Doubt served a purpose, but it also prevented me from trusting anyone or anything. Without trust, how could I ever be happy?

One night, after an argument with John about some green beans that I hadn't cooked to his liking, I left the house where we were staying, walked the short distance to the Yamuna and sat alone on the bank. It was then that I felt how much affection I had for this place. Just its ether was soothing. The soft night breeze, the silky river, the gentle sounds and exotic smells, the devoted people, all felt rarefied and all embraced me.

If that dancing woman of faith was an ever so slight softening of the heart, an allowing, an opening, an acknowledgement of a possibility, then it meant I was stepping out of my skepticism into … what? The impractical? The unbelievable? The unknowable? It was bewildering.

Prabhupada's students had established centers in Calcutta, Delhi and Bombay. When they traveled between them, Vrindavan, ninety miles south of Delhi, was a natural stopping point. Since John and I knew which ashram they would stay in during their visits, we'd go over regularly to see who'd come. One day Brahmananda Swami, a burly young man in the renounced order, was there. Brahmananda invited us to join him for *parikrama*—a walk on the path that encircles Vrindavan. While John, who didn't enjoy walking, stayed back to photograph Vrindavan's downtown area, I joined Brahmananda. As we went I asked him about a Bhagavad-gita verse where Krishna says to Arjuna, "Never was there a time when I did not exist, nor you, nor all these things."

Brahmananda said, "No, no, that's not how it goes. Krishna says, 'Never was there a time when I did not exist, nor you, nor all these *kings*—not things.'"

"What does that mean?"

"Bhagavad-gita was spoken on a battlefield where kings had assembled to fight. Krishna was telling Arjuna that he, Krishna, was eternal, and that Arjuna and all the warriors on the battlefield were also eternal."

"They're eternal in the sense that the soul never dies?"

"Yeah."

"But I think that things are also eternal—their form may change but the elements that made them are never lost," I said, more to save face than to argue philosophy.

54   CHAPTER FIVE

"That's another point," Brahmananda said. "In the verse you're talking about, Krishna's talking about the existence of the soul beyond the demise of the body."

"Oh, okay."

Another of Prabhupada's students who visited was Giriraj das, who had a childlike simplicity that belied his intelligence. After graduating cum laude from Boston's Brandeis University, Giriraj had joined the Hare Krishna movement, much to his parents' dismay. His parents had offered him a million dollars if he would leave, but Giriraj was not allured. He remained firmly convinced about his path.

The gaunt Subal Swami was a distant, dour, taciturn twenty-year-old who avoided company and had a wide-eyed stare that seemed to harbor some secret fear. I kept a distance from him.

One especially hot day, Yamuna Devi (who'd screamed when she'd seen me in Bombay and who, like the others, was visiting Vrindavan for a few days) and I sat like water buffalo in the cool waters of the Yamuna River. With heartfelt gratitude, Yamuna spoke of Prabhupada and his teachings—how a spark of divine presence was within every living entity and how understanding this presence unified all beings, breaking barriers caused by gender, race, religion, nationality, economic status, and species. Spiritual life, she said, was inclusive. Yamuna spoke of how Prabhupada was complex yet simple and how he embraced unity along with diversity. Prabhupada, she said, loved Krishna.

At another time and in another place, on hearing such a rhapsody I would have countered with severe questions: "But how do you *know* a divine spark is present? Have you ever seen it? Has anyone ever seen it? What's the evidence?"

But this day, with only our heads bobbing over the broad expanse of the clear, dark water, as temple bells and gongs sounded in the distance and scents of dinners cooking over open cow-dung fires drifted past and a few merry children ran along the riverbank flying small paper kites, I let it go.

Yamuna, next to me, broadly smiling, straightforward, expressive and earnest, coaxed a laugh out of me—she somehow made me laugh at my own reluctance. "When all was said and done," I thought, "what do I know, anyway?"

Oddly—very oddly—it felt good to say, "I don't know, I just don't know." I hardly knew what I thought about anything.

One afternoon, Yamuna, John, and I were together in Loi Bazaar, Vrindavan's shopping center, when Yamuna, smiling sweetly, shamelessly (her word) said to John, "I saw gorgeous little deities in a shop; could you buy them for me?"

Without much hesitation, John benevolently said, "Okay."

"Wait a minute," I thought, "how much do they cost? What do we get in return? Are we being taken advantage of?" But before I could say anything, Yamuna had taken John to a deity shop a few steps away and brought out the deities she'd chosen and set aside. In another few seconds, they were Yamuna's and she was so gleeful that I didn't find the heart to voice my concerns.

"We want to publish a book of appreciation of Prabhupada for the occasion of his upcoming seventy-sixth birthday. Can you two go to Calcutta to oversee the book's design and printing?" Gurudas, Yamuna's husband, asked John and me after he'd learned that we had publishing experience.

John readily agreed but I was less inclined. I had a pleasing daily routine of grocery shopping and cooking, exploring and photographing different aspects of Vrindavan, and in the evenings, both John and I loved sitting under the stars with our elderly English-speaking Vrindavan friend and relishing parathas, fresh mangoes, and hot milk. We'd never eaten anything so tasty and satisfying. As we ate, we'd gotten to know our friend a bit. He'd told us that before moving to Vrindavan he'd been a successful businessman in Kanpur and had had a large bungalow and a large family.

"I have three sons, two daughters, and nine grandchildren now—everything I have," he said. "But I gave it up to live here alone, in Krishna's village."

"Why?" I asked.

"I'm old," he said. "I'm going to die soon enough. And when I do I'll be leaving them all behind anyway. They can't save me from dying."

"Yeah, those things can't save you, but your family can make you more comfortable. They can be with you and take care of you."

He chortled. "God is with me, God is taking care. At the fag end of my life I want to center on him. Family is good, but such a distraction!"

I couldn't at all relate to what he was saying, but he was so consistently carefree and jovial I had to think his choice might be working for him.

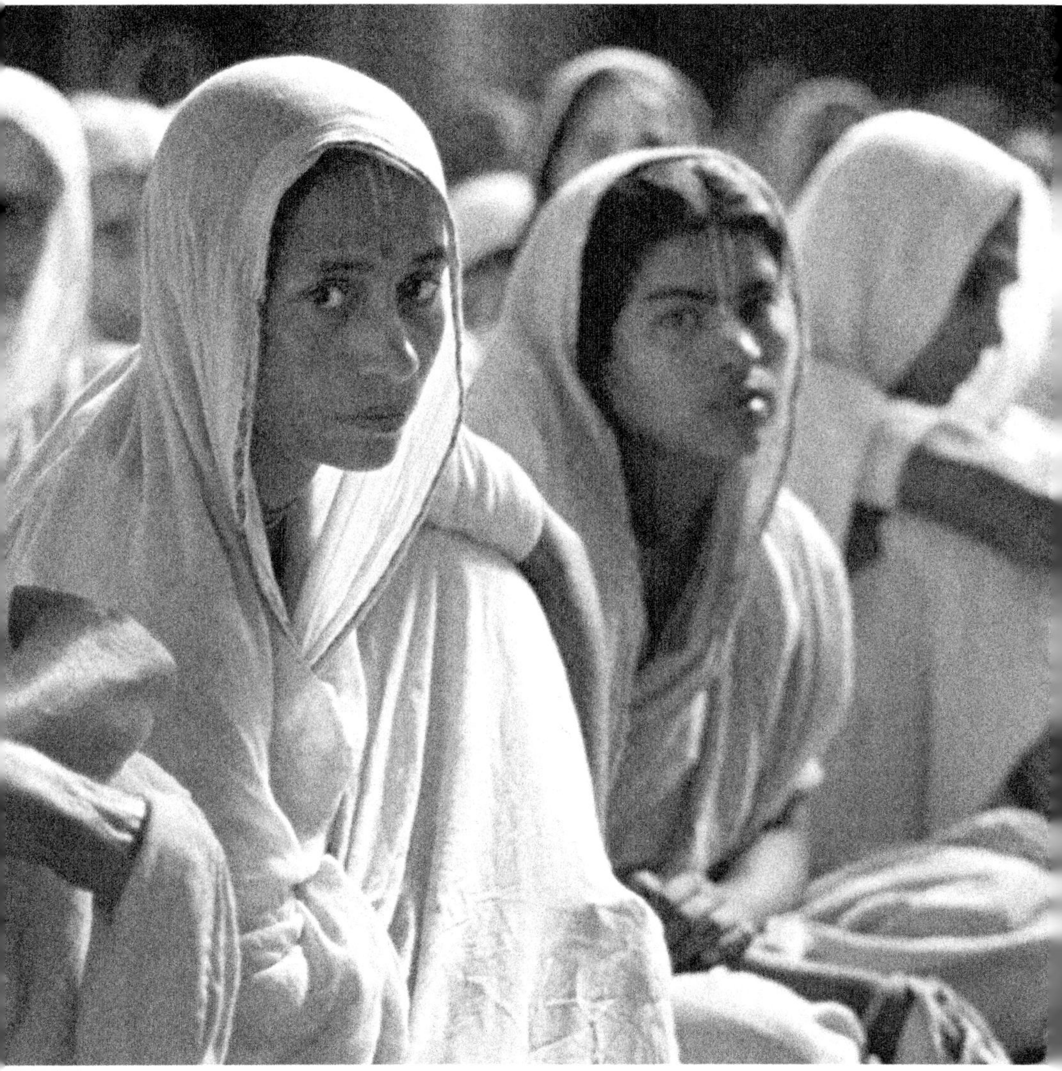

Another reason not to accept Gurudas's invitation to go to Calcutta was that Krishna's grand birthday celebration was coming, and converging on Vrindavan were hundreds of the most curious-looking, photogenic pilgrims: some had chiseled ancient faces, some had stiff matted hair hanging from their heads in long, thick ropes, some carried bizarre walking sticks, many held peculiar bundles made up of their meager possessions and all were startlingly serious about being in Vrindavan for the occasion.

"We can come back to Vrindavan for other festivals," John said. "Now it's time to move on." Reluctantly I agreed. We boarded a cramped, worn tonga drawn by an emaciated, bullied horse to go to Mathura where we would catch a Calcutta-bound train.

Leaving Vrindavan's warmth, my spirits were high. Peacocks were calling and parrots chirping. The sky was as translucent as water. Vrindavan had seemed to freshen the wellsprings of some clear energy in me that made the laboring wheels of the tonga cart and its straw seats and grizzly driver vivid and cheerful. Even the smell of the horse honed my appetite for life, and the world spread out around me was clearly a paradise. I'd begun to care more about creeping and crawling things and for the beauty that met me at every turn—in melodies, in flavors, in scents, in leaves and shrubs and petals, and even in the roadside hogs that nuzzled and scoured for food. Living in Vrindavan had penetrated and sweetened my whole being, and I felt kinder and elated with everything.

The pilgrims walking toward Vrindavan had springy steps that were full of intent—they were trekking to the holy land—and tenacity—they had to endure crowds, heat, decrepit shelters, questionable water and scarce food. I was charmed and inspired by them, and impulsively felt close to them.

CHAPTER SIX

Atlas's Burden

On the night of the 25th of March 1971, the Pakistani military junta based in West Pakistan launched Operation Searchlight to systematically kill nationalist Bengali civilians, students, intelligentsia, religious minorities, and armed personnel in East Pakistan. East Pakistan responded by declaring war on West Pakistan. Over its nine month duration, this war witnessed large-scale atrocities, the displacement of 30 million people and the exodus of 10 million Bengali refugees. When John and I arrived in Calcutta—250 miles southwest of East Pakistan—the war was five months old and a million refugees had taken shelter in the city. (The same month we arrived—August—former Beatles lead guitarist George Harrison and Indian sitar master Ravi Shankar responded to the plight of the East Pakistani people by organizing the first-ever supergroup benefit concert, which included Bob Dylan and Eric Clapton, at Madison Square Garden in New York City.)

To exit the Howrah train station, we wended our way along a foot-wide path between blankets spread on the station floor. Each blanket was a home for a family and their possessions—stoves, pots, dishes, produce, clothing, toys. Riding from the train station to the ashram, we saw roads lined with refugee families living in makeshift burlap tents, in five-foot-diameter abandoned concrete drainpipes, under awnings, in hallways, on sidewalks.

Any and every area large enough to be occupied was a home. The city was a gargantuan extended family with all manner of household activities going on: people bathing at street hydrants, cooking over small cow-dung stoves, squatting in semicircles eating meals on battered aluminum plates, men shaving, women braiding their yard-long hair, students studying, people cleaning their ears and brushing their teeth and sleeping, adults disciplining children, girls picking lice out of each other's hair, boys playing with marbles and chasing hoops with sticks, the elderly relaxing and chatting on wooden beds with woven coarse rope mattresses; we saw idleness and industriousness, mischievousness and piety, we heard laughter and playing and fighting and innumerable conversations. By comparison, teeming Bombay was deserted. Having never even imagined so many people living in such a way, I was aghast. What if a war had forced my family and me to leave our Great Neck home, perhaps never to return, to go to a foreign country with only the things we could carry? It was hellish just to consider.

The Hare Krishna ashram where Prabhupada's students lived was one of 69 such ashrams scattered throughout the world—in just a few years, Prabhupada's teachings and personal example had sparked a veritable Hare Krishna explosion. The Calcutta ashram was on a back street slightly removed from the city's hubbub and across from a small park with a lake. The building had remnants of classic British elegance—a sweeping wooden staircase, spacious double doors, high ceilings, large rooms, and a wide, long, marbled veranda that overlooked the street. Walking into the ashram, which occupied half the second floor, we were immediately in the temple room—significantly larger than the one in Akash Ganga. An interior room, it had no windows, but five doors—the main one we'd just walked through, two on the left leading to the veranda, and two on the right to the office and the cramped and blackened kitchen. Small, framed prints of paintings by Indian artists hung on the walls. The overall effect was homey and lived-in.

"You can stay in the women's quarters," I was told by a thin, saffron-robed young man, who showed me through the temple room, the office, the bathroom, and down a short servant's hallway, finally indicating that I should climb up a narrow, metal spiral staircase.

Sooty and exhausted, I did as directed, lugging my backpack with me. The quarters were large and adequately ventilated, but dingy. My roommates were Yamuna, who had gotten there a few days before, Kaushalya (a forceful young American who wore a white sari to indicate she'd separated from her husband), and motherly, soft-spoken Chitralekha, also a young American. I tried to reciprocate the welcome these women extended, but felt thoroughly displaced. While I had admired the Vrindavan residents' devotion, I was most definitely not a devotee myself. I started calculating how many days I'd have to endure these conditions. A week? Two at the most? I didn't think I could survive more than two.

We slept on straw mats on the floor, and the next morning Kaushalya woke me at two so I could join her and the other women in the temple room for japa. I'd never gotten up at two before; it never occurred to me that a person could or would get up at such an hour. I felt as if I hadn't slept. "Oh my god," I thought, "this is crazy!"

But in the spirit of being a worthy guest, I somnambulantly went downstairs, bathed, went back upstairs and located a sari. Due to its having been left to dry in a heap, this particular sari, which was the only one I could find, had innumerable wrinkles.

For a consummately practical person, the sari is not the dress of choice. I'd found an inadvertent description of it while reading a chapter in the Bhagavad-gita about God's Universal Form: "There is no beginning, there is no middle, there is no end to all this." I was about to don a piece of cloth that was six meters long! Another craziness.

I'd been watching women wrap saris around themselves on and off for a year, and I thought I understood the procedure. But watching and doing are two quite different experiences. In the wee hours of my first morning at the Calcutta ashram, with a mix of grogginess and gameness, I placed the faint blue sari before me in a pile on the floor. From its folds and twists it could have been water gushing from an artesian well. On my knees, I located a corner of it, stood up, tucked that corner into my slip and spun a quarter turn clockwise, tucking in the edge of the sari as I went and allowing its width to cover my slip and fall to my ankles. I continued turning and tucking in what could have been t'ai chi movements until I'd completed 360 degrees. Most of the sari was still on the floor, but now a stream of it wound around me and flowed back to its source. As a test, I tried to take a step. My legs separated six inches and caught, bound like a geisha's. I turned counterclockwise, undoing the sari as I went, and redid it, this time adding a generous gathering at the waist. Better. Now my legs could separate fifteen inches before binding. Buoyed by my progress, I made five-inch folds for the front pleats—but how many pleats? Five, six, seven, eight? As they bulged over my stomach, I felt like I was in the last months of pregnancy. Finally, there was the last remaining bit of sari—the end piece—did it go under or over the arm? And which arm? Whatever way I wrapped it, it refused to remain on top of my head.

There was no mirror for me to check my work. Feeling like I was ready for Halloween, I crept downstairs, through the bathroom and into the office that was situated between the bathroom and the temple room. Devotee men, asleep on mats all over the floor, were breathing heavily and snoring. Dead tired, disheveled and grumpy, I gingerly tiptoed past the sleepers by the light of a single candle, faintly recalling that I'd forgotten to brush my hair.

Suddenly, just before I entered the temple room, Yamuna, whom I hadn't noticed, stopped me. She looked straight into my eyes and with a Colgate smile said, "You'll look even *more* beautiful if you put on tilak."

"And I'm considered sarcastic?" I thought, as I peered back at her in the dimness. To my surprise, she meant it. I took the tilak—a small ball of holy clay—a little container of water, and the small mirror she handed me. I'd often seen devotees in Vrindavan apply tilak, but I'd never done it myself. It was more difficult than it looked. I made the paste too watery, the forehead lines too thick and a dandelion shape on the bridge of my nose instead of the graceful lotus-petal shape. When I finally plopped down on a mat in the dark temple room, it was with a substantial sigh of relief and one clear thought: "I hope no one thinks I'm going to do this tomorrow!"

Japa meant softly chanting the maha-mantra (Hare Krishna Hare Krishna, Krishna Krishna Hare Hare, Hare Rama Hare Rama, Rama Rama Hare Hare), while fingering wooden beads, not unlike a rosary. Vrindavan residents chant japa daily, but for me it quickly became tedious, and I passed time by observing the fervor of my companions. Kaushalya, sitting on a slight mat, eyes shut, back straight, swaying rhythmically as she enunciated each word of the mantra, was impassioned. Chitralekha's japa was as focused as Kaushalya's, but sweeter and slower. Yamuna's style made the words of the mantra into an intense song with alternating pitches (someone commented that her varied intonations and rhythms made her japa sound as captivating as a mockingbird's song). Observing these women helped pass time, but I couldn't possibly do the same thing ever again. It felt too machine-like. Where was individuality and creativity in japa? When John appeared hours later, Yamuna told him of my activities as if I'd been a willing participant. I didn't interject, perhaps from sleep deprivation.

One hazy morning a few days after we'd moved in, the other ashram residents and I were sitting in a circle on the spacious veranda. One by one, each person was taking a turn reading a passage from Prabhupada's *Bhagavad-gita As It Is* and briefly commenting on it. Usually during such sessions, out of a combination of unbelief and diffidence I'd excuse myself, but this day I stayed. And for me, on this day a bomb dropped.

The final reading of the morning was one of Prabhupada's purports in the Gita's first chapter:

> According to the sage Chanakya Pandit, women are not very intelligent generally, and therefore not trustworthy. So the different family traditions of religious activities should always engage them, and thus their chastity and devotion would give birth to a good population.

Outraged, I exploded inside. "So this is another patriarchal religion that oppresses and represses women," my mind screamed, "keeps them barefoot and pregnant, cooking and cleaning!" What was I doing in a place where women were denigrated and subjugated? I wondered about Yamuna's and Kausalya's and Chitralekha's sanity.

The class over, I immediately leaned over and asked Kausalya, "What's with this 'less intelligent' statement? It makes no sense—in my school, the girls did as well as boys, sometimes better." Even as I said it, I thought of my brilliant brother. But he was exceptional.

To my surprise, Kausalya threw her head back and laughed her carefree, cast-off-all-problems laugh. "I had the same reaction when I first heard that," she said. "I was ready to forget the whole philosophy. But then I went a little deeper. There are different types of intelligence, and so in Sanskrit there are different words that are translated as 'intelligence.' One is *'buddhi,'* which refers not to a person's IQ but to his or her ability to discriminate between matter and spirit. *Buddhi* means having analytical, discerning knowledge and is associated with male intelligence. But another Sanskrit word for intelligence is *'medha,'* which refers to mental vigor and power, wisdom, prudence and nourishment. *Medha* means 'the intellect illumined by love' and is associated with female intelligence."

"I don't know," I said, looking closely at her. "Are you trying to rationalize away sexism and male chauvinism?" Instead of answering right away, Kausalya flipped to a statement in one of the Gita's later chapters where Krishna says, "Among women I am *medha.*"

"Women's thinking tends to be less analytical than men's," she said, "and in general women work more on an emotional level, more with their hearts. Women often have a quality of heart and a type of intelligence men lack, which is why women often take more interest in spiritual matters than men."

I was still doubtful. Was I being appeased? Was this an extension of my high school days where cruel, mean students killed the life in me every day with their scorn and smugness? Only now women were confusing men's condescendence for transcendence.

Kausalya laughed again. "I was in exactly the place you were," she said. And with that she showed me another purport in another book where Prabhupada had written, "The Lord is so kind that he does not show special favor only to one who is a great philosopher. He knows the sincerity of purpose. For this reason only, women generally assemble in great number in any sort of religious function. In every country and in every sect of religion it appears that the women are more interested than the men. This simplicity of acceptance of the Lord's authority is more effective than showy insincere religious fervor."

"But still," I said, "won't describing women as 'less intelligent' be taken in the wrong way? Won't women be angry, just as I was, and won't men get the wrong idea?"

"Yeah, both those things happen, unfortunately," Kausalya said. "They happen too often."

The next morning my fears and her words were confirmed. Again we were sitting in a circle on the veranda taking turns reading Prabhupada's Gita, when Chitralekha received the book. Immediately, Revatinanda Swami said, "I'd rather not hear from a woman," got up, and sauntered out.

"Prabhupada wants women as well as men to speak," Achyutananda Swami said to Revatinanda's departing back.

Confusion ensued. Our group reading came to a sloppy end and the devotees dispersed, leaving me sitting alone on the veranda, confused and disgusted. Was this man so weirdly uptight because he thought himself superior to women? Did his unbearably patriarchal understanding come from thinking himself 'more intelligent?' What did his attitude have to do with spiritual life? I looked for Chitralekha, but it wasn't until several hours later that I found her.

"What did you think about that reading session?" I asked.

Chitralekha was petite, had a full-moon face and gentle, large, thoughtful eyes, beautiful in their truthfulness.

"Prabhupada encourages all his students to be all that we can be for Krishna. His mood is the opposite of the repressive, oppressive, suppressive, compressive mood of some of his followers," she said.

"Where did you go after the reading?"

"I went to pick flowers to make a garland for Prabhupada." She spoke with warmth and a delightfully confidential and enthusiastic tone.

"What an extraordinary response to sexism," I thought.

Revatinanda Swami was grave, scholarly, austere, and hardworking, and always either instructing others or busy setting a good example. He was also a young man attempting celibacy. Women threatened him and he responded, it seemed to me, by pretending that sexism was spiritual staunchness. Struggling to silence his secret voice of lust, camouflaging his weak and flabby ego with haughtiness, he was evading his countless fears and force-feeding himself into believing his own lie—that he was an honorable renouncer. How stressed he must be! I felt sorry for him, disturbed by what he subjected the devotees to, and dismayed that no one checked him.

Another Swami in the ashram, on the other hand, was rude to women and men alike. He'd come to India two years before Prabhupada's other students, and had lived in ashrams with Prabhupada's godbrothers, learned traditional rites and music and become fluent in Bengali. Initially thin, this young man was on his way to gaining a hundred pounds. He specialized in a quick and biting wit, sometimes at his own expense ("I gained my hips in Hyderabad, my thighs in Madras, my stomach in Bombay …") but more often at others' expense. If someone wasn't playing a musical instrument to his liking during kirtan, he'd say, "Gimme that thing," and grab the offending instrument. That only happened when he was the lead singer, as he only attended temple programs when he led them.

Besides personality challenges, there were also personnel challenges. Indian stoves, fuel, utensils and ingredients were so unusual for Westerners that cooking was knotty. Even shopping for ingredients was knotty, as Indian merchants automatically overcharged Westerners. So, devotees hired a local person to shop and cook. Although Calcutta was home to a large number of excellent cooks, the hired ashram cook wasn't one of them; the ingredients he bought and the way he prepared them were substandard. The devoted Giriraj was the first to get sick and weak. Others followed.

Although there was a hired ashram cleaner, the ashram was never convincingly clean. And the devotees argued. A week after John and I arrived, the two top ashram leaders walked from the office through the length of the temple room yelling at each other, slamming the veranda doors behind them. I expected to hear blows. There were arguments about money and books and donors and positions and behavior and worship; arguments about subtle philosophical points, Indian politics, Prabhupada's desires. No topic was exempt.

I couldn't understand why these people stayed—why they voluntarily suffered the daily indecencies of humiliation, tension, and posturing.

And I wanted no part of it. I had things to do. I didn't spend years protesting prejudice and discrimination against black people to put myself in a humorless enigma of inequality and enmity. More and more in my life I was questioning why I should do something, and staying in a sexist ashram made no sense. If John stayed, that was his business. I was leaving for good—after we'd finished the book of appreciation for Prabhupada that we'd agreed to produce.

Each morning John and I traveled miles to the printer to proofread and design the pages. One day, on the way, we discovered a famous Bengali sweet shop that specialized in *misti dahi*—a thick yogurt made from cooked-down milk sweetened with the juice of date trees. The sweet maker made the *misti dahi* in the clay cups he sold it in, and each cup had a stiff, heavy crust of frothy golden cream atop the cool, smooth, heavenly yogurt. From our first taste, *misti dahi* became our daily delight and one small respite from Calcutta's tribulations. Then, in the grimy, airless printer's office, I'd read the devotees' appreciations and feel uncomfortable with their hyperbole. Prabhupada was a learned gentleman, a perceptive and inspired person, but the devotees' words of praise were frenetic sentimentalism. Was it healthy? Was it cultish? Anyway, it wasn't my concern.

I dug out crumpled Rochester Institute of Technology admission forms from a neglected pocket of my backpack; I would rejoin the Bachelor of Fine Arts program. Just flattening the pages and filling in the little boxes on them was a breath of sanity. I was too late for the fall semester, but I still had time for the winter. Chitralekha, who knew my drift, said, "You can't leave now! Prabhupada is coming! You have to wait and see him!" That mantra, "Prabhupada's coming!" kept me hanging on in the Calcutta ashram by a frayed thread.

The morning of October 29th, 1971, Prabhupada arrived.

He got out of the black Ambassador carefully, cane in hand, and glanced up at the second-floor ashram veranda. His eyes were dark and encompassing, his expression kind, his posture erect but not rigid. When he saw us waiting for him in the street in front of the ashram, he smiled and, while still holding his cane, put the palms of his hands together in a gesture of respectful greeting. We followed behind as he entered the building and walked up the grand, ten-foot-wide staircase. In front of the temple room door, he slipped off his shoes, entered, walked before the altar and bowed down, lying prostrate before it as he had taught his students to do. Then he stood, looked at the altar, walked around the perimeter of the temple room, observing the various small paintings on the walls, and finally sat on the raised seat reserved for him at the back of the room, facing the altar. As we sat down in front of him, cross-legged on mats on the wooden floor, he more carefully observed us, his bedraggled Calcutta crew.

He said he was happy to see us again. And, he said, the first benediction of chanting the Hare Krishna mantra was that our hearts became cleansed. Later, listening to the recording of his talk, I wrote down how he defined a clean heart:

> There is no more such consciousness that "I am this," "I am that." The only consciousness is that "I am Krishna's." That is cleanliness of heart. As soon as we come to this platform, that "I am Krishna's" … Just like the *gopis*—all the inhabitants of Vrindavan—they were thinking, "We are all Krishna's." The central point is Krishna. That is the beauty of Vrindavan. All the inhabitants of Vrindavan, the elderly cowherd men, the boys, the girls, the trees, the river, the birds, the beasts—everyone—they are simply thinking, "I am Krishna's." This is Krishna consciousness. And as soon as we think otherwise—"I am Indian," "I am American," "I am this," "I am that," that is material consciousness. … Accidentally I have got this body in America or India or Africa or in hell or heaven. That is accidental. Or by my karma. But actually, I am not this body.

Sitting before him, tired and disgruntled, I was surprised. He'd tied the Vrindavan mood that I'd so appreciated to the essence of spiritual life. And that essence was simple: beneath all externals was a throbbing pulse of real life. Prabhupada's simple message—that we are ultimately spiritual beings—easily resonated with me. And it attracted me.

Then commenting on the book we'd compiled, Prabhupada thanked us and said, "My spiritual master knew that alone I could not do this great work. Therefore, he very kindly sent you all to help me in this task. Therefore, I accept you as representatives of my Guru Maharaja playing as my affectionate disciples. It is said that the child is father of the man. Kindly therefore continue to help me and act as my young father and mother in my old age."

From my years of high school experiences, I was hypersensitive to haughtiness and condescendence. And from some of Prabhupada's writings about women, I was on the lookout. But I felt nothing like that from him. More than appreciative, I felt his affection for all of us, even for me.

Stumbling down the steep mountainside of the life I'd known, I was peeking at the realm Prabhupada lived in, through his implicit faith in his guru and in the line of gurus that came before his guru, and ultimately in Krishna, God. My orientation shifted slightly away from college and from being the world's next great photographer to somehow hearing more from the diminutive endearing elderly gentleman I was sitting before.

I hadn't planned on being moved by Prabhupada, neither did I especially *want* to be moved by him, yet I was. He seemed so genuinely humble, so genuinely grateful. Seemingly effortlessly, Prabhupada opened a new window on the world and the breeze that blew in stirred something in me; it cleared some of my heady complexities and gathered my jumbled, inchoate thoughts and feelings into fragments of a cogent and compelling design.

After breakfast the next day, Prabhupada asked all of us to come to his room. We filed in and sat on the thin, sheet-covered mattresses, facing him. I sat in the corner farthest from the door and from Prabhupada, with no idea what to expect.

Prabhupada first noted that Chitralekha was absent and sent Revatinanda Swami to find her. When they were both present, Prabhupada spoke, his voice concerned yet confident. He talked not of the particular difficulties we faced but of basic spiritual knowledge, just as he had in the temple room the day before. At first his words seemed irrelevant—he wasn't addressing the very real tensions before us. But as I sat and listened, I discovered that his words were quite pointed.

Prabhupada said again that we were spiritual beings, eternal souls. Our body, mind, and intelligence cover the soul and were animated by the soul, but unlike the soul, were temporary.

The soul is eternal, Prabhupada said, and God—Krishna—is also eternal. And our relationship with him is eternal. That relationship is one of bhakti, devotional service to Krishna.

Prabhupada urged us to focus on our spiritual nature and not on the soul's transient coverings. He encouraged us to engage in spiritual activity—bhakti—by dedicating our mind, words, and body to Krishna's service without material motivation. Only in that way, he said, would we find lasting happiness.

Prabhupada's words hit me as unsentimental truth. He wasn't trying to impress us with his knowledge or seniority or even really win us to his point of view. He was telling us what he perceived as the truth. He didn't speak directly to our issues but gave us a framework with which to solve them. And he did it without making us feel guilty or ashamed or foolish. He appealed to our higher nature—*my* higher nature, too—a nature he knew beyond a doubt we had. His words were simple, clear, direct, and based on the Bhagavad-gita's teachings—knowledge that had been passed down from spiritual master to student and made relevant for each generation for millennia. He seemed sure that if we applied it, we'd overcome not only our immediate troubles but *lifetimes* of trouble. How was it that I found myself starting to take him seriously?

As he spoke, the mood permeating the room slowly shifted and the hard collective knot choking his students relaxed.

Prabhupada went on to say that the world is a place of suffering; suffering was impossible to avoid. Those who wanted to make spiritual progress tolerate. They forgive. They put aside their differences to serve a higher cause.

Prabhupada told us of his own trials when, at sixty-nine, he'd first left India to come to the U.S. (Sometime later I learned that during his ocean passage on a cargo ship he'd suffered two severely painful heart attacks. And after arriving in New York City he'd rented an office, which he also lived in, on 72nd Street and supported himself with great difficulty by selling his Bhagavatam books to bookstores. "New York is a very expensive city," he'd said, "but I am a poor man." That winter, of 1965–66, was the coldest in forty years and Prabhupada, who had never before even seen snow, was with-

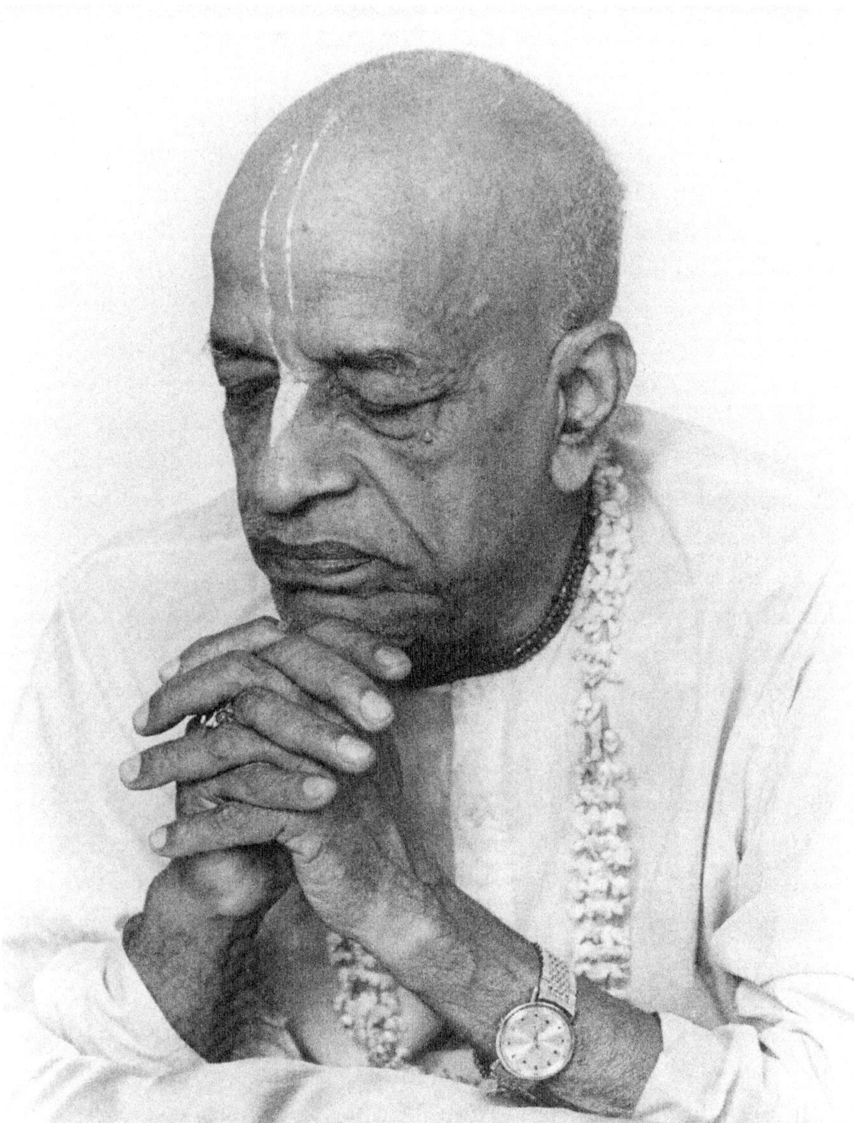

out proper cooking facility. He was eating only one meal daily and felt, he said, "night starvation." One day he'd returned to his office-cum-bedroom to find it had been robbed and his only valuables—his typewriter and tape recorder—stolen. Then, at the invitation of an acquaintance, he moved into a Bowery loft where, unfortunately, his roommate was a mentally unstable drug addict. This young man became crazed at one point and "showed some ferocious features" to Prabhupada. With nothing but the clothes he was wearing, Prabhupada had run down four flights of stairs and into the street to get help.)

At this morning gathering, Prabhupada didn't bring up any of the major and sometimes life-threatening difficulties he'd had after he left India. Instead, the example of suffering he gave from his own life—from his first months in the U.S.—was that he had to share a refrigerator with someone who kept meat in it. Although I'd only been vegetarian since I'd arrived in India six months earlier, Prabhupada said the word "meat" with such palpable disgust that, sitting in the corner listening, I got some glimmer of the weight of that austerity for a person of Prabhupada's caliber. Even the *idea* of eating meat was repugnant to him, what to speak of the smell and sight of meat near his food.

Despite every setback, Prabhupada had kept going. He was focused on fulfilling the desire of his spiritual master to give spiritual knowledge to English-speaking people. And we could also rise above trials, he said, but it would require our enthusiasm, confidence, and patience.

Prabhupada's message was so forthright, so real, so powerful and clear, so simple, practical, and earth-shaking—and so in my face—that he reached past my pettiness, grabbed hold of me at my core and tugged. He aroused some sleeping understanding in me where humankind is lovable and nature divinely beautiful. It was like seeing a splendorous view from a pristine mountaintop where pure air vaporized your mental troubles and allowed the soul to expand. I'd entered Prabhupada's room weighted down like Atlas carrying the world's burdens, but I left it floating. Blaming, accusing, and complaining, whimpering, bickering, and despair did not become us. We were meant for so much more. Prabhupada had lifted me above trivia, shown me that none of it mattered, and given me an inner vision strong enough to see everything in a different perspective. Hope brightened my horizon. If I stood on my toes and stretched my fingers I could touch the sky. My heart danced a little jig.

Except I wasn't the kind of person whose heart danced jigs, and it wasn't long before I was back to questioning who I was and whether I wanted to become someone else.

When I went upstairs to the women's quarters, I was surprised to see Yamuna there, sitting on her mat and furiously writing in a small book. Usually Yamuna's days were so full she didn't have time to even come to the women's quarters. As I entered, she looked up at me and said, "Jean, that was the most extraordinary talk I've ever heard! I'm trying to write everything Prabhupada said in my journal."

"Yes," I said, appreciating her seriousness. "It was transforming, that talk."

Later, I started wondering what had happened to me in the corner of that room. Other than Prabhupada's experiences with the drug-addicted hippy and the meat, I hadn't heard anything I hadn't heard before. But this time I was deeply moved. Why? Prabhupada's no-nonsense approach appealed to me. I liked it that he didn't pander to my sentimental ideas about happiness and how to pursue it, but that he installed the idea of how to find happiness on a whole new foundation, basing it on the Bhagavad-gita's teachings. Prabhupada was uprooting and moving a mighty mountain range of skepticism and emotional defensiveness to new bedrock. In such a process there would be wobbles, muddles, massive misunderstandings. It was to be expected—and it was bearable due to the outrageously defiant novelty and unparalleled momentousness of his message: concentrate on what's lasting, become less absorbed in what's transient. Perfectly logical conclusions—*if* the soul and Krishna existed.

The world I'd been living in, devoid of soul and God, was imploding. When I allowed for their existence I felt euphoric, rapturous, exhumed. Did that intimate that they were true? No. But I couldn't ignore the darkness and dread on the one side and the happiness and optimism on the other.

Before I came to India, John had experienced the transforming effect of Prabhupada's words and, not long after Prabhupada's talk that morning, decided to become initiated. I was surprised and unsettled.

"Are you sure? Why do you want to do that?" I asked.

"I just feel it's the right thing for me to do," he said. That was a vague and unsatisfying answer for me but, not wanting to get in his way, I didn't try to dissuade him.

I photographed the morning initiation ceremony in the temple room, nervously dashing here and there like a squirrel, capturing a variety of perspectives. Prabhupada always gave his students names that would remind them and others of Krishna, and John received the spiritual name Yadubara Das, meaning servant (das) of the best (bara) of the Yadus. Krishna had been born in the Yadus' dynasty (in what is today known as India) and was the best of them, so Yadubara was actually a name for Krishna.

For the occasion John had shaved his head, leaving only a small tuft of hair in the back (a *sikha*) like a young Vrindavan sage. In the temple room, kneeling before Prabhupada, John looked innocent, his Roman nose and angular jaw more pronounced without the rounding effect of hair. His eyebrows made a line over his sky blue eyes as he gazed at Prabhupada with expectancy.

John made his solemn vows, received japa beads that Prabhupada had chanted with and bowed down. He made a commitment to Prabhupada and to his spiritual life. He didn't press me to do the same, but I felt pressed. If I turned away from Krishna and Prabhupada now, I'd also be turning away from John—no, from Yadubara Das. The stakes were higher. I would wait and watch. My life was coming to a major juncture, but not yet. Could I dismiss the part of me who distrusted all that was invisible and intangible? Could I accept that God existed and this unusually earnest person, Prabhupada, could bring me to him?

Saraswati, the three-year-old daughter of Malati and Shyamasundar, regularly re-created a temple ceremony on the veranda just outside Prabhupada's room and would come into his room with the offered ghee-wick flame so Prabhupada could honor it by passing his hand over it and touching his forehead. No matter what else he was doing or who he was speaking with, Prabhupada respectfully did this whenever Saraswati came in, and complimented her on her dedication. Once, I watched from the doorway as Saraswati forcefully threw a fistful of pink rose petals at Prabhupada, seated five feet away, reading. The petals landed on the floor hardly a foot in front of her. Prabhupada looked up and, amused, said, "Not so hard!" The candid love between Prabhupada and this little girl charmed me.

Turning to me, Prabhupada said, "You are looking very nice in sari," his unexpected, loving words touching me like an awareness entering a dark, silent space.

"Why am I so moved by such simple praise?" I thought. Ordinarily, praise landed like a thud in me, but these words from Prabhupada softened and encouraged me. Something luminous in them entered me despite myself and lit me up just a little. I regarded him blankly, feeling a hope I'd never felt before; feeling a stiffened heart soften.

Pishima, Prabhupada's younger sister, who looked startlingly like Prabhupada, often came to our Calcutta ashram. She had lively eyes and was gentle, soft-spoken, and genial. "When we were children," Prabhupada told us, "my sister and I used to daily visit the Radha-Govinda temple across the street from our home."

"How diametrically different from what I did as a child!" I thought.

"We were standing for hours together seeing the Krishna deity," Prabhupada continued, "and that is the inspiration of our devotional life." He explained that his father worshiped a deity of Krishna in their home and, "When I was five or six years old, I requested my father that, 'Father, give me this deity. I shall worship.' So father purchased for me little Krishna, Radha, and he gave me, and my sister and I were imitating. Whatever foodstuff we got, we'd offer to Krishna and eat. In this way our lives developed. What I am doing, it was all taught in our childhood by our parents, my family."

Clearly, from their foundational years, Prabhupada and Pishima were imbued with godliness, just as I was imbued with godlessness during my foundational years. I wasn't obliged to accept my old foundation. But was this new world I was dallying in real or mythological? Would I get cheated and hurt in it?

Prabhupada said that whenever he and Pishima encountered obstacles in their play, they would pray for help. "I used to fly kites with Pishima when I was young," he said. "Her kite always flew higher than mine and that made me angry. One day I flew my kite from the roof. My kite flew higher than hers until she started chanting, 'Govinda, Govinda, help me!' Then her kite flew higher than mine." Envisioning young Pishima's and Prabhupada's convivial childhood play, I was delighted.

Pishima loved Prabhupada dearly, not only because he was her brother, but also because he'd given us spiritual shelter. In our tiny ashram kitchen, she expressed her love for Prabhupada and for us—her spiritual nieces and nephews—by cooking. Her dishes were delicious except for the traditional

Bengali ones that contained mustard oil. Those had an overpowering mustardy taste that didn't appeal to me. Prabhupada told Pishima that he liked everything she made but her mustard oil dishes were difficult for him to digest. I laughed when I heard Pishima reply, "You can digest nails if you want to!"

Pishima hid a bottle of Ganges water under a fold in her sari and often produced it to cheerfully splash us with holy water. Because I usually had my camera with me, around Pishima I was always on guard, ready to try to protect it from her divine deluge.

Yadubara and I went into Prabhupada's room to meet with him, just as we had in Bombay when I'd first arrived. Yadubara asked Prabhupada if he should complete his master's thesis for Rochester Institute of Technology (RIT).

"How long will it take? Prabhupada asked.

"Three or four months."

"Yes, why not?" Prabhupada said. Then he asked me about my parents.

"They're both atheists, Prabhupada," I said.

"Do you have a brother?" he asked.

"Yes, and he's an atheist too, and a communist."

"How did you come to be here?"

"By your mercy," I said because it sounded like the right thing to say, if only partially true—after all, it was by Vrindavan's and Yadubara's influence, too. Yet, sitting before Prabhupada, I knew that neither Vrindavan nor Yadubara had evoked my excitement for spiritual life the way he had.

"No," said Prabhupada, "it was by Krishna's mercy that you came."

Krishna's mercy notwithstanding, neither Yadubara nor I liked living in the ashram. In spite of Prabhupada's stirring talk and some practical improvements made under his direction—like augmenting our diet with cheese—ashram life was difficult. To transform theory into practice was a slow, tricky, and often halting process. Yadubara explained our feelings to Prabhupada, who commiserated: the Calcutta ashram was not the best place for newcomers. "But," Prabhupada said, "isn't it more difficult to live outside the ashram?"

"Well," I thought, "it wasn't more difficult in Vrindavan, but in Calcutta, yes, it would be. Renting a place here would strain our finances and, unlike Vrindavan, our neighbors' habits would be a disturbance." But we didn't need to consider alternatives—along with Prabhupada and most of the other Calcutta devotees we were going to Delhi on November 10th for another pandal program.

I was being tossed by a turbulent sea: attracted to Prabhupada yet disturbed by some of his followers, wanting to pursue my chosen path yet aware of its shortcomings, attached to Yadubara yet unsure of his choice of Krishna consciousness. I hadn't thought of telling Prabhupada, but I'd mailed in my RIT admissions forms, and Delhi was a little closer to RIT than Calcutta. I'd made no commitment to Yadubara or to Prabhupada, and was open to options.

On his arrival in Delhi Prabhupada was greeted like a homecoming hero, garlanded and escorted from the plane to a seat of honor by Delhi's Mayor, Lala Hansraj Gupta (known affectionately as Lalaji), and other dignitaries. Sitting cross-legged on a small raised wooden platform on the tarmac just yards from the plane, Prabhupada addressed his welcomers who, in business suits and with solemn official expressions, sat before him on plastic chairs. Squinting under the winter sun, Prabhupada spoke of the spiritual culture that lived beneath the surface of present-day India and explained that birth in India was accompanied by an obligation: its people were meant to offer their wealth of transcendental knowledge to others.

A little later, he sliced through the vagueness of demigod worship and impersonalism (the belief that the supreme is a force without form or personality), both of which pervaded the thoughts of the pious in India, to present Krishna to press reporters:

> Reporter: So, sir, are we rightly understanding that by "Krishna" you mean some eternal principle, not as …
>
> Prabhupada: Not principle. A person—like you, like me.
>
> Reporter: A person?
>
> Prabhupada: Yes. Just as you are talking with me and I am talking with you—you are person and I am person. Similarly, Krishna is a person.
>
> Reporter: Person in the ordinary sense of the word, or …?
>
> Prabhupada: No. He is the Supreme Person.
>
> Reporter: Supreme?
>
> Prabhupada: Yes. Just like, we are sitting here in Delhi. Now, here is Lalaji. He is supreme personality, the mayor. [The reporters laugh.]
>
> Reporter: So, we can see and feel and touch him.

Prabhupada: No. I am giving an example: in India, the president is the supreme personality. You have to admit it. You may accept him or not, but officially you have to admit it. So, in this cosmic manifestation, there must be a Supreme Personality. That is Krishna. That is confirmed by Krishna and the Bhagavad-gita, *mattah parataram nanyat kincid asti dhananjaya*: "There is no superior personality than me," and we accept it. That is our Krishna consciousness: "Oh, Krishna is the supreme person." Our knowledge is very easy. We don't research. Krishna says that he is the supreme personality and we accept it. That's all. It is very simple.

Reporter: Can we see him, just as we see Lalaji?

Prabhupada: Why not?

Reporter: But with these eyes or the …

Prabhupada: Yes, with these eyes. Simply you have to purify yourself. Just like we can see Lalaji here, but if he goes in the street, nobody may recognize him. So, if a person does not know Lalaji, then even if Lalaji meets him, that person does not see him. Why?

Reporter: Question of eyes and knowing, sir.

Prabhupada: Yes. Then he has to prepare his eyes to see Lalaji.

Reporter: So, sir, how do we prepare our eyes to see?

Prabhupada: It is easy. It is easy. Suppose you say that, "I have never seen Lalaji," and if I say, "Here is Lalaji. Why don't you see?" and if you accept, what is the difficulty? If you say, "No, I cannot believe you. I don't think that he is Lalaji. Why is Lalaji walking on the street? He must be in a big, nice car." If you put all these arguments, then it is very difficult for you. But if you believe me that "Here is Lalaji," then the matter is very simple.

Reporter: The question is faith versus the …

Prabhupada: It is not faith. When I say, "Here is Lalaji," it is not faith. It is fact.

What Prabhupada presented hit me like a tsunami. Somewhere in the watery depths of my faithlessness an earthquake was erupting, sending massive tremors racing toward the shores of my consciousness. I could sense the swell, but didn't know where to run or what to do. Something far beyond my capacity to grasp was emerging in front of me, unasked for, irrepressibly beautiful, unreasonably reasonable, overwhelmingly compelling.

Prabhupada said:

> If you study yourself as a sample, a little sample of God, then you can understand God. Just like you take a drop of Pacific Ocean water, and you chemically analyze the constituents of that drop of water, then you can understand

what the constituent ingredients in the Pacific Ocean are. God and we individual souls are of the same quality. It is the quantity that distinguishes us. Just like we have got creative power and God has also got creative power. By your creative power, you manufacture an airplane to fly in the sky, but by God's creative power, millions and trillions of planets are floating in the sky. That is the difference between God and me. God is great. How great? Nobody is equal to him and nobody is above him. Everyone is below him.

But there remained that persistent nagging in me: the universe was a pointless, nature-made machine, and all beings were insignificant by-products that would be swallowed by the oblivion of death. There was no God. There were only atoms and the forces of nature. Yet, even while those dry, dismal thoughts hounded me, Prabhupada beguiled me. His powerful, logical arguments and absolute conviction were attractive, and even beyond those was his seemingly selfless caring. Formerly, I would have thought that people who didn't have power, fame, wealth, comforts, prestige, and sex as goals— people like the Nepalese monks and Vrindavan widows and Prabhupada—were fictional characters. But now for me to deny their existence might just be shirking reality. And for me to deny my attraction to Prabhupada would also be shirking reality. I could feel that attraction loosening atheism's grip on me.

In Delhi we were joined by the former temple president (i.e., charging rhinoceros) of the Brooklyn temple, who was on his way to becoming insufferably arrogant. One afternoon I overheard him telling a few others, "If Yadubara doesn't start wearing saffron cloth [indicating that he's unmarried] then I'll rip those white clothes off him and put saffron on him myself!" Fortunately, Yadubara, more uncertain than usual but unfazed by such talk, remained his friendly, easygoing self.

I marked how the former temple president's approach to the relationship between Yadubara and me was a diametric contrast to Prabhupada's approach. The previous month, when we were in Calcutta, Prabhupada had spoken about marriage several times during his morning lectures. Once he leaned forward on his seat, his eyes closed in concentration, and said:

> This man and woman living together, unmarried, this is not civilized life. This is animal life—no commitment, no loyalty. In the Twelfth Canto of Srimad-Bhagavatam, this boyfriend-girlfriend is mentioned: it is a symptom

of this age of quarrel and hypocrisy. Human life means that the boy and girl must get married and live together peacefully in Krishna consciousness.

Listening to Prabhupada then, I had a fuzzy feeling that what he was saying was relevant to me, but I never talked about it with anyone, and although he had ample opportunity, Prabhupada never said anything to John or me. One morning in Calcutta, when we were discussing something else in Prabhupada's room, John had casually said, "Maybe Jean and I should get married." Prabhupada, also nonchalant, said, "Yes, that is a good idea." After that, the subject of marriage hadn't resurfaced.

Before long, we were immersed in another pandal, much like the one we'd done in Bombay. But before it began, Yamuna, who'd made all the preparations for the worship at the pandal, became gravely ill. To recuperate she moved into a six-foot by four-foot walk-in closet that adjoined the room where the devotee women were staying. One morning I went to visit her in that closet. She was lying on her back on a thin mat on the floor of one side of it, and on the walls near her head she'd put black-and-white photographs of Prabhupada that I'd taken and given to her. I sat next to her cross-legged, and as we discussed what I could buy that might help her, suddenly she rolled over to offer her prostrated obeisances. I looked up and saw Prabhupada, barefooted, walking through the unoccupied women's room toward the closet where we were. He peered in the closet, his eyes shining like two black lamps, and said, "Yamuna Prabhu, you are not feeling well?"

"I'm always thinking of you, Prabhupada," Yamuna said.

"And I am always thinking of you," Prabhupada said. "You need to have a place with air and light so you can get better." Later that day, Prabhupada arranged a small room with a window where Yamuna could rest. Prabhupada was speaking before tens of thousands of people twice daily, managing an international society, and guiding his worldwide students; he was also lovingly reciprocating with one student's—Yamuna's—ardent love. I felt sheltered by his personalism.

Each evening at the pandal, a prominent guest—the Canadian High Commissioner, the magistrate of the Delhi High Court, the mayor of Delhi, the Indian defense minister—introduced and spoke a few words of appreciation about Prabhupada and his mission. And every evening, seated on the stage, Prabhupada lectured. The opening evening he told the audience how, before Krishna had explained the Bhagavad-gita to Arjuna, he had spoken it to the sun god, Vivasvan. Vivasvan had explained the same thing to his son, Manu, and Manu to *his* son, Ikshvaku. Krishna had told Arjuna that the system of knowledge described in the Gita came through disciplic succession—from spiritual master to disciple—but how in course of time it had been lost. Krishna was speaking the same knowledge to Arjuna, because Arjuna was Krishna's devotee and friend.

"Oh, no!" I thought. This harked back to God lifting Govardhan Hill with the pinkie of his left hand and a fetus learning of transcendence. Sun gods? Prabhupada unhesitatingly and unabashedly integrated the uplifting excitement of profound and sensible spiritual revelations with what was to me outlandish, bold contradictions of scientific knowledge and truths. Yet what smacked of mythology to me left the Indian people—and Prabhupada's Western students—unfazed. It made me question the line I drew between sweet transcendental vistas of reality and what I thought of as fanciful or mythological stories. Who was I to draw such a line? And how had Prabhupada developed such unflinching faith in an unseen order? How had his students crossed that line?

When I dismissed much of what Prabhupada said, at first I felt smug and superior in my understanding and reasoning abilities, as in "How could educated people believe such phantasmagoria? *I* certainly couldn't believe such stories." But on hearing Prabhupada present logical, profound understandings juxtaposed with those fantastic statements, and on seeing how Prabhupada's disciples and the Indian people accepted statements I summarily dismissed, I quickly felt growing and painful confusion. After a while I was in a churning sea of doubt about my former convictions.

One evening a young Westerner got on the stage with the devotees, took a microphone and challenged Prabhupada.

> Man: The Bhagavad-gita you are quoting is only 1500 years old …
>
> Prabhupada: You are speaking of the Bhagavad-gita. Do you know the process for understanding the Bhagavad-gita?
>
> Man: According to the research here [he holds up a scholarly-looking book], not only the Bhagavad-gita but also the Puranas [histories] were written down 1500 years ago …"
>
> Prabhupada: [raises his voice] You may accept the version of this scholar or that scholar, but for ourselves, we accept the words of Vyasadeva, the

compiler of the Bhagavad-gita and the Puranas. We accept the words of Sukadeva Goswami, the reciter of the Srimad-Bhagavatam, we accept the words of Krishna and Sri Chaitanya Mahaprabhu, the Supreme Personality of Godhead.

The young man did not budge from his position and began yelling at Prabhupada, who continued to respond strongly. Then, in front of 20,000 onlookers, devotees escorted the young man off the stage. I was in the audience with some Life Members and they began buzzing, "Oh, your guru became angry. It is not right for a saintly person to get angry." "A saintly person is always peaceful but your guru isn't." I looked at Prabhupada wondering what to make of the incident.

Giriraj, nearby, said to these Life Members, "Prabhupada just illustrated the process of how to understand the Gita: one must approach a spiritual master with an attitude of humble inquiry and service, not a challenging attitude. Prabhupada isn't sentimental and has little patience with people who only want to assert their own ideas. He's interested in protecting the foundation of faith, and some stereotyped idea of passiveness as saintly behavior is not going to stop him from doing that! He used anger as Hanuman, the great servant of Rama, used it—to serve the Lord." The Life Members were quiet and respectful. Giriraj added, "Anger has its place. As a sculptor might use a forceful tool, Prabhupada used anger—as a tool he could put down as fast as he'd picked it up."

Well, maybe, I thought. Or maybe Giriraj was making excuses for Prabhupada? I'd read about cults in which the leader does things that his followers attempt to rationalize and explain away. At the same time, what Giriraj had said made sense.

A few of the devotee men at the Delhi pandal vied for the honor of leading the singing. Prabhupada observed this jostling without comment until the last kirtan of the evening, which he wanted Yamuna to lead. One evening, Yamuna, who had told me that she was increasingly dismayed by the intensity of the men's eagerness, indicated to Prabhupada that her throat was sore and she couldn't lead. Although her point was clear—I certainly understood it—Prabhupada ignored it and, with a slight nod of his head in Yamuna's direction, repeated that she should sing. They were seated on different sides of the stage and again Yamuna, through sign language, indicated that she couldn't sing. Again Prabhupada ignored her message and indicated she should begin. Yamuna led the chanting.

During the final kirtan on the last evening of the Delhi pandal, Prabhupada put his small hand cymbals down, got up from his seat, and clapping in time, began joyously circumambulating the deities on the stage. When he came in front of them, he raised both his arms, making a sweeping, graceful arch, and began to dance, effortlessly jumping up and down in time with the music.

I was in the audience, transfixed. My camera dangled around my neck and a pragmatic voice inside my head said, "Lift your camera, put it to your eye and photograph. What are you doing! Don't be an idiot!" Another part of me, the larger part, was immobile. For enchanted moments I held my breath as an ineffable lightness, a discernible clearing of the ether, an opening of treasures to come uplifted me.

There are no photographs of that moment.

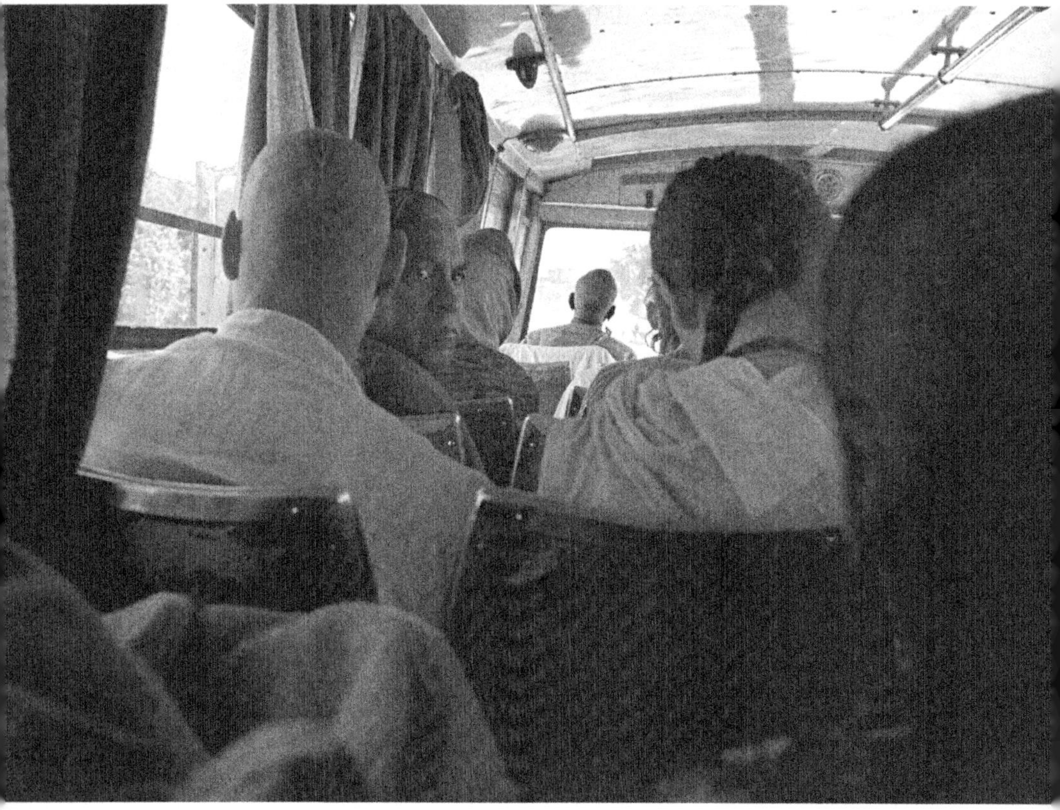

CHAPTER SEVEN

An Aristocratic Lady

Thirty-five of us rode a chartered bus to Vrindavan. We stayed at Saraf Bhavan, a large home a mile from the town center, and went on daily pilgrimages with Prabhupada — to Varsana, Radha's place on top of a hill; to the Yamuna River for bathing; to Govardhan, that hill Krishna had held aloft.

While looking at the protruding boulders, peculiar bent trees, and soft grass that decorate Govardhan, my nemesis, I heard Prabhupada say, "If Krishna has all strength, is it very difficult for him to raise a hill on his finger? That is the definition of God: all-powerful. So why should I think, 'Ah, this is all a story'? It is not a story. It is fact. If he is all-powerful, what is the difficulty for him to lift a mountain?"

Now, instead of dismissing his words, I found myself struggling to understand them.

I was intrigued. "God," Prabhupada said, "is supremely beyond our comprehension, and is surely able to perform amazing deeds that defy and even mock our comprehension."

But what was happening within me surpassed logic. Prabhupada's selfless and complete dedication to a pure devotional path—to bhakti—was kindling in me a desire to do whatever I could to please him. For the first time, I was starting to trust someone deeply. It was scary to open up, to make myself vulnerable. It was also uniquely uplifting and thrilling.

Not having faith, I thought, might just be missing out on a reason to live.

When Prabhupada's Ambassador car broke down he shifted to the front seat of our bus. During the long, bumpy rides, Malati, puttering in the back seats, would magically emerge to sway down the aisle with plates of colorful refreshments. Without complaint, Malati would serve, laugh, and offer apropos insights about this motley group of wandering believers I was part of. While we visited holy sites, Malati stayed back to cook. Once, when we were having lunch on the porch of an ashram, two hungry, snarling street dogs wandered near. Malati was about to shoo them off when Prabhupada stopped her, tore his bread in two and threw the pieces to the dogs, saying, "No living being should go hungry in Krishna's place." Prabhupada's caring delighted me.

I got swept up in the momentum of the pandal and this unique tour. Clutching the vine of faith, I found myself swinging into a mysterious realm of spirit, my eyes alternately wide open in amazement and shut tight in fear, hoping against hope that I would survive the ride, that I was doing something right and reasonable. *(Reasonable? To be a devotee of Krishna? No, I don't think so!)*

The faith I had in the unbelief, skepticism, and suspicion I'd inherited from my parents was becoming a noxious squatter who lived in my heart as if it owned me. Spiritual faith, I discovered, could not be trifled with. She was like an aristocratic guest in my home. If I was hospitable, if I made her feel welcome, if I respected her, she'd gladly stay and offer me a life so filled with varieties of loving relationships it was beyond my imaginings. But neglected or taken for granted or in the company of unpleasant people, she was gone—along with a sense of how small things depend on great things and how I cannot comprehend much in this world. When faith left, my sense of the mystical left with her.

Yet, faith was more than a house guest—she was a permanent resident within me who'd long ago receded to an inner room. As she slowly emerged, doubt was edged out along with his tasteless and flagrant decor. Faith began decorating with tenderness and beauty, warmth and impeccable good taste. A child's candor and wonder began to return to me—the unspoiled vulnerability and verve of innocence.

Faith carried me over a threshold: from material to spiritual causality, from the fantastic idea that life originated from matter to the fantastic idea that a supreme being was the cause of all life and all things. The atheistic and theistic concepts were both beyond comprehension, but when I looked at them squarely, the theory that matter combined to become conscious of itself and to form endless varieties of creation was not just farfetched, it also eradicated its purpose; it created a vacuum of meaning.

When I accepted a supreme being, the creation I formerly saw as devastatingly empty and purposeless filled with the extraordinary, like a barren field that's covered overnight in spring poppies, or a ravenous person sated by a hearty stew on a winter day. Faith explained why there was something instead of nothing as science and reasoning could not. And faith's explanation embodied joy. It affirmed that the everyday world I experienced was not all there was. Behind it all was the mystery of God's presence. That presence and the soul's presence could not be confirmed or denied by experiment, verified or nullified by empirical research, but the effect of my acceptance of them was palpable and good. I could not ignore that. That warm feeling and the satisfaction of my mind and heart did not prove spirit's existence. Then again, nothing disproved its existence either.

On my first visit, the piety of Vrindavan's residents had captivated me. This time, under Prabhupada's tutelage, I was captivated by the sweet, bottomless mystery of Krishna, the supreme cause of everything, who was a mischievous village child and who charmed his devotees—agrarians and cowherds. And who was to stop him? Who was to claim that God can't or shouldn't or wouldn't? Which audacious person could bar God from being among those he loved and who loved him without reserve? From doing whatever he wanted? I now shrank from taking that proud and foolhardy role. In Vrindavan with Prabhupada, the concept of an inconceivable all-attractive person made perfect sense. Certainly that person had created everything and was playfully enjoying himself. Certainly I was something more than matter and could have a deep relationship with that all-opulent person. Why not? I felt that Prabhupada's experience of Krishna was beyond faith and belief. Prabhupada was experiencing Krishna. Prabhupada was with Krishna. And his love for Krishna was evident.

Perhaps that person who effortlessly lifted a hill was also kindly lifting my doubts. I was not sad to see them go.

On the cold gray morning of November 29, 1971, two couples married: Mani-bandha and Kanta, recently arrived from America, and Yadubara and his girlfriend, Jean. Jean was also initiated.

Did Jean remember that only five weeks earlier she was prepared to leave ashram life for good? No, not really. Although her faith was dim and pliable, she was propelled by the euphoric impetuousness of youth. Did she grasp the tradition and culture she was entering? Vaguely. Jean was caught up by the place, by the circumstances, and by Prabhupada. Did she consider entering other religious traditions more natural to her upbringing? To her, the path mattered less than the guide. She'd found a guide. This was a singular moment, a silent sounding of inconceivability.

Before handing me my japa beads, Prabhupada asked, "What are the rules and regulations?"

"No eating of meat, fish or eggs, no taking of intoxicants, no gambling and no illicit sex," I said.

Four simple no's—but how revolutionary! This rare standard separated Prabhupada's movement from almost every other organization on earth. Had I stumbled into something crazily depriving? Or was it authentic? Something that would disappoint me or benefit me? Was I following my head or my heart? Or neither? Or both? It was dizzying.

I realized that observing the four prohibitions Prabhupada requested of all his students could avert untold suffering—the adverse health and ecological effects of meat eating, the wasteland of addiction, the emotional damage of sex out of wedlock. My thoughts were simplistic: "Why blur the senses, why cloud the mind, why be lust's lackey when just by abstaining I can attain God?" With uncharacteristic optimism I skirted the seriousness of these lifelong vows and the struggle inherent in bucking the entire thrust of modern life and plunged in. I would compete in the greatest of all contests: the inner frontier, the struggle against lust and greed. I would define myself against the temptations of an age.

Flushed with the beauty and consistency of Krishna consciousness, with the promise and potency of Prabhupada's presence in my life, I had unstoppable hope—I *could*, I *would* follow these rules and regulations for the rest of my life. Krishna, irresistible Krishna, was Prabhupada's. Prabhupada had the power to give him to me.

I accepted my vow to chant the maha-mantra with the same easy optimism.

Prabhupada, solemn, looked directly at me, his eyes as deep as a woodland pond. Full of guileless wisdom, those eyes that knew the secret of a rich culture penetrated the many layers covering me. I wondered what he saw in me and wished it was better; but anyhow, he was accepting me. Although he already had hundreds of disciples, at that moment it was just him and me. A long-lost individual was making a momentous, fateful promise. My soul glowed, my heart trembled.

"And how many rounds of japa will you chant each day?"

Nervous yet confident, I said, "Sixteen."

With that same direct look, Prabhupada said, "*That* is the minimum," and handed me my shiny, dark brown, smooth beads made from the holy tulasi tree from the holiest land of Vrindavan, the place where Prabhupada had once directed us and where my spiritual journey had begun.

As Prabhupada watched, Gurudas performed the marriage ceremony, intoning Sanskrit mantras and pouring clarified butter over a small fire in a two-foot square, sand-filled box. As part of the ceremony I put drops of water on my right palm, and the red mehndi lines Malati had drawn on my hand (a traditional art, but Malati hadn't used the traditional water-resistant henna dyes) started to run. Red water ran through my fingers, onto my wedding sari and spread into a six-inch Rorschach inkblot over my knee. I thought my knee had somehow started bleeding. Malati ran for a cloth, I dried my hands and swabbed the mess. Expressionless and without comment, Prabhupada solemnly observed.

Gurudas concluded with a talk on the relationship between husband and wife, saying that the husband was duty-bound to protect his wife. Hearing this, I squirmed inside. To me, "protection" sounded like a bedfellow to "restriction" and "repression." What was I getting myself into with this marriage?

But it was as if Gurudas heard my qualms. He went on to say that protection was not suppression. It was not stifling growth, as with a topiary, but freedom from disturbance so a woman could grow without hindrance. A protected woman was loved, honored, championed, cherished, and motivated to offer service to God according to her unique ability.

"I dunno about this," I thought. "But I guess Dad protected Mom. He paid for our apartment, food, clothing. He gave Mom the space to do things she loved to do." I sighed, relieved by the thought. Then it got worse again.

Gurudas continued, saying that the wife was subordinate to her husband. "Oh no, where's he going with this one?" I thought.

He explained that beneath its surface, women's subordination held weighty implications. As a source of inspiration to men, her subordination was a wellspring of strength where the inspirer was more powerful than the inspired. Gurudas quoted Prabhupada, saying, women 'are accepted as a power of inspiration for men. As such, women are more powerful than men.'

I wasn't interested in power and wasn't sure about a wife's position in a Krishna conscious marriage, but my trepidation lessened. I understood that marriage was a complex dance between two individuals and for Yadubara and me to learn the Krishna conscious steps to that dance would take some time. For now, at least, a successful marriage seemed doable and even an exciting way to offer service to Krishna.

We then threw whole, unpeeled bananas onto the fire, signaling the end of the ceremony, and kirtan started. The end of Yadubara's shoulder wrap and the end of my sari were ceremonially tied together, and we joined everyone else in circumambulating the altar, which housed the small brass Radha Krishna deities Yadubara had bought at Yamuna's request when we were in Vrindavan five months earlier. Smoke rose from the fire, the kirtan beat picked up, and Prabhupada stepped into his room. Sitting relaxed, he observed us through his open door. As I jumped and clapped and sang with abandon under his gaze, I felt my lingering reservations and old perceptions and the rationality that had previously directed my worldview all slip away. I was investing my heart and mind wholly in spirituality. I felt unbelievably present.

Now with the spiritual name Prabhupada had given me, Visakha Devi Dasi, servant of one of Krishna's Vrindavan companions, I had officially entered an unknown frontier with a leader who knew the tricky terrain. To do anything else, to go anywhere else with anyone else was unthinkable. Something inside me that had begun to yawn and stretch and twist since I'd arrived in India had become unshackled. Unabashed hope was dawning in my heart. I felt sheltered. I was completely alive and burned with desire for more life. The toxic vacuum of atheism no longer sucked all the special value from me and from how I viewed other beings. The universe was no longer awash in purposelessness. For the first time in my life I was completely happy. I was so happy I felt nothing could or ever would cloud my happiness. I was now Prabhupada's spiritual daughter. No one and nothing could ever break that relationship.

My feelings were so varied and intense I couldn't really deal with them. I was embracing all the glee, all the wonder that resided in everything. I looked at everyone present and they were beautiful. The blazing sacred fire filled my eyes with tears. Deep inside me gates were opening, one by one, revealing a vital area I couldn't afford not to reveal; releasing my love for that irresistible Person within yet well beyond my reach.

Not one family member or relative had attended my initiation-marriage, and except for Yadubara, no one from my school days. The only guests present were those who happened to be there—we hadn't invited anyone. Yet I missed no one. I had stepped out of my past so completely that I hadn't even informed those who'd been in it. Neither did I think of my future. The present filled my existence, and I wanted nothing but more of it— of Prabhupada, of the reality he presented, of the culture he propounded.

Now that I was not Jean but Visakha, not single but wedded, a flood of paradoxes floated through me—I was bound to vows, mostly ones contradictory to my upbringing—and I was suddenly afraid of the karmic consequences of breaking those vows, plus I never wanted to shame myself before Prabhupada and his students. But mostly I was thrilled by the possibility of spiritualizing myself and my life, although I wasn't particularly clear what spiritualizing meant.

Meanwhile there was Prabhupada, so elderly and wise yet so fresh and youthfully innocent. Excited by Krishna and exciting us about him. Steady yet unpredictable. I was so infused and ignited with hope that I overlooked the magnitude of my goal. Commune with God himself? Become a godly person? Me? Yeah, sure. Yet Prabhupada said we could—*I could*—do just that. It seemed impossible, unrealistic, pie-in-the-sky, but I believed him *(why? because he was believable)* and became filled with enthusiasm.

If I *could* do this immense thing—become closer to God—how could I do it? The only possible way was to come closer to Prabhupada, the person who made the promise, who was telling me how to get there, who knew so much and was so earnestly giving me what he knew, who didn't seem to falter in his God conscious mission and behavior. Galvanized by the possibilities Prabhupada confidently placed before me, I wanted to take every opportunity to hear him, and when I couldn't do that, be ever eager to hear about what he was saying and doing. Gone were my aspirations to be a world famous photojournalist. Prabhupada would now be the subject of my photographs. In a sense I wanted to be subsumed by him, not to lose my self, but to find my self, my centering, my identity. I wanted to be one in purpose with Prabhupada.

Both my parents had rejected religious ritual as meaningless; under Prabhupada's tutelage I embraced it as a window to reality. They had both abruptly left their tradition-filled heritage; just as abruptly, I left the tradition-less heritage they'd bequeathed me.

The tsunami of new thoughts, values, attitudes, priorities, diet, dress, schedule, and habits, hit the shore. Other than character barnacles like quietness and aloofness, my old life was behind me.

The hyperbolic writing about Prabhupada that had made me cringe in the stinky printer's office in Calcutta just months before no longer seemed so hyperbolic. I now knew that Prabhupada's other disciples were expressing their gratitude for something substantial he'd offered them, something that transported my consciousness from a grim world to a glorious one, from a place of suffering to a place of sweetness. I also felt that Prabhupada wasn't exploiting us; the regulative principles he followed with his students distinguished him from an exploiter, as did his emphasis on scriptural validation and the succession of spiritual masters he was part of, a succession traced back through centuries. Prabhupada, steeped in the tradition he propounded, was offering, in his words, "a cultural presentation for the respiritualization of the entire human society." He wanted to respiritualize society and he wanted to respiritualize me too. Somehow, I was eager to be respiritualized.

I was growing past the tiny story of my life, past the stories of my nationality and gender and race to an awareness of the sacredness of *life*—mine and all others'. Blind to this sacredness of my own eternal, beautiful existence, I'd been blind to it in others—I'd failed to see the common bond between all that lives. The Gita explains that all beings are spiritually equal and that our natural state is to see them equally. The implications were stunning.

In December 1971, India allied with East Pakistan in the war effort. When our group returned to Delhi that same month, it was under siege from nightly West Pakistani bombings.

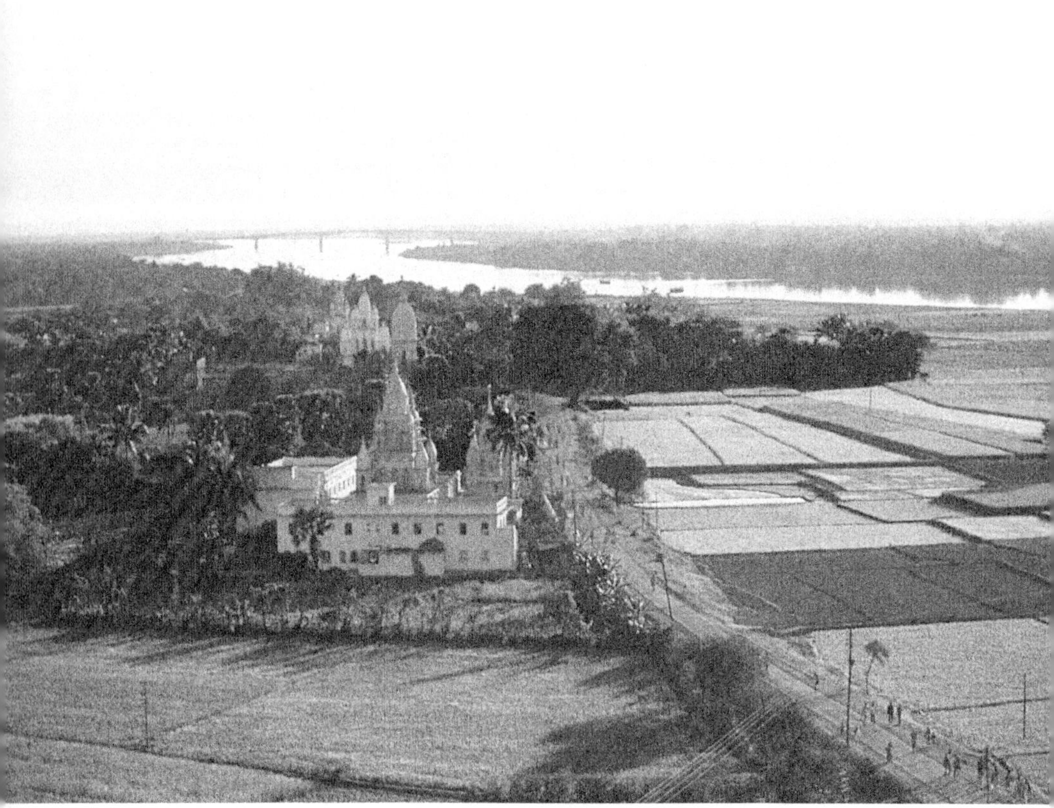

CHAPTER EIGHT

Honeymoon

We stayed in Kamala Nagar, New Delhi, in an unadorned, two-story cement ashram with a large courtyard. I, just initiated—a spiritual baby—and married only days before, was with my husband and thirty others in a besieged city. Since Calcutta, Yadubara and I had been living separately: he in the men's quarters and I in the women's. And now, even though we were husband and wife, we continued to live in the same way—as did all the married couples.

Long before dawn the day after we arrived, I was happy to run into Yadubara on the dark veranda just outside the temple room.

"How'd you sleep last night?" I said.

"I was cold. I had to put my chaddar on top of my sleeping bag to keep warm. You?"

"I was okay in my sleeping bag, but the room was so cold I didn't want to get out of it even to go to the bathroom."

"Yeah, me too."

"There's no heating system in this place!"

"I know. And no hot water either."

In the women's ashram, the other ladies and I used an immersion heater—an electric metal rod with coils at one end and a hook at the other—to heat our water. After the first austere morning, I started a system of filling a bucket of water the night before, placing a stick across the top of the bucket, hooking the immersion heater to the stick so its coils hung suspended in the middle of the water, and placing the bucket with its heater near an electrical outlet close to my sleeping bag. When I woke in the morning, the first thing I did was to reach out and plug in the immersion heater. Then I'd snooze for the ten or fifteen minutes it took for the water to warm up. This system had a learning curve, though. Once I bumped the immersion heater so its coils touched the side of the plastic bucket. A few minutes later the heater melted a hole in the bucket and warm water from the bucket was spilling through the hole onto the floor of the ashram and the smell of melted plastic filled the room. Another time in a dozy state, I touched the water before unplugging the heater and got a 220 Volt electric shock that left my whole arm tingling. More than once, I'd lay in my sleeping bag as steam rose from the very hot water, thinking I could heat the room that way. It never worked. I didn't bemoan these daily mishaps and difficulties but accepted them as if they were somehow inevitable and there were no alternatives. In fact, I'd already stopped looking for alternatives. I wasn't being stoic or austere but making do, doing the needful, surviving, and even having some fun with it. It was an adventure.

Somehow, both Yadubara and I stayed healthy. And both he and I were constantly wrapped up in and exhilarated by our new discipleship and all it entailed. My center of gravity had spontaneously shifted from Yadubara to Prabhupada and Yadubara's had similarly shifted from me to Prabhupada. The present-moment buzz of spiritual life engulfed us—so much so that, amazingly, it didn't occur to either one of us that we would now normally be on our honeymoon. Before the prospects of spirituality—before Prabhupada—all else paled. Considering that Prabhupada was a simple, humble, elderly person with a penchant for philosophy, from one perspective it was odd that Yadubara and I and so many others had dedicated ourselves to him and his teachings. But to me it didn't feel at all odd. It felt completely right.

Just before dawn on our first Delhi morning, my dear friend, soft-spoken and smiling Madri, said to me, "Prabhupada's going for a walk! Let's go with him."

I ran and got my camera, and Madri and I bustled off to join Prabhupada, who was with a few others, as he left our compound to walk the still dark streets. Stores were shuttered, sidewalks deserted, and traffic minimal in bone-chilly Delhi. An eerie and menacing foreboding hung over the city. Prabhupada, wrapped in a reddish wool chaddar, his head and ears covered with a thick beige cap that tied under his chin, quiet but alert and observant, set a brisk pace, his legs pressing against his thin saffron robe. Delighted to be walking with Prabhupada, I ignored how cold I felt, dressed only in a cotton sari and a thin wool chaddar. Prabhupada paused at a newspaper stand to read headlines on the war's progress, his face gentled with concern. He walked on, commenting, "On the 12th December 1942, there was heavy bombing all night in Calcutta. Everyone vacated. Calcutta was a city of no man, but somehow or other, I had to remain there. I was just eating and there was siren of bombing. *Chee-kyam!* Like that, so many bombings. So what can be done? There may be so many dangers in our life because it is the place only full of dangers."

"Oh my god!" I thought. "I wouldn't be able to eat while bombs dropped around me."

After half an hour we turned back, the rhythmic, crisp sound of Prabhupada's cane on the cobbled pavement rising above our muffled footsteps. Beneath our coats and cloaks we fingered japa beads as we individually chanted the maha-mantra, collectively making a bee-like murmur.

Once inside the ashram again, Madri said to me, "That was wonderful! I wouldn't have missed that for anything. Let's go every morning!"

Without a moment's hesitation I agreed.

That evening I gathered with thirty others in a large, whitewashed ashram room for worship, kirtan, and Prabhupada's lecture. I'd started taking notes during his lectures, but due to Delhi's total blackout, the windows were covered with blankets and the only light was a solitary candle on the altar. Even sitting as close as I could to that candle, the light was too dim to write by. The batteries in my tape recorder were dead and stores were sold out—no wartime batteries. So, in this scared and suspended dark city, I sat on the hard floor cross-legged and erect and listened with rapt attention. I felt a vivid expectancy, a yearning: as much as I'd ever wanted anything, I wanted to understand spiritual life. I was ready.

When he spoke, Prabhupada made no attempt to entertain. He expected me to listen because I was human, and as a human I had a responsibility to grasp the import and urgency of his message. His forty-five-minute talk, delivered easily, extemporaneously and without haste, cascaded around me with a melodious, comforting quality my ear effortlessly received. Something about his words magnetically attracted me and drew me in to what he was saying. I longed for his revelations to unlock my realizations, for his extensive knowledge to profoundly affect my thoughts and attitude. Like a person who'd crossed a desert and come to an abundant oasis, I rejoiced in his words and drank them in with gratitude. I felt close to him—to the person he was. Those special qualities that stirred within him became visible to me. Prabhupada was giving me what I craved.

He so spoke to my inner thirst that I wanted only to sit and hear him, to learn from him. He had begun to hydrate me, a person dying of dry empiricism, with a vision of a world so irrepressibly full of color and joy and diverse loving relationships that it was irresistible. Prabhupada said I could access that world at any time and in any place, even in the most disturbing, apparently unfavorable situations of this world, like a war torn city. I wanted to do that.

When I left that dark room I felt nourished, enriched and a little fortified from the illusory temptations of this world. In the women's quarters, Yamuna, who'd been nursing a sick devotee and couldn't attend the talk, asked me what Prabhupada had said. I opened my mouth to speak but was blank. Despite my attentive listening, I couldn't remember a single point; I couldn't even remember what topic he spoke on. What happened? The next day, redoubling my efforts to hear with attention, I could feel his words penetrating the rusted barbed wire of my mind and entering my heart, where they evoked a warm glow that spread everywhere. But when Yamuna again asked me what had been said, the result was the same. Zero. What was going on? I couldn't figure it out.

Yamuna told me that medicine hadn't been effective for the sick devotee and Prabhupada had told her to give *charanamrita*—holy water from the bathing of the deities—instead.

"That's risky! She's really sick. We should try some other medicine. Or maybe we should take her to the hospital," I said.

Yamuna said, "Actually, since we gave her *charanamrita*, she started improving for the first time."

Would she have gotten better anyway or was my faith lacking? I wasn't sure. I was flitting like a fruit fly, sometimes accepting the limitations of my understandings and the inconceivability of God's potencies, and at other times believing only in mundane cause and effect. My flip-flopping, I realized, had to do with the condition of my heart at any given time.

In becoming Yadubara's wife I suddenly had many new relatives I hadn't yet met, and in becoming Prabhupada's spiritual daughter, his other disciples became my godsisters and godbrothers and I lived with them, although in an ordinary social milieu I wouldn't have spent time with them. But in this ashram-fortress in this mirthless city I was around them all day, mostly to my dismay: the blustering carpenter/cook, whose gruff voice resounded throughout the building from the rooftop kitchen, where he toiled for recognition; another, his trounced yet dutiful wife; a third, our exacting and clever ashram commander, driven by limitless ambition; and a fourth, his rooster-pecked wife who was otherwise a delightful devotee. Yadubara and I, just entering this odd arena of personal eccentricities mingled with mystical possibilities, were trying to figure out our place in this new family while also surviving in it. Together, all of us tried following a rigorous schedule: rising early, attending temple programs, doing lengthy chanting meditations. None of this was what I'd envisioned for my life and in uncertain moments, like when I first awoke, achy from the hard straw mat I slept on and forgetful of Krishna and his world and Prabhupada's message of bhakti, I'd wonder, "What on earth am I doing here? Why am I putting myself through all this?" Then the spirit of the great transcendental adventure I was on would return and, gripped by that spirit, I'd be ready to go on, to bend as Prabhupada wanted me to, to endure whatever was necessary. The promised land was ahead.

Krishna consciousness, it occurred to me, was like trying to improve my posture. When I managed to do it, it felt right, it felt great, it felt like that's exactly how it was supposed to be. But then in no time I'd forget and go back to slouching, back to my old materialistic mentality.

Early one morning the small group of us were sitting with Prabhupada chanting on our beads when the newest member of our group pulled his beads out of his bead bag and held them up, revealing a large knot. His string of beads had gotten tangled in itself, something that also regularly happened to my beads.

On seeing the tangle Prabhupada commented, "That means you are not concentrating."

"Wait a minute, it doesn't mean that," I wanted to say. "It means the string coming out of the head bead got caught on the other beads. That's all it means."

But I was quiet. I considered how my linear, reductionistic, Western-trained mind was being challenged on every front by Prabhupada's teachings and how that mind had only brought me confusion and dissatisfaction. I sat with the concept of tangled beads indicating a lack of concentration and felt it. Certainly I regularly failed in the concentration arena. Why not take my tangled beads as a wake-up call? Why not see Prabhupada's meaning behind incidents that perhaps were not mechanistic? In the days that followed, as I experimented with accepting his explanation my beads tangled as much as before, but their tangling humbled me. I took that as a good thing.

One evening, instead of giving his usual lecture Prabhupada asked his disciples to speak. Sudama Vipra Swami, a lanky young renunciant said, "We may see a leper or some other diseased person and feel sorry for his suffering, but a pure devotee feels sorry to see any living entity without God consciousness. A pure devotee sees that anyone lacking spiritual knowledge is in a suffering condition."

At this point Prabhupada, who had been listening with closed eyes, opened them, looked at Sudama softly and gave a hum of appreciation that seemed to say, "This boy has understood something."

Another evening, after his lecture Prabhupada asked for questions. I asked, "What happens to the soul of the vegetable or flower that's been offered to Krishna?"

"That soul becomes liberated," Prabhupada said.

"What form does that liberation take?"

"It means that the soul enters a human body to continue devotional service to the supreme person, Krishna."

It was a whole new vision. I needed my aristocratic lady friend, faith, to help me grasp it.

A small group of us were scheduled to go with Prabhupada to meet Kenneth Keating, the U.S. Ambassador to India. I'd heard of Keating and was looking forward to photographing him and Prabhupada together. On the morning of the appointment I was getting my camera, lenses, and film ready when the Delhi temple president asked me to cook breakfast for the devotees. I explained to him this wasn't a good day for me to cook but, to my distress, he failed to see my point and insisted that I cook. Since Prabhupada was so accessible, without much thought I burst into his room and blurted out my difficulty. From his usual vantage point—seated cross-legged on the floor behind a small table—Prabhupada regarded me. Even while I was in the middle of my first sentence I thought, "This is dumb! Why on earth am I bothering Prabhupada with such a petty issue?" And from his expression, it seemed Prabhupada was thinking similarly. I left his room, now doubly flustered, to find that in the meantime the temple president had enlisted someone else to cook.

Relieved, I packed into a car with the others, including Shyamasundar and his daughter Saraswati, and we all drove to the American Embassy where we were graciously welcomed by Keating and his wife. Sitting with them in a posh room in the Embassy, we were each served a tall glass of fresh coconut water as Prabhupada explained to the couple how the body is a dress, just as our clothes are, and that the person, the living force or soul, is within the body, just as a person is within his or her clothes. The soul is massless, invisible, and indivisible, yet more essential than any aspect of our physical nature. It is our identity.

As I photographed I was surprised to hear Mrs. Keating say, "That's very interesting. I believe in the transmigration of the soul."

"It is a fact," Prabhupada said. "Just like this child," he said as he indicated Saraswati, "is transmigrating from one body, one kind of body to another body. So in the same way, when I give up this body I transmigrate to another body. This is the science. Unfortunately, there is no university, no education, no culture of this great science."

Prabhupada pointed out how the soul's nature is to serve and therefore everyone is serving, whether one's boss or family or pet or oneself. He said, "Suppose I say that I don't serve. That is not possible. That being our constitutional position then, just like my finger, it is serving, always, sometimes doing like that, sometimes doing like that, sometimes doing like that. The finger's business is to serve. As part and parcel of my body, the finger's business is to serve the whole body. Similarly, we are part and parcel of God. Our essential business is to serve God. How do you find this argument? Do you refute this argument?"

Again, Mrs. Keating surprised me with her acceptance. She said, "You serve and you share."

Prabhupada: "Yes. By serving I share. Just like this milk. The hand helps me, brings it here. I drink, and as soon I drank, the benefit is shared by all the parts of body. Is it not?"

Ambassador Keating: "That's true."

Prabhupada: "Just like you pour water in the root of the tree. The energy immediately, I mean to say, distributed to the leaves, to the tree, to the flowers, to the fruits, everything, immediately. Similarly, there must be something which is the root of everything. That is God."

Prabhupada's confidence seemed effortless and his words, resonating within me, encompassed layers of common sense as it stretched those layers too. Hearing from him I could imagine I was a spiritual being—a soul—inhabiting a body. And I could feel why my mother's answer to my question a decade earlier, "What will happen to me after I die?" had frustrated me and left me empty. (*"Nothing happens. You're buried or cremated. That's it,"* she'd said.) I wanted to live a life built on the premise of the soul's presence. That premise made sense out of life; it gave meaning and shelter to my existence. And it just could be true.

I was thrilled to hear Prabhupada speak the basic tenets of the philosophy and see him interact with people; as far as I could tell, he didn't calculate, plot, or scheme, but stirred their consciousness—*my* consciousness—with the clarity of his message and his simple mood, full of vigor and emotion and faith.

I was enamored of a 76-year-old who was four inches shorter than me and had no material assets! How could I ever explain such a thing to my friends and family in the States? How could I explain it to myself? Yet as strange as it looked and as unexpected as it was, not only did it feel completely natural, but I wanted it to happen. I'd wandered into a traditional guru–disciple relationship of mutual service and love and was held by its possibilities, by how it opened me up. After all, I thought, ultimately what is love but the way a person makes me feel, the intense affection I have for that person; love is not the proper subject of arguments.

As Prabhupada's teachings and his very being filled my gaping vacuum, inside me there was a whoosh, the whoosh of newly found reasoning and logic, the whoosh of fresh analysis and analogy, the whoosh of spiritual duty, and most of all, the whoosh of the possibility of love for God, the beautiful, delightful, playful person Krishna. Krishna was complete in himself yet yearned for my love as I, underneath everything else, yearned to love him. White water rapids of hope had swept me up and were carrying me downstream toward an ocean, my head bobbing on their promise.

Prabhupada had entered a barely noticeable clear spot in my heart and stirred something that affected me as nothing else in my life had. What had happened to my lifelong skepticism? Would my feelings for him last? Was I being duped?

After the meeting, Keating accompanied us to our waiting Ambassador and watched politely as Prabhupada sat in the front passenger seat next to Shyamasundar, the driver, and the other seven of us crammed into a back seat meant for four. I was sitting on someone's knees, the back of my neck pressed against the car's ceiling and my elbows and camera case pinned in by the people wedged beside me. We were young and products of the '60s and besides, stuffing as many people in a vehicle as humanly possible was quite Indian. Prabhupada and Keating continued chatting.

By mid-December, West Pakistan was decisively defeated and peace returned to India. As the pall over Delhi lifted, I noticed that all of us breathed more easily and smiled more readily.

In January, in cooperation with the Queen of Jaipur, Kaushalya and Srimati, another American devotee, arranged a pandal program for Prabhupada and his students in Jaipur. Our group shifted to Jaipur, the capital of Rajasthan, home of the Radha Govinda deities who'd been worshiped in the Queen's compound for 450 years. For the few days that we were there, I and a few others on our party joined the hundreds of townspeople who daily gathered at the temple's locked gates in the morning dark. When guards opened those gates at 4:30 a.m., these exuberant devotees ran across the expansive lawn crying, "Jaya Radha Govinda! Jaya Radhe! Jaya Govinda!" I had intended to walk to the temple, but as I was surrounded by sprinting people, I started sprinting too, thinking "Wow! They do this every day! Such heartfelt enthusiasm!"

Yadubara had to return to Calcutta while I continued traveling with the small group that accompanied Prabhupada. Before we parted, Yadubara told me, "I really wanted to go with you but there're just too many things I have to do."

"So we can meet up later, when you're done?"

"Yeah, we should be able to meet in Calcutta." With that assurance, I'd gone on to Madras, our next stop, where Giriraj had organized a pandal program. Now the South Indian tropical weather replaced the cold dryness of the north, the curvy sounds of Tamil replaced Hindi's coarseness, urad dal and rice combinations—idlis, dosas and wadas, served with spicy coconut chutney—replaced whole-wheat chapatis and mung bean soup. The gradually and gracefully bulging temple spires of the north were replaced by the south's huge gabled roofs covered with ornate, colorful bas-reliefs of gods and goddesses on the temple domes. Even the South Indians had a different quality about them—more settled and patient.

Mr. K.K. Balu hosted us in his home for our weeklong stay. A typically squat, slick-haired, pious businessman, Mr. Balu, always dressed in black pants and a starched white business shirt open at the collar, was a courteous if flamboyant host. Daily he drew a thin black vertical line in the center of his forehead, from the bridge of his nose to his hairline. I'd seen a few people in Vrindavan with the same mark and hadn't known what to make of it. One afternoon Prabhupada asked Balu, "Why do you wear that line on your forehead? Such a mark is not mentioned in any scripture."

"My guru asked me to wear this mark," Balu said.

"He may ask," Prabhupada said, "but it must be confirmed in the scriptures."

Prabhupada was respectful yet piercing. He spoke to Balu as a professor would speak to a student during lunch—they were comrades in negotiating life's questions, but Prabhupada knew more; he was wiser.

"I follow my guru blindly," Balu said.

"No, no. What the guru says must be confirmed by the great saintly persons and the scriptures: guru, sadhu (holy person), and scripture. The guru cannot say anything that is not confirmed. If he does, then he is not guru."

"I know nothing but the words of my guru."

Our host wouldn't budge. I worried that Prabhupada's challenge had disturbed him, but it hadn't. He left the room with a contented look. Prabhupada explained to the few of us remaining that guru, sadhu, and scripture were an invincible triumvirate, an ongoing litmus test for life choices that would keep spiritual seekers secure on their path. The guru-sadhus-scriptures, I understood, were a kind of communion with the inner strength of the tradition and civilization to which I now belonged, an inner strength that was indestructible.

I was not well educated in the guru-sadhu-scripture wisdom that Prabhupada consistently used to analyze and evaluate. In Balu's blind following of his guru I saw myself blindly following Prabhupada, and that made me uncomfortable. My ignorance weighed on me. I didn't know enough to measure the quality of my guru. Neither did I know enough to know what to do and what not to do in my spiritual life. If I could learn, I'd become a responsible follower. I'd have a standard measuring stick, a solid basis for discernment. Yet I was a little surprised to realize that I wasn't worried that Prabhupada might be bogus. He'd already won my heart. And the fact that he wanted us to question, to weigh what he said against the words of sadhu and scripture, to become knowledgeable and perceptive, made me feel protected. Prabhupada's openness to examination evoked my trust and helped assuage my pesky and lingering doubts about my life choice. Prabhupada, I felt, was not giving us "his" wisdom, just wisdom.

I received a letter from Yadubara, sent from Calcutta:

> It seems most of the time everything in Krishna consciousness is rushed. I am rushing around trying to put the Bengali BTG [Back to Godhead] together for the Mayapur program. I am now discouraged and am far behind schedule, but by Krishna's grace, we may finish.
>
> I am glad that you are enjoying yourself in Madras and I wish I could attend the program but I have much to do here ... I hope to see you in Calcutta and we can have some *misti dahi* together. I'm going to rush off again.

I encouraged Yadubara, helped him when I could, asked little of him and didn't get in his way. He did the same for me. At least for now, he and I were like electrons separately but happily spinning around the nucleus of Prabhupada. Our lives were full.

One morning, a few of us went with Prabhupada to the home of Dr. Sarvepalli Radhakrishnan, an elderly Indian scholar and a former president of India who, in his commentary on the Bhagavad-gita had written that it was not to the person Krishna to whom we should surrender but to "the unborn, beginningless, eternal who speaks through Krishna." When he had heard this statement in 1966 at the first Hare Krishna ashram on Manhattan's Lower East Side, Prabhupada had called Radhakrishnan an impersonalist, someone who thinks God's form is material and beyond God is the formless, senseless energy of the supreme Absolute Truth. In Radhakrishnan's view God was subordinate to that energy.

Impersonal philosophy, according to Prabhupada, was akin to atheism. In Bhagavad-gita Krishna says he is the supreme person. His body, mind, and self are spiritual, and everything and everyone is subordinate to him, including his all-pervading, effulgent energy, his white light. Krishna asks for surrender to him, the supreme person, not to his effulgence. To deny God's form and personality was to deny God his completeness.

Referring to Radhakrishnan, Prabhupada had spoken strongly, "This rascal commentator says it is not to the person Krishna that we should offer obeisances but to the soul within Krishna. Just see how ignorant he is! He does not know that for Krishna there is no such division between his self, or soul, and his body. This fool is rascal number one, and yet he has written a commentary on the Bhagavad-gita and is accepted as a scholar. And this nonsense is going on all over the world."

After a few minutes' wait at Dr. Radhakrishnan's home, a slight, short, bent old man with a cane in one hand and the other resting on the arm of a prim nurse, entered with shuffling steps. With his nurse's help he sat near Prabhupada, wordless. Prabhupada leaned forward and gently addressed the doctor, explaining how he was traveling widely to present the teachings of Bhagavad-gita as it is throughout the world, and receiving a good reception. People were hankering for this knowledge, taking it seriously and becoming devotees of Krishna, Prabhupada said. Prabhupada quoted Krishna in the Bhagavad-gita: "I am the source of all spiritual and material worlds. Everything emanates from Me. The wise who know this perfectly engage in My devotional service and worship Me with all their hearts."

Krishna, Prabhupada went on, is a person. Not a person like us, for we are embodied souls; Krishna's form is all spiritual. We could personally relate to him by serving him with love and devotion.

As Prabhupada spoke, Dr. Radhakrishnan raised his head and looked at Prabhupada attentively. Then, after just a few minutes, his nurse interrupted, "The doctor is tired now and must rest. He thanks you for kindly visiting him." With his nurse's help Radhakrishnan stood and shuffled to a back room.

To me, an appeal, a bright desperation amid much sorrow was in Dr. Radhakrishnan's eyes. Inside the lonely prison of his body something was alive and hungry. I felt his hunger, for I had been similarly hungry. But now, somehow or other, Prabhupada, unassuming and uncomplicated, was offering me nourishment, making Krishna's presence known, making his culture accessible. And Prabhupada was offering his gift—Krishna—to others as widely as he could.

In Madras, caste brahmins dominated religious and governmental posts and excluded non-brahmins regardless of their qualifications. Prabhupada adamantly challenged this caste system that, he said, had destroyed Indian culture. According to the Bhagavad-gita, Prabhupada said, one's occupation is not based on one's birth but on one's proclivity. In Krishna's words, one's work is determined by "one's qualities and activities," not by birth.

For an American like me, the brahmins' position was untenable. Birth was secondary; why should my career be determined by the family I was born into? But for them, birth was not secondary. Birth was all-important, and one accepted it as divinely ordained fate and conducted one's life accordingly regardless of one's qualities or activities. With this philosophy, it was easy to take one's birth in a high caste as well-deserved, and if one lacked knowledge, as a license to oppress lower castes. That mood of superiority and oppression, however, was the antithesis of an actual brahmin's mood: an actual brahmin was humble and wanted to elevate others, not repress and oppress them; an actual brahmin wanted others to be all they could be for God's pleasure.

The brahmins in Madras criticized Prabhupada for creating brahmins from lowborn, unqualified Westerners. Prabhupada replied, "This is not my philosophy. I am simply acting on Krishna's words in Bhagavad-gita. These students have given up their bad habits and come to the brahminical standard, so they are qualified and must be accepted as brahmins."

The Bhagavad-gita's teachings, I understood, were Prabhupada's warp and weft, his grounding, the bottomless sacred well where he drew his strength and courage. Bhagavad-gita was where his spiritual master and the spiritual masters before him had also drawn divine potency. I couldn't fathom how much the Gita's 700 verses contained, but I was moved by their antiquity and the ease with which Prabhupada drew on their wisdom.

The evening we were to leave, Mr. Balu and his wife asked Prabhupada to recite the *rasa-lila,* the pastimes of Krishna with his cowherd girlfriends in Vrindavan, described in Srimad-Bhagavatam's Tenth Canto. The Srimad-Bhagavatam, also known as the Bhagavata Purana, is considered the ripened fruit of all Vedic texts and the postgraduate study of the Gita.

Prabhupada said, "Only a person completely free of material desires is fit to hear the *rasa-lila*. Otherwise we will confuse it with worldly affairs."

"No, Swamiji," Balu said, "my wife and I are very keen. You must recite *rasa-lila*."

"To understand the Srimad-Bhagavatam we must begin from the First Canto, the lotus feet of the Lord," Prabhupada said, "and then gradually progress to his smiling face, the Tenth Canto." Prabhupada explained how God's greatness had to be grasped by God's mercy. It was not mundane. "When we're completely free of all material attachments to wife, family, home, and money, then we're ready to hear Krishna's pastimes in Vrindavan."

Balu folded his hands, "Swamiji, my wife and I plead with you. Please recite *rasa-lila*."

"Well," Prabhupada said, "you may be fit to hear *rasa-lila*, but I do not feel qualified to speak it."

It occurred to me that an appreciation of Krishna's activities was incredibly precious. His affairs were his private, sanctified pleasure and an understanding of these was available on his terms only. Balu's trying to bulldoze his way in or approaching with a sense of entitlement disqualified him from being invited in. He was missing out on the sweetness of a relationship with Krishna, of this supreme, independent being choosing to reach out to him. Occasionally, I got a sense of an ambrosial relationship before me, a relationship I could enter simply by my willingness. But that willingness, I found, was deceptively elusive. It could be present and then gone like a whisper.

Prabhupada said some people foolishly think Krishna embraces cowherd girls as an ordinary man embraces young girls; they think Krishna allows sex indulgence. He said what we called love in this world was in fact lust. Spiritual love and material lust were opposites—one was about giving and the other about getting. Love meant being controlled by the other person's desires; it meant that person's desires came before mine.

I could easily get confused and lose my tender grip on the teachings and lifestyle I'd so recently accepted. I could quickly ignore what I'd learned about who I was, who Krishna was, what my relationship with him was, and how to act in that relationship. I could make the divine commonplace and let the entire concept of transcendence slide away like raindrops down a window. From day to day I was faced with a choice. In Prabhupada's company I felt strong and cared for, freed from every sort of distraction from my spiritual practices. It was easy to make the right choices. But sometimes I wondered, "What would happen to me when he went on to travel the world without me?" I knew it was only a matter of time before that happened and I was left to serve him from a distance. Would Krishna still be real? What would happen to me when his clarity and concern were not encircling my life?

In Visakhapatnam, on the coast of the Bay of Bengal halfway between Madras and Calcutta, Prabhupada's godbrothers hosted us at their temple. Here we were neither the "dancing white elephants" (Prabhupada's phrase) before thousands at city pandals nor the gawking pilgrims of Vrindavan nor the disqualified low-borns of the Madras brahmins. Rather, here we were taken into the bosom of the Gaudiya Vaishnav tradition, of which we were a part, and warmly welcomed. For one heavenly week, staunch Gaudiya Vaishnavs reveled in encouraging us and in praising Prabhupada's accomplishments in introducing us to bhakti culture. From their acceptance it was clear that Prabhupada's movement was a flower in the Vaishnav bouquet—an exotic flower, no doubt, and sometimes a pungent one, but also a prominent one, of which they were proud.

Between his public lectures, Prabhupada relaxed and joked with his godbrothers. Once, I passed his room and saw him squatting, washing his dhoti Indian-style. Any one of the twenty students present would have gladly done it for him, but it seemed he wanted to do it himself, that he took pleasure in it.

Both in the West and in India, devotees had converted rented apartments or buildings into temples, but the Visakhapatnam Gaudiya Math had been designed and built as a temple and so was, from its very architecture, centered on the deity and service to the deity. It radiated the well-worn character of a culture kept vital by genuine feeling. The temple functions went on with mature assuredness, with efficient, reverential jolliness. We twenty young, rowdy, voracious, vivacious, semi-trained Westerners descended on this idyllic seaside ashram with our idiosyncratic demands (Nanda Kumar was on an all-fruit diet) and sincere misunderstandings (Malati tried to give Prabhupada a donation she'd received, but Prabhupada told her to use it for her three-year-old daughter, Saraswati, who was traveling with us). We were surely a burden for these lifelong resident sadhus. But, smiling, they let us know we were a burden of love.

Here we were united with two dear spiritual uncles, both in their sixties: B. V. Puri Maharaj, the wispy, energetic, irrepressible, warm-hearted, wise sadhu, brimming with appreciation for Prabhupada, who graciously overlooked our shortcomings; and Anand Maharaj, the robust, alert, jovial sadhu who spoke no English but relished cooking and serving us elaborate feasts. His life, dedicated to helping others, welled of satisfaction. I became a great fan of both of them. They were cheerful, fresh examples of high ideals lived; their lives conveyed a message of godly and selfless service, their acceptance of us assured me, and their devotional enthusiasm humbled me. Whatever aches I felt from my recent, bumpy conversion—a choice that in India had made me even more of a spectacle than I had been as a Western tourist—were soothed by the affirmations of these residents of the Visakhapatnam Gaudiya Math.

Each day we walked with Prabhupada along the nearby beach, accessed by a rough road. One morning, Gurudas was late, and in his rush to join us, he was barefoot. We saw him hobbling over the rocks, obviously in pain, as he caught up.

"Why aren't you wearing shoes?" Prabhupada asked.

"I'm trying to be austere."

"Then why don't you be austere by cutting your throat?" We laughed, unsure, and then Prabhupada pointed out that austerity did not mean inflicting unnecessary pain on the body; austerity was meant for spiritual advancement. Mindfully chanting the names of God was the spiritual austerity most suited to us.

After a week in Visakhapatnam, we again boarded a worn-out, noisy train and continued north to Calcutta where we joined Yadubara, who had succeeded in publishing the second Bengali *Back to Godhead* magazine (a feat for someone who spoke no Bengali). Prabhupada, pleased to see the magazine, looked through it page by page, praising Yadubara for his accomplishment.

Yadubara and I, glad to be reunited, piled into a bus along with the traveling group and headed further north. For four bouncy, lurching hours we filled each other in on what had been going on in our lives. As the road became narrower, more poorly maintained and ever more likely to be filled with lumbering bullock carts and riders on antiquated bicycles, our bus slowed to a jerky crawl, and excited, bare-chested and barefoot children, seeing our white faces in the bus windows, ran after us giggling and shouting. Now open fields replaced Calcutta's sprawling, cramped metropolis, and the typical thatched-roofed Bengali villages got progressively smaller and more separated by farmlands until, when we rolled into Mayapur, lush rice fields stretched to the horizon, broken only by temples—Gaudiya Maths—scattered along the main road. That road was Bhaktisiddhanta Marg, named after Prabhupada's spiritual master, the Gaudiya Math's founder. He and his spiritual forefathers had wanted Mayapur's importance broadcast widely. Prabhupada wanted that too, and he had arranged for us to arrive in time for Mayapur's grandest festival of the year, Gaura Purnima, the anniversary of the appearance of Sri Chaitanya.

Prabhupada often spoke of Sri Chaitanya. He told us that Sri Chaitanya Mahaprabhu's appearance in this age was predicted in Srimad-Bhagavatam. "Sri Chaitanya comes especially to deliver the fallen souls," he said, "who are always planning something for material enjoyment. He gives the people of this age the advantage of being able to chant the Hare Krishna mantra and thus become fully pure, free from all material contamination."

Once again, I felt the need for my aristocratic lady friend, faith. Everyone in the world had heard of Krishna, renowned speaker of the famous Bhagavad-gita. But even Indians outside of Bengal hadn't heard of Sri Chaitanya. How could he be God? But Prabhupada was insistent. To support his insistence, Prabhupada, as always, quoted scripture. As I listened, day after day, my skepticism waned somewhat.

"In the Srimad-Bhagavatam it's described that Sri Chaitanya is Krishna himself in the form of a golden-complexioned devotee who always chants the Hare Krishna maha-mantra and is always accompanied by His associates. Unlike Krishna, Sri Chaitanya doesn't tell us to surrender. Sri Chaitanya says we can make spiritual progress simply by chanting the Lord's names. Anyone can do it, anywhere, anytime and without cost."

Prabhupada repeatedly called on the triumvirate of guru, scripture, and sadhu to establish the position and importance of Sri Chaitanya. Sri Chaitanya, he said, was described not only in verses of the Srimad-Bhagavatam but also in the Puranas, Mahabharata, and other places. Faced with Prabhupada's faith I tried to summon my own.

It was Sri Chaitanya's teachings, I found out, that were the basis of Prabhupada's emphasis on chanting Hare Krishna, and Mayapur was Sri Chaitanya's place.

The only cement structures on our newly acquired three-acre Mayapur property were a small storage building and an even smaller building for the enchanting, two-foot-high, brilliant, brass deities of Sri Sri Radha Madhava, as well as a captivatingly graceful, wood-carved deity of Sri Chaitanya. Their priest, a survivor of the early Calcutta days, was Jananivas, a good-natured Englishman who had been Revatinanda Swami's assistant and had moved to Mayapur to focus entirely on serving the deities.

Prabhupada was quartered in a straw-and-mud thatched cottage near the main road. He told us, "You can build me the biggest palace, but still, I'd prefer to live here." When I went inside I could see why: it was cool and tranquil and seemed built of virtue and purity.

The devotees' quarters were two separate large tents, one for the men and one for the women—the women's complete with twenty-four-hour fluorescent lighting (we never did find the "off" switch for those lights). Mayapur was infested with mosquitoes, and from dusk on our first day we were fending off hordes of oversized, undeterred attackers. My friend Srimati and I were on the side of the women's tent that was just ten feet from the open *chattai* window in Prabhupada's cottage, and while still under my mosquito net hours before sunrise on our first morning in Mayapur, I heard Prabhupada's voice in the fresh, calm air. He was speaking into his dictaphone, translating the Sanskrit scriptures into English and giving purports based both on commentaries from previous spiritual authorities and his own realizations. These recordings, which he made every morning wherever he was, were later transcribed, typeset, and printed as the Srimad-Bhagavatam.

I could not imagine Prabhupada's daily task of harnessing impetuous, impassioned, untrained young men and women to an international society with a selfless spiritual mission. In 1969, Prabhupada had written one of his disciples, "If all problems come to me, even personal problems, then it becomes a heavy task for me. I received your letter, full of problems; Gargamuni's, full of problems; Rayarama's, full of problems, and similarly ISKCON Media's, full of problems. If everyone's problems are sent to me, then who will solve my problems? I have divided these departments to solve problems, but if in the end they are all sent to me and I have to tackle, then just imagine what is my position. The best thing would be to stop all activities and simply chant Hare Krishna."

How restoring it must have been for Prabhupada, in the silent mornings long before the rest of us—his problems—arose, to gradually fulfill his guru's desire for spiritual literature and, in solitary communion, to deeply reflect on Krishna and his energies. Prabhupada's translations and commentaries on the Srimad-Bhagavatam, "the ripened fruit of all scriptures," were a daily flowering of grace offered to a world in critical need of that grace. Lying on my side under the glaring fluorescent lights listening to his voice, laden with Krishna, I felt a sanctuary in the strength of his determination, in his devotion to his divine duty. My feelings soared and before I knew what was happening my eyes were moist. I realized how little I normally felt, how numb I was to what he gave one small person—me.

The other temporary structure on the property was a pandal set a hundred feet from the road, not quite in the middle of the land. On its high wooden stage the devotees chanted and danced and Achyutananda Swami lectured in Bengali to visitors.

One afternoon, a stocky, muscular American devotee sat squarely before a microphone in the center of the stage and chanted the maha-mantra while accompanying himself with a plain, pounding drumbeat. His voice was more than gruff; it conveyed hardness and ruthless self-assertion. Loudspeakers were everywhere, and the volume was up. There was no escape from this disconsolate chant. I hid my irritation at being subjected to it, because after all, God's holy names were being broadcast and God was nondifferent from his names (that's what Prabhupada had always said). Sri Chaitanya himself had prescribed chanting as the method for attaining God consciousness and assured his followers that there were no hard and fast rules for chanting. I was supposed to appreciate the singing—I was practicing bhakti, after all—but I loathed it. So, even while resenting this vibrational affront, I retired mentally, determined to say nothing, show nothing, betray nothing, determined to pretend to be a neutral, undisturbed devotee. After all, spiritualists are undisturbed, aren't they? I walked around full of aggravation and annoyance, as well as a barely controllable urge to destroy the blaring sound system. The singing went on, flauntingly, the crass voice with its dire need to be heard infiltrating everywhere without mercy. The afternoon went on. Distraught and baffled, I entered Prabhupada's cottage, sat down, and listened to him speak with Bob Cohen, a young Peace Corps teacher in India. Finally, the singing ended. An unspeakably sweet silence ensued.

Leaning back on his bolster, relaxed, not looking at anyone in particular, Prabhupada said, "Good. He has stopped."

I was startled as if from a dead sleep. Had I heard that right? Yes. Exhilaration. Catharsis. My cognitive dissonance, my jumbled, clashing, only semi-suppressed emotions dissipated like fog in the morning sun, and the few of us sitting on that earthen floor before Prabhupada burst into relieved laughter. By doing it himself Prabhupada had just given us permission to express our feelings candidly, humanly, and without apology.

From his spiritual attainment, I later thought, Prabhupada could perceive his disciples objectively and occasionally, as he'd done this time, he'd indirectly express what he perceived. (On another occasion he'd accepted a nickname Dr. Patel, his walking companion in Juhu, had given one of his leading disciples: Major-Domo.) But from my position, although I sometimes strongly felt certain things, I wasn't sure what to do with those feelings—whether they were valid or unnecessarily critical; objective or offensive. After all, so many of his disciples were senior to me and had accepted lots more responsibility than I had. Who was I to call them arrogant, angry, antagonistic, harsh, misogynistic, or anything else? Yet sometimes it felt obvious that they were one or more of those.

After this Mayapur kirtan experience, I tried to take Prabhupada's cue: I respected and supported his followers and at the same time, also respected my own feelings. Although Prabhupada's cue wasn't easy to follow—it took a degree of maturity I didn't always have, and in certain cases I thoughtlessly fell into disrespect—it was balanced. Wholesome. Uplifting, even. By following it, no one was quashed.

One evening, I was again listening to Prabhupada explain Krishna consciousness to Bob Cohen. He was talking about Krishna's separated material energies when Malati entered with a glass of hot milk. Prabhupada said, "Just like this milk is the separated energy of the cow," and, struck by the stark simplicity and clarity of his analogy, I laughed.

Another evening, Prabhupada dexterously used a knife to peel the outer skin of an orange, keeping the peel in one piece. Holding up the limp spiraling peel he said, "Perfectly packaged by Krishna." Hearing that, my heart swelled with a wave of fresh appreciation for Krishna, who so dexterously wraps his gifts before giving them to us.

In the morning after a simple breakfast, Srimati, Dinadayadri (a shy and talented seamstress from the U.S.), and I left the property, turned left onto Bhaktisiddhanta Road and walked ten minutes until we came to a cluster of huts near a sixty-foot-high jackfruit tree, its two-foot-long, olive-green jackfruits dangling perilously from branches high overhead. There, chattering, welcoming, curious villagers gathered around us and asked questions in a language we couldn't understand. We said, "I come from America," or, "I'm American," and invariably got a wide-eyed expression of awe and a Bengali-style repeat of the word "Aameeriicaa," "Aameerriicaan," as if that was the last place on earth anyone could have come from. We turned right onto a narrow path through the fields and fifteen minutes later came to the fine-sanded beaches of the magnificent Ganga, the broad, strong, clear Ganga that carried its sanctified waters from far beyond the Himalayas, offering it to countless farmers, industrialists, and the pious.

Although only recently I'd clutched a vine of faith and swung into an alien realm of spirit, now in Mayapur that vine entered a bucolic, divine scene. Although my faith was tender, the devotees' faith cradled me. In this setting, the entire aspect of spiritual life and the spiritual world became more than plausible. It was positively alluring. Along with my companions I marveled at our inconceivable good fortune at being by the Ganges River in Mayapur with Prabhupada for Gaura Purnima. On the bank of this river of redemption that plied through Mayapur's verdant paddy beneath a horizon of blue-black cumulus clouds, our gratitude swelled.

The air in Mayapur seemed rarefied (was it due to the high ion content from those ominous clouds?), but near the holy Ganges it was even more special: here we sensed the pure, moist ecstasy of the river. How could anyone explain such a thing? But we didn't need it explained; we celebrated it. How many future cycles of death and rebirth were we undoing, how were we advancing spiritually by being here now, by entering this peculiarly soft, glistening water? We replaced our saris with sarong bathing suits, offered respects to the river and gingerly entered her clear water, silky soft silt squeezing between our toes, ripples caressing our legs, then waist, then arms, and then we pushed off and swam steadily against her current. If we didn't resist it, the might of that current would carry us to the Bay of Bengal, seventy miles south. It was the force of another current, the current of the holy names, of Sri Chaitanya, of Prabhupada, of holy food and company and philosophy, that we wanted to stop resisting, that we wanted to give ourselves to and be carried away by. We were young, carefree, filled with irrepressible optimism—*we were going to God*—or rather, *Prabhupada was taking us to God*—and nothing else mattered, nothing could stop us. We coated ourselves with the silty-mud and lay down in the sun until it crusted on our skin like a dried-up cake and hindered our movements. Then we ran, cracking our mud coating, into the water and rubbed it all off. Our skin was as soft as a baby's.

A mile away, in the town on the far shore of the river, we saw houses and the pinnacles of the temples of Navadwip, the town that Sri Chaitanya had roamed when a boy and taught in when a young scholar. There were sacred sites throughout the area: where Sri Chaitanya and his devotees had gathered in civil disobedience against the local Muslim ruler who had tried to ban the chanting of the holy names of God, where they had held nocturnal kirtans, where Sri Chaitanya had befooled some would-be thieves, where he had begun the congregational chanting of the holy names. How momentous for us to be in a place with such transcendent history!

February 29, 1972, was Gaura Purnima, the celebration of Sri Chaitanya's appearance, and ten of Prabhupada's godbrothers joined us on the pandal stage before a large audience of Bengali pilgrims. Yadubara and I received a second initiation from Prabhupada, giving us the privilege to chant the holy *Gayatri* mantra. I photographed Yadubara receiving instructions on the mantra from Prabhupada, and Yadubara photographed me doing the same. Prabhupada patiently showed me how to count the mantras on my fingers and, in his distinct way, pointed to and recited each sacred word written on a small piece of paper as I repeated after him so that my pronunciation was distantly correct. Later, when the smoke from the fire ceremony drifted into Prabhupada's face, I tried to redirect it, using a banana leaf as a fan—the photographs made it seem as if I were hitting Prabhupada with the leaf.

Prabhupada lectured in English, encouraging us to understand the science of God and to again return to our position of attachment to God.

Prabhupada envisioned Mayapur as the international headquarters for his society and so had arranged a ceremonial opening for the large temple he wanted built there. After his lecture, he went down a bamboo ladder into a fifteen-foot pit and placed a gold, ruby-eyed deity of Ananta Shesha on the cornerstone of the Mayapur Chandrodaya temple, the future world headquarters where we would forever more worship Sri Chaitanya and Sri Sri Radha-Madhava.

The five-day festival ended the first annual grand Mayapur Gaura Purnima celebration. It had been a year since I had arrived in India. Looking back on the consumer-driven mindset I was surrounded with growing up, I now saw it as stuffy, banal, confining. Somehow I'd entered a brightly colored, blooming, fragrant, diverse, and lively world where, however unknown and strange it was to others, I felt invigorated.

Prabhupada said, "First of all, understand the maha-mantra. Hare Krishna, Hare Krishna, 'O Krishna, O the energy of Krishna, please accept me.' This is the prayer: now I am engaged in this material service; kindly accept me in *your* service."

I was trying to understand. The world was the same. The way I viewed it was changing.

CHAPTER NINE

Under a Bombay Mosquito Net

The moment I'd been oblivious to—partly denying it could ever come and partly dreading it actually would—was finally upon me: Prabhupada was leaving India for a six-month world tour and I wouldn't be traveling with him. How I would miss his unpretentious presence, his ability to gently go straight to the heart of any matter, his tireless corrections of abounding misconceptions, his kindness, his humor. Prabhupada wanted to establish permanent spiritual centers in as many places as possible and before leaving, he had either purchased or was arranging to purchase land in Mayapur, Vrindavan, and Juhu. The small group of us who'd been traveling with him scattered to these and other places. Along with a few others, Yadubara and I started for Juhu.

The forty-eight-hour Calcutta-Bombay train ride elicited our Indian-train-survival mode: we brought prasad (vegetarian food offered to Krishna) with us—strange-sounding fare like *dokra, chidwa, kakri, bindi subji*, achar, parathas—and augmented it with local fruits from train-station kiosks. After eating our fill we'd climb into our roiling bunks to read, chant, and sleep, and when roused again, have another meal, starting the process over. The noisy clanking rhythm of the trains, the unending flat miles of farmland, the grungy, banged-up, trash-filled towns, the loud grating station catcalls of *"Chai! Chai! Chai!"* our chattering fellow passengers,

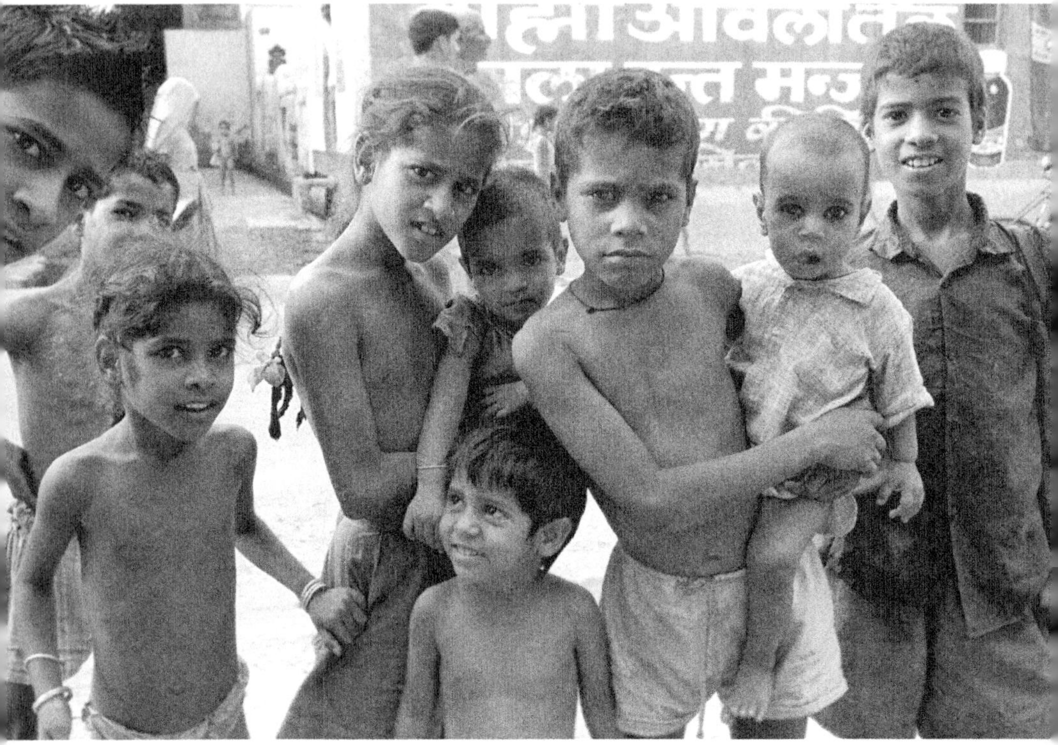

the dust-soot laden air, the increasingly distracting smells from the bathroom (looking down the toilet I saw the blur of railway ties race by), was our sensory fare. In my bunk, lying on my back abstractedly, I luxuriated in the knowledge that life was operating all around me while for the time being I was removed from it—I was obligation-free. When we finally arrived at Bombay's Victoria Station, dirty, crumpled, disheveled, and with sea legs, the ashram routine once again appealed to me.

A few months before—in December, 1971—Prabhupada had seen a four-acre parcel of land a quarter-mile from the ocean in Juhu, a suburb of Bombay, and negotiated with Mr. Nair, its owner, signed a deed and given a down payment to buy it. None of Prabhupada's senior managers had been enthusiastic about the property, but Prabhupada, sensing potential, had us shift from our modern, comfortable, centrally-located Akash Ganga apartment to Juhu, twelve miles north. Even as we were moving, Mr. Nair began a protracted and complex battle to cheat Prabhupada out of his down payment and the land.

The front section of the Juhu property—now called Hare Krishna Land—was next to the road and had been an unkempt tropical jungle locals had used as a dump. Six separate, two-story apartment buildings grouped in a large rectangle took up the rear portion. Although Prabhupada had possession of the land, under Indian law tenants had the right to remain in their apartments. So we set up a large tent—a walled-in pandal—in the open area in the center of the apartment complex where we worshiped, cooked, ate, chanted, read, and shared our space with rats, mice, snakes, and varieties of insects, mostly large ones that flew. The tent was also the men's ashram, and Yadubara, the project's secretary, slept there. I chose to sleep on a straw mat under the fronds of the swaying palm trees that shaded the flat rooftop of a tenant building.

When we were in Akash Ganga, Rishi Kumar was the ashram treasurer. Shortly before his Indian visa had expired we were on a walk one morning when Prabhupada told us that Yadubara should take Rishi Kumar's place and I should assist him. For three days before he left, Rishi Kumar explained his duties to us. Then we were on our own.

Three days later, Yadubara and I went to Prabhupada's room and told him, "This treasury service is giving us too much anxiety."

Without a moment's hesitation Prabhupada replied, "Then don't do it," and until he found someone more suited than us, Prabhupada himself was treasurer.

Now as secretary, Yadubara was more properly situated and regularly reported to Prabhupada by post. He began his first letter:

> My ignorance is so great that sometimes I think that I will never advance beyond the mechanical routine of someone who has just taken to devotional service. This philosophy is so subtle and difficult to understand that only by the mercy of the spiritual master can we hope to understand this greatest of all sciences. Therefore, I am ready to take birth after birth situated as I am now in the modes of ignorance and passion, only praying that I may be engaged in your service.

Both Yadubara and I had accepted the idea that the body is a temporary vehicle for the eternal soul and, after the body's demise, the soul would enter another one. With this and other basic spiritual knowledge, which to me was still revolutionary, Prabhupada was helping me find a road through the wildness of my experiences and understandings. Viewed through the lens of his teachings, my life was starting to make sense.

In Juhu, Yadubara printed Krishna conscious magazines and small books in Hindi and Gujarati and kept Prabhupada abreast of the local Life Membership program, in which a family paid a one-time fee to receive all of Prabhupada's books, a subscription to the monthly *Back to Godhead* magazine, and a pass to stay at any Hare Krishna center for three days for free.

But all was not running smoothly in Juhu. Prabhupada wrote to Yadubara:

> Today I have received a telephone call from Giriraj, and he has informed me that there is some disagreement among you leaders there in our Bombay center. This is not at all a pleasant situation for anyone. I am entrusting this huge task to all of you for working together cooperatively for doing something wonderful. I can understand that you are responsible and cool-headed along with the others, so you take the hand in reconciling all differences.
>
> I have just now written to Gargamuni, Mahamsa, Nara Narayana, and Giriraj as follows: "It is my request even you do not agree on some points, Giriraj is in charge, so please follow his direction and that will please me. I am very much anxious to see the progress at Bombay center, and I want it shall become the first-class preaching center in the world. Please help me in this ambition. If we can manage successfully, we will be attractive for the whole of India. Our task is very heavy. Do not neglect by paltry disagreement. I hope Krishna will bless you to understand my heart and oblige.

Although Yadubara and I stayed apart from it, many of Prabhupada's men were fighting. Sometimes physically. In Calcutta this raw reality had nearly sent me scurrying back to college, but this time it was different. I'd made a commitment to Prabhupada and to my spiritual life. In Juhu I watched as leaders passionately took up Prabhupada's mission according to their understanding of it and sometimes clashed with others so vehemently that they became Prabhupada's "problems." Personality traits were so ingrained, opinions so ineradicable, that collision seemed inevitable. Dismayed, I decided to take Prabhupada's cue to comply with the ashram president's direction—in this case Giriraj's. Fortunately, Giriraj was a level-headed and concerned manager. I also tried to see disputes as "paltry," although sometimes they were confrontations between titans. It seemed to me that the mere fact that we were all trying to be devotees was a symptom of Prabhupada's potent, unrelenting commitment to his spiritual master's desire. And the fact that projects progressed despite our disagreements was mystical in itself.

At the end of his letter to Yadubara Prabhupada wrote,

> N.B. I have just now got one letter from Achyutananda Maharaj from Mayapur, and his plan is to photograph all of the original manuscripts of Bhaktivinode Thakur, which are held by his son, Lalit Prasad Thakur, in Birnagar. This is a very, very important work, so I think you are just the right man for going there with Achyutananda to make photos of each and every page of the old manuscripts, as they are in very bad condition.

When we had been in Mayapur a few months earlier, a small group of us had gone to Birnagar to meet Lalit Prasad Thakur. Unlike Mayapur, Birnagar was a tropical forest, and Lalit Thakur's ashram, folded within it, was a few typical, flat-roofed, single-story, well-worn cement buildings. In one of those simple buildings Lalit Thakur, in his nineties and hunched with age, sat cross-legged on a taut white sheet that covered a thick, firm mattress on a wooden bed so high it was even with the windowsill. His blue eyes were alert and animated, his face expressive. He wore a plain white tee shirt and a white cotton wrap around his waist. Holding his japa beads between the thumb and middle finger of his right hand, he inaudibly chanted the maha-mantra, touching one bead and then immediately moving to the next in a rapid, continuous motion. This was something new for us, as we meditated on and recited the complete sixteen-word maha-mantra on each bead before moving to the next.

Lalit Thakur's upper body was stocky, and when he spoke he used his long thin arms to emphasize points, often punctuating them with grins. He explained how the *gopis'* (Krishna's Vrindavan friends) days are divided into many parts and subparts, with the *gopis* performing specific activities during each part of their day. We listened politely, not knowing what to make of this information; like his chanting method, it was foreign to us.

Later, beneath arching jackfruit and banana trees, we sat on straw mats in the open courtyard and had a traditional Bengali lunch. One dish included chewy cooked jackfruit, which had a mildly sweet, earthy flavor. Maybe it was the flies that swarmed everything, but that afternoon I got even sicker with diarrhea than I'd been in Brussels, although it didn't last as long.

For eight days in July, I covered Yadubara's secretarial duties in Juhu while he photographed 3,000 pages of original, handwritten manuscripts by Prabhupada's great predecessor teacher, Bhaktivinode Thakur. Bhaktivinode Thakur's follower and son, Bhaktisiddhanta Saraswati Thakur, was Prabhupada's spiritual teacher. This was the lineage that linked us with our spiritual heritage. A vital part of Prabhupada's distinction was his connection and unswerving loyalty to this succession of exalted teachers.

After Yadubara returned, Prabhupada wrote to him,

> I have been very much encouraged to see some advertisement booklet printed by Air India wherein the theme is exclusively dedicated to Krishna and Vrindavan. With this idea, the Air India Company is enticing tourists to come to India simply to experience the spiritual life around Krishna. So in

the future, I expect that our Bombay project will be one of the most important showpieces in the world for foreign tourists to actually come and get actual experience of Krishna consciousness or the real Vedic culture. So, with this idea in mind, work very vigorously and with renewed spirit to do the work very gorgeously and raise up first our temple and later on the apartment houses as you have planned.

Regularly, Yadubara and I went with Giriraj to encourage families to become Life Members. Being quiet by nature and afraid of saying the wrong thing, I rarely spoke. Late one night after one such expedition, Giriraj said, "I'm thinking about starting a small magazine with articles on spiritual life and advertisements from supportive businessmen."

"How come?" Yadubara asked.

"The revenue from the ads could cover the magazine's printing costs and also contribute to the temple construction." Prabhupada's vision for the Juhu property was ambitious and expensive.

"There are so many supportive businessmen in Bombay, I bet we could generate a lot of ads for that magazine," I said.

"Yeah, I'm sure we could," Giriraj said to me. "I can canvass for the ads. Would you like to be the editor?"

"Me?"

That was a complete surprise. I thought about it and said, "Yeah, I'd like to do that!"

Thrilled to be entrusted with this project—a magazine, *The Hare Krishna Monthly*, to single-handedly edit, produce, and print—I made the flat roof where I'd been sleeping into my work space by placing a large plywood board over a corner of the three-foot high protective wall so I had a shady spot for my straw mat and mosquito net. Settled there, I began to systematically read Prabhupada's books—the *Bhagavad-gita As It Is*, *Srimad-Bhagavatam*, *Teachings of Lord Chaitanya*, *The Nectar of Devotion*, and the *Krishna* book—to become fit to write for and compile this new publication. Sometime before, to get relief from the substandard living conditions on Hare Krishna Land, I'd accepted an offer from a Life Member who lived nearby and moved into an empty bedroom in his home. Prabhupada had me move back, saying, "To live in someone's home as a guest for more than three days is an imposition."

Now on a rooftop on our own property, I relished the ocean breezes that swayed the coconut trees and my mosquito net, relieving the enervating 90-degree temperatures and helping me stay alert. As days passed and pages turned, I became astonished at the scope of Krishna consciousness—how it included the minutiae and the magnificent, how it saw magnificence in the minutiae, how it saw an integral whole and purpose behind all beings and all things. It was a philosophy that at once reached into the smallest details of daily existence and beyond the bounds of the universes. Prabhupada's books described the height of human achievement in terms of sublime character, qualities, values, and love. Without apology they also described lowly aspects of human consciousness that prevented spiritual progress.

The implications stimulated me even while they eluded me. Krishna consciousness was individual, practical, logical, and apparently simple: the foremost purpose of existence was self-realization, the full awareness of and proper attitude toward the Absolute Truth, whose divine intelligence directed all life with goodness and justice as an ordered, elegant whole that followed divine laws. Serenity was to steer our lives in harmony with the will of that Truth.

Once I'd glimpsed this reality I felt I wouldn't be satisfied until I'd experienced divinity or at least something close to it. When I thought of the life I'd left behind, a life caught in a web of pettiness, a life warped by ceaseless pressures to conform to questionable standards, I felt more and more distant from it. I wanted to follow my own path, to reinvent myself. But was this path I'd chosen—Krishna consciousness—just another way to delude myself? Was it a false path that I'd chosen simply to escape reality?

I had to think about that. If I *was* deluding myself, the culture and tradition still went back thousands of years. It had been carried forward through the chain of spiritual preceptors of which Prabhupada was a part and of which I was a part through him.

Prabhupada, I learned, hadn't declared himself a spiritual teacher. As the disciple of another teacher, Srila Bhaktisiddhanta Saraswati Thakur, he was part of a long line of spiritual teachers that were supposed to trace back to Lord Krishna Himself. It was Bhaktisiddhanta Saraswati who had asked Prabhupada to present Krishna consciousness to the English speaking people of the world. So Prabhupada's mission was not of his own making but was his dedication to a divine desire; it was his offering to his great spiritual lineage. Although he had no resources or backing, after a lifetime of preparation Prabhupada got free passage on a cargo ship and had come to the United States to fulfill his spiritual master's request. The knowledge and practices Prabhupada and his preceptors offered were based on scriptures like the Bhagavad-gita, arguably the oldest of all known scriptures, and confirmed by genuine sadhus both past and present.

While seagulls hung in the flawless summer skies I read stories portraying the rich spiritual soil of those scriptures: stories that rooted me in a distant past and summoned the aspiring spiritual self within me. Through his careful translations and commentaries, Prabhupada would not allow Krishna consciousness to roll off me like water off a lily leaf. He willed it to enter my mind and intelligence and to alter my consciousness. To the extent that I was present to the power of Prabhupada's words, I found I was not a distant observer of spiritual life but an eager recipient of it. And, as far as the women's issue, when I thought about the hundreds of thousands of Prabhupada's words that I'd read and about the spirituality he was inviting me and others to join, it was fully inclusive. Any woman was able on her own right to pursue that spiritual journey—and not necessarily under the protection of her husband or any other male.

The culture of Krishna consciousness, pulsating beneath the skin of life in India, held a comprehensive and richly nuanced worldview scarcely known in the West, at first glance unappealing in its hierarchy, yet with its own uniquely attractive equity, peace, beauty, companionship, relevance, and strong emotions. It seemed to me Krishna consciousness and the culture embodying it weren't my personal escape from reality. But was it a collective escape? I guessed anyone could say that about any religion or ideology.

Sitting on my straw mat on that rooftop, I wondered at Prabhupada and his books. Like him, his books were elating. They were encompassing. They charmed me. The more attention I put into reading them, the more enjoyable they became. They were beyond my capacity to fully comprehend or convey.

I wondered why I was taking this knowledge so seriously, allowing it to alter the direction of my life, to contradict everything I'd learned growing up, to change my sense of self. My grandparents, none of whom I'd met, were certain they were souls and spirits, and the society they lived in had reinforced their faith. Was their faith based on peer pressure? Old wives' tales? Empty hopes? Or on lackadaisically following cultural norms? Did my parents reject the ideas of a soul and spirit because they rejected the rituals associated with those ideas? Because being faithless was more intellectually proper? And why had faith dawned in *me*? I didn't know the answers to these questions, but I knew the potency of faith was momentous. Without it and a tradition that embodied it, everything was impermanent and in flux. It was like building a home on silt.

To follow this path others had carved out was to simultaneously surrender to my spiritual predecessors and to rebel against societal norms. My choice had made me more aware of my ability to choose, more alive to my senses, more conscious of my identity and more determined to push forward, as the effort itself was valuable. Being on this pristine path meant I too could be pristine, regardless of my past follies and foibles. The clarity of Krishna consciousness included me. Somber and elated, as the sun glimmered through the palms, brightly reflecting off the chipped marble rooftop floor even through my mosquito net, I was swept by a sensation I realized I'd bottled up: a view of reality that was coherent and beautiful because there was a person behind it.

Krishna consciousness was a rigorous alternative, a philosophy to help me understand and address the failings I saw in and around me. It was philosophy that gave the calling of my heart clarity and focus and a means to improve myself. It was straightforward, highly interactive and provided me with a map of reality, allowing me to examine the world intellectually as well as emotionally and to accept the mystery that makes the world meaningful—the mystery of God's presence. I was obliged to that mystery for seeking me out.

The weather turned so hot I spent the daylight hours away from my rooftop, but eventually completed a long, disjointed article in praise of Prabhupada for the new *Hare Krishna Monthly*. In May, shortly after I'd turned 22, I wrote to him:

> Actually I have no understanding of this Krishna conscious philosophy, and my brain is so dwarfed that I cannot hope to be enlightened in the future. I long for the understanding that will make this most perfect philosophy a coherent reality, but Krishna has endowed me with such an obstinate subtle body that, although following your instructions, I do not feel the least bit surrendered. I must simply hope against hope that your potency will deliver this floundering soul and enable me to taste a portion of a drop of the ocean of nectar, about which I have heard so much.

Giriraj Prabhu has requested me to inform you of my activities here in Juhu ... Recently I wrote an article entitled, "Prabhupada: India's National Hero." Please find a copy enclosed for your surveillance ...

Prabhupada replied from Mexico City on June 6, 1972:

My dear Visakha,

Please accept my blessings. I am in due receipt of your letter from Bombay dated May 24, 1972, along with the very nice article, "Prabhupada: India's National Hero." I am very grateful to you for your kind words about me, but I do not think that I have done anything, but I am only delivering the best message as it is. Actually, anyone who is a sincere devotee of Krishna and who is rendering service by preaching His message is to be considered as hero. So, you are all heroes of your country and your humanity. Hero means someone who others want to follow as example of the best type of person. So you all become like that, perfect examples of Krishna conscious heroes and heroines, and preach the message exactly as I have taught it to you very seriously and being fully convinced, and others will automatically come forward and join us. We shall all be like one great army of heroes for Lord Chaitanya Mahaprabhu.

Your ever well-wisher,
A. C. Bhaktivedanta Swami

I felt like the luckiest person in the world to receive Prabhupada's letter, to read his understanding of what a hero meant, and to learn that he wanted all of us to become an army of heroes and heroines. It was an elating view I hadn't considered.

Some months later, after an evening discussion in his Juhu room, Prabhupada suddenly said to me, "I have read your article. You have written nicely." Surprised he remembered it and more surprised that he was commenting on it, I mumbled something approaching "Thank you."

"Of course, it is not yet perfect," Prabhupada continued, "but if you go on writing it may become perfect."

I wanted to say, "What are the imperfections? Let's go over them one by one," but I didn't dare ask. Looking at Prabhupada, I was electric with hope. How unexpectedly, mysteriously wonderful it was to receive his encouragement.

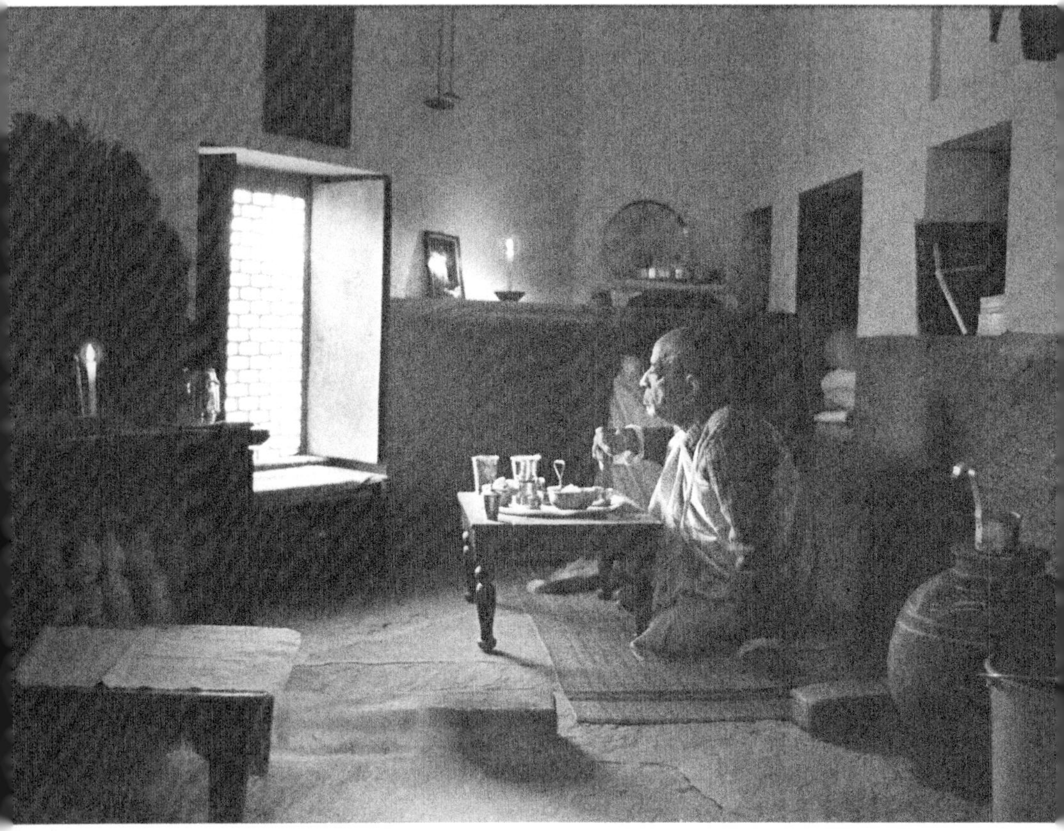

CHAPTER TEN

Relativity On Pause

I enjoyed the challenge of editing and producing *The Hare Krishna Monthly,* and even traveling from Juhu on packed trains to oversee the printing in downtown Bombay was an adventure in austerity. But on hearing that Prabhupada would be in Vrindavan from mid-October to mid-November, I felt compelled to drop everything and join him. Reading his books and following his directives were no comparison to the magic of being with him; practically, he was my Pied Piper. Yadubara didn't need my help in Juhu, and the *Monthly* had a flexible, Indian-style, laid-back schedule, so on October 15, 1972, I went to Vrindavan.

Riding a bicycle rickshaw from the train station with my camera gear on my lap and my arm draped protectively over my luggage, I saw the monsoon had left Vrindavan in a luxuriant wake of greenery and sentience. The peacocks' calls were more vibrant than I remembered them (years later, Prabhupada would say that the peacocks' calls were their chanting), the monkeys' chatter more bubbly, the dogs' wails more piercing, the hogs more robust and the donkeys toiling under huge loads not quite so miserable. Velvety white cows with humps on their backs and long eyelashes peered at me with jet-black eyes. My old Vrindavan acquaintances were cheered to see me in a sari. I felt light yet grounded, in the right place at the right time yet unbound.

Prabhupada and thirty-five of his international students were gathered in the courtyard of Rupa Goswami's medieval Radha Damodar Temple when I arrived. This was where Prabhupada had lived before he'd gone to New York in 1965. As I entered, Dr. O.B.L. Kapoor, a long-time Vrindavan resident, was greeting everyone: "This is really a rare moment in history, because for the first time in the history of the world, for the first time at least in living memory, Vaishnavism, the message of Vaishnavism, the message of Sri Chaitanya, the message of devotion and of pure devotion has been carried to the West and carried so successfully."

Prabhupada responded, "So blessings of Dr. O.B.L. Kapoor. He is a Vaishnava. Although by age he is my younger brother, we are godbrothers, and for the last forty years perhaps, since he was a student at Allahabad and I was doing some business there, we are known to each other. So his association is a great blessing for us. But this reception is actually not my reception. It is the reception of my foreign students."

Prabhupada was being recognized because of us, his American and European followers, but the fact was that without him, there was no way we—or at least I—would be in Vrindavan or interested in anything remotely spiritual.

For this month, Prabhupada would live in the same two rooms he'd occupied before coming to the U.S.—a small bedroom-work space and a separate and smaller kitchen-dining area, which adjoined the Radha Damodar Temple. All of us lived a half mile away in a large red sandstone palace on the bank of the Yamuna River at Keshi-ghat. My roommate was Ganga-mayi, a hardy devotee from Britain with a laugh full of gusto. She and I hung a clothesline across our room, put our straw mats on the floor, and, although it was late and we were tired, lay awake too excited to sleep.

The next morning she and I rose at 3:30 a.m. and silently went down the back steps of the palace into the cool, black waters of the Yamuna. At this time the area was hushed, and we could hear the current's ripples lapping the stone steps, momentarily caressing this consecrated place before continuing to join the great Ganges River. We took a full bath and then, wet and chilled, returned to our room, got ready, and at 4:30 gathered with all the other devotees to worship small brass deities of Radha and Krishna, the same deities that, in July of '71, Yadubara had bought on Yamuna's request and, four months later, had presided over my initiation and Yadubara's and my wedding. Now almost a year after that, I, all of 22 years old, stood reverently before them with other devotees, singing beautiful Sanskrit prayers that described the spiritual master's activities and mood. In that rarified atmosphere, the prayers' refrain, *vande guroh sri charanaravinda*, seemed to penetrate past my mind, past my intelligence. Prabhupada's love, I felt, along with Krishna's and his devotees' love, permeated the very ether around me. I wanted to deeply inhale the rare fragrance of such unexpected love.

At five, Achyutananda Swami led us in a kirtan procession through Vrindavan's dark, empty lanes. We had to walk gingerly to avoid stepping into the six-inch-wide, open, concrete, canal sewers that ran along the edge of the roads. Moving in a cluster while singing and playing drums and hand cymbals, we helped each other stay safe. Dawn found us three miles away at our newly purchased Raman Reti property on the town's outskirts. Peppered with deep holes that had multiple wisps of rebar swaying from them like patches of scrawny bamboo shoots, construction of the Krishna-Balaram Temple was underway, supervised by Subal Swami. Minutes later we turned around, this time following the bank of the Yamuna, to reach the Radha Damodar Temple just before seven—after two hours of walking.

In the back of the temple on the right was a tree-covered area with a small memorial marking Rupa Goswami's place of worship and another, similar memorial marking his tomb. We sat in the speckled shade between these potent shrines. The air had shed the heat of summer and had yet to succumb to winter's cold; it had an in-between tartness just suited for patient hearing.

Prabhupada sat facing us with his back to an old brick retaining wall. He played hand cymbals and sang *Jaya Radha Madhava*, deeply focused, his eyes closed and his head tilted in attention. Coming again into his aura after months of separation, I felt at once resuscitated and humbled and thrilled. And concerned, too. My attraction to Prabhupada seemed unreasonable—even like the dawning of fanaticism—and that gnawed at me. Certainly he was my teacher and I his student, but that didn't mean becoming a zealot, a blind follower. Yet my reservations about this elderly Indian gentleman were dissipating. I, a skeptical New Yorker who was repulsed by even a waft of hypocrisy, was becoming hopelessly attached to and subsumed by Prabhupada.

Prabhupada didn't seem particularly charismatic to me, but he had something I craved—something I suddenly discovered I needed so much that I couldn't live without it. No doubt part of his magnetism was his exotic knowledge, but it was more than that also. It was that his whole being, I felt, expressed his confidence in God—confidence I sorely lacked. More and more I wanted to be with him, to please him, to follow him, to understand him, and to be understood by him. Part of me knew that the more I opened up to Prabhupada, the more vulnerable I'd become, the more I could be hurt. I was scared yet at the same time, compelled.

Almost a year before, Prabhupada had spent a week taking us on pilgrimage to Vrindavan's holy sites; now for a month he would be sitting and speaking to us each morning and evening. In this topmost of all holy places I expected him to divulge details of Krishna's intimate trysts with the *gopis*. But he didn't. He spoke on the basics. He said, "All efforts to understand Krishna are hopeless because no one can understand Krishna unless Krishna personally reveals himself by enlightening us from within our heart. We need to *feel* what he is telling us." *Feeling* the teachings was exactly what I lacked, I thought. I was accepting them from the head: I found some of them logical, some interestingly analytical, some relevant, some hope-giving. But I wasn't experiencing them in my heart. I wasn't emotionally affected but disappointingly cerebral.

When Prabhupada said "we need to *feel* what Krishna is telling us," my spark of hope for spiritual progress morphed into a wildfire of earnestness to hear more about Krishna, for if I heard his teachings deeply enough to *feel* the philosophy, I could become the devotee Prabhupada wanted me to be. I felt like an adolescent—uncertain of herself and her life's direction, but completely sure that she wanted to please her dear father.

I understood that, if Krishna allowed it, I could awaken to his divine presence and also realize my own divinity. The knowledge Prabhupada gave was profound and I'd never before experienced the enchanted sense of elation that it evoked. Willingly in the grip of this elation, I felt an almost ecstatic tug of possibility: I could become peaceful and wise and giving by living to serve God and his creation; I could be drawn upwards and outwards by extraordinary, unearthly realizations about the unlimited yet personable, playful Absolute Truth. Life sparkled. Everything glowed with meaning.

Bhakti, devotional service, was so much more than memorizing verses and performing rituals; it was about me becoming aware of who I was—of realizing my actual, lasting, joyful identity as a spiritual individual.

Prabhupada decided to speak on the Srimad-Bhagavatam's First Canto, second chapter, "Divinity and Divine Service," starting with text 5: "O sages, I have been justly questioned by you. Your questions are worthy because they relate to Lord Krishna and so are of relevance to the world's welfare. Only questions of this sort are capable of completely satisfying the self."

As we listened, pilgrims wrapped in plaid wool chaddars circumambulated the temple grounds and us as well, occasionally ornamenting Prabhupada's words with a mellow "Jaya Radhe." Monkeys in the area bickered, flocks of birds in the dense branches overhead twittered, and the words of Srimad-Bhagavatam entered my ears, replenishing pools and freshets of faith in transcendence—simple faith that had begun as an experiment and which I now wanted to experience more fully and to make more fixed.

Prabhupada said: "So Srila Rupa Goswami, in front of whom we are now speaking, he gave us the definition how one can make progress in spiritual life."

Just before coming to Vrindavan, I'd read some of Rupa Goswami's many instructions for spiritual progress, among them to "reside in a holy place like Vrindavan." That, I thought, was Prabhupada's first instruction to me: "Best that you go to Vrindavan." My life had not been the same since, which was, to me, a testimony to the validity and potency of Rupa Goswami's words.

Prabhupada continued, "Everyone is blind after material way of life. So the mission of human life is to get out of these clutches of maya [illusion]. That is the real mission of life. We are missing the point. We are accepting this body as everything. And the modern civilization means to enjoy bodily comforts as much as possible. That is perfection of civilization. No. That is not perfection of civilization."

"My god," I thought, "practically everyone in the world has gone astray!" Then, soberingly, I realized, *I'm part of the problem—I like comfort and pleasure as much as the next person.* Yet at the same time, I could feel my desires and goals shifting. I was valuing simplicity as something helpful for Yadubara's and my lives together. Waste of any sort was becoming distasteful and disturbing. I was beginning to look askance at what was labeled modern "progress." I could clearly see how the existence of cars, for example, was questionable progress. By using cars people were, no doubt, getting to their destinations faster than they had by horse or bullock or on foot, but car exhaust fumes had poisoned the air in Delhi and many other cities. City traffic jams were notorious, traffic noise was disturbingly loud more or less everywhere, parking was a nightmare, horrible car accidents were prolific and, on top of all that, hundreds of thousands of people were stressed by the heavy costs of owning, maintaining, and driving their cars. Plus, how many miles of rich earth had been covered with asphalt to accommodate traffic? How many people suffered to manufacture these cars? To sell them? To repair them? This was progress?

I found I loved Prabhupada's logic and pragmatism and how he made everything relevant and easy to understand.

He continued, "Here, in this very sacred place, all the Goswamis used to study Bhagavatam under the leadership of Rupa Goswami and his elder brother, Sanatan Goswami. This is the most important place in the world. So, you have got this opportunity. At least for a few days, let us sit down here and under the protection of Srila Rupa Gosvami and Jiva Gosvami, we are not going to imitate them, but we want a place under the shelter of their lotus feet to discuss something of their contribution. Then our life may be one day successful."

To me, success was having a good relationship with Yadubara and the other devotees. It meant doing my photography service well, and it meant that I and my photography were being recognized and appreciated by Prabhupada and his followers. To be an anonymous, unknown face among a mass of devotee faces was not, to me, success.

"Honestly," I thought, "I've given up a desire for success and recognition in the photojournalistic world for a desire for success and recognition in the smaller devotee world. What kind of devotee am I, anyway?"

Prabhupada's teachings surged and throbbed ceaselessly against my old, barnacled mindset like ocean waves pounding a concrete pier. I accepted his teachings to some degree, but I kept to my old ways. Then I accepted them again, but kept to my old ways. Again and yet again. Still, the more I listened, the softer I felt myself becoming; I was slightly less ready to criticize myself and the other devotees, slightly more ready to try to grasp and apply what he was saying.

After his talk, Prabhupada invited questions and an Indian guest asked how we can become peaceful. Prabhupada said we needed to understand three principles: that Krishna is the supreme proprietor, the supreme enjoyer, and everyone's best friend. He added, "So if you want friendship, make friendship with Krishna. And because he's the proprietor, he'll protect you. He'll satisfy you in all respects."

Prabhupada expected me to become friends with God! For Prabhupada, that was a practical and realistic goal. But how could *I* do that? I was filled with skepticism and ego. Yet I was feeling some of those instinctive standards called ideals slip past my reservations. Prabhupada was promising that if I reached for those ideals, I could enter God's playful, nuanced, jubilant company.

But … I found it preposterous to think that I, of all people, could become God's friend. How absurdly arrogant! Besides, if God was my friend, did it mean that he could treat me as other friends had, that he could become impatient and angry with me? That he could decide to stop talking to me?

After the questions and answers, Prabhupada returned to his room for a breakfast prepared by his dear Yamuna Devi, a chef par excellence. Yamuna's singing stirred the heart, her deity worship was meticulous and stunning, she was friendly and, it seemed, without pride. In the Akash Ganga temple room some months before, I'd observed Yamuna sitting cross-legged, spine erect on a mat on the floor, listening to Prabhupada speak. Her eyes were closed and tears were streaming down her cheeks and dripping onto her sari. I'd never seen anyone react to words that way, and it made me long to hear what she was hearing. Now in Vrindavan, Yamuna wasn't sitting with us for the talks but was busy with service.

One morning Yamuna said to me, "You want to come buy some yogurt for Prabhupada with me?"

"Sure," I said. As we walked the short distance to Loi Bazaar, Yamuna reviewed what she'd be making for Prabhupada's lunch that day. "He hasn't had toor dal for a while, so I've soaked some toor dal to make a soup, with of course chapatis on the side. I have some fresh okra so I'll make that with shredded coconut, and I'll make dahi vadas as well," she said. Dahi vada, fried and spiced urad dal puffs soaked in creamy yogurt, was what had inspired our mission. "I have everything I need except the yogurt," Yamuna said as we entered Loi Bazaar and turned left toward the throbbing heart of the market.

By this time of day, Loi Bazaar was in full swing, bustling with shoppers, bicycle rickshaws with their piercing horns sounding, shop owners peddling their wares, haggling customers, children laughing as they skipped to school, and a few cows, dogs, hogs, and monkeys peppered here and there. Yamuna and I, now going single file to wend through the crowds, passed shops selling deities of Radha and Krishna along with paraphernalia to dress and decorate them, shops selling traditional Indian dress (dhotis, kurtas, colorful saris, and woolen chaddars), shops with japa and neck beads made of sacred tulasi wood hanging from dozens of hooks that covered their walls and ceiling, fruit and vegetable stands, stores selling medicines, electric wares, jewelry, souvenirs, garlands, holy books, and sweets, until we finally came to a six-foot-wide place that I'd previously overlooked. Its speciality was milk and milk products.

The middle-aged man squatting on the ledge where the store opened to the street seemed like he'd just stepped out of a shower. His black hair glistened, his face and skin were smooth and clean and the red and blue lungi he wore seemed new. He was smiling broadly at Yamuna as he swayed, still squatting, to the container of fresh yogurt and removed its woven dried leaf covering. The flies seemed less interested in this store than in other sweet and milk stores.

"This is the place Prabhupada used to get his milk when he was living alone in Vrindavan before he came to the U.S.," Yamuna told me.

"Really! And is this the same person who was there then?"

"No, this is his youngest brother."

"Oh!" Suddenly everything about this store and the man in it seemed special.

"*Dahi,*" Yamuna said to the man.

"*Kitna?*" he replied.

"*Doh. Bara,*" Yamuna replied. The man examined two large rinsed clay cups to insure they were clean and deftly filled them both with thick yogurt, re-covered the large yogurt container and then covered both cups with leaves. Yamuna, smiling, paid him and, now she and I, each carrying a cup—one hand under and the other over it to keep its leaf covering in place, walked back the same way we'd come.

Just before we reached the Radha Damodar Temple kitchen area, a large and aggressive male monkey jumped in front of us, stood up with teeth bared and began to lunge for the coveted yogurt. Yamuna, who had a dramatic bent, instantly screamed her mighty scream, threw her cup of yogurt high into the air and ran into a nearby room. As the clay cup hit the ground, broke, and the yogurt splattered, the monkey was momentarily distracted. I, decidedly undramatic and intent on protecting Prabhupada's yogurt, covered my cup more tightly, curled my body over it to hide it from the monkey, and also ran into a room. Hearing of Yamuna and my differing reactions to this little misadventure, Prabhupada chuckled and commented, "Just see the different natures."

I had a light breakfast and afterwards, camera in hand, wandered my old haunts, but this time with tall, thoughtful, brooding Hayagriva, an English professor from Ohio State University, who was writing a book he was calling *Vrindavan Days*. I would later read his description of me: "introverted, ectomorphic, taciturn, and stone-faced." Hayagriva, whom Prabhupada sometimes affectionately addressed as "Professor Howard Wheeler," was refreshingly free of the desire to control things, laconic, and occasionally made astute and wry observations. His old friend, Achyutananda Swami, was our guide and translator. I was his photographer.

Hayagriva described one of our first adventures:

> Her face set like a Mount Rushmore President, Visakha walks up the seven steps to the altar. There are no less than three sets of Deities in the dim alcoves: the Deities belonging to Chaitanya Mahaprabhu's biographer, Krishnadas Kaviraj; expansions of Jiva Goswami's original Radha Damodar Deities; and Jayadev Goswami's Deities. These Deities are guarded by strict *smarta*-brahmins, and photographs have never been allowed.
>
> Before the pujari can protest, Visakha takes five pictures. The lamp flashes like a strobe at the Avalon Ballroom.
>
> "No photos! No photos! No! No! No!" the pujari shouts, waving his arms. The temple goswamis jump to their feet, but it's too late. Visakha is already walking out to the street.
>
> "Good shots?" I ask.
>
> "Yes," she says, giving a tiny smile. That's all. Just a typical Visakha smile, lips closed.

More and more I was using photography, a skill I'd started honing since I was seven, as my primary way to serve Krishna, Prabhupada, and their followers. By photographing temples, devotees, and devotional activities, I was transforming what I loved to do into a devotional activity, into bhakti-yoga, by doing it to please God and his devotees. Through this pleasant discovery—that by utilizing my existing skill I could progress spiritually—I was beginning to find my niche and stride in my new life. On Vrindavan's dusty streets something welled up in me: I sensed that I was made for devotional service—that I could find myself and God through my photography.

Granted, at present I was far from God, and the person I thought I was—a young American woman, a photographer—wasn't actually me. I was a soul, an eternally joyful part of God. I realized I wanted to stop measuring my self-worth in terms of how others saw me. It would be a spiritual disaster for me to rest content with my exterior identity, with my expertise, with my past accomplishments. Was my existence validated because I'd honed a skill? Because I'd published a book? Were those safe indications that I existed?

But by using my skill in God's service as attempted acts of devotion, I could get closer to him and to myself; I could be lastingly happy. I wanted my photography work to not be driven by ambition for fame or prestige but to be my worship, my passage to reality, my path to pleasing Prabhupada and his followers. I began questioning my mundane motives and tried penetrating my many disguises. Perhaps one day little quiet unassuming me could become qualified to be seen by God himself?

As the three of us roamed from holy place to holy place, it seemed a glow of animation filled Vrindavan, as if hundreds of gaily talking persons occupied its homes, streets, and lanes. Every nook and cranny teemed with sated and irrepressibly positive life. I walked with a lightened heart, a heart that threw off old sorrows and at least some concerns about becoming a zealot, a heart warmed and alive with more certainty of the mystical.

Around lunchtime I usually returned to my home at Keshi-ghat to join the others for Malati's nourishing rice and bean stew *(kitchari)* with chapatis and yogurt, and then relax. But on this day, instead of going to Kesi-ghat, I went back to the Radha Damodar temple where Yamuna was preparing Prabhupada's lunch, now with half the amount of yogurt that she had planned. Her mood amazed me. She was constantly absorbed in cooking, something I hardly ever thought about. From early morning, Yamuna would shop for, clean, and cut vegetables and fruits; pick out foreign particles from the dals, rice, and spices; soak and marinate; make *chaunces* and fresh pastes; and consistently clean the utensils, kitchen, and eating areas. The loving intensity of her absorption was a wonder to behold and, sampling the exquisite preparations she made—all healthy and varied traditional yet subtly flavored Indian fare—I could only think they'd descended directly from the spiritual world. Yamuna, deferential to Prabhupada and attentive to his needs, seemed continuously appreciative of the gift of bhakti he offered.

On this afternoon, I stood nearby as Yamuna placed Prabhupada's lunch plate on the small table before him and said, "Would it be all right if Visakha makes a photograph of you as you take your lunch?"

Prabhupada glanced from her to me, ready with my camera, and said, "Yes, that's all right."

To get the best angle, I squatted in the small area where Yamuna had cooked, which adjoined the eating area where Prabhupada sat, now meditatively looking out the latticed windows toward the tomb of the great 16th century devotee, Rupa Goswami. I felt a surge of warmth in my heart for this was one of Prabhupada's two original rooms at the Radha Damodar temple and it was at this same spot where, in the years before he'd come to the U.S., Prabhupada had looked out that same latticed window and deeply contemplated his own spiritual master's directive to him to bring spiritual life to the English-speaking people of the world. The scene felt momentous.

In the early evening we gathered at Radha Damodar again for Prabhupada's second talk, this one on *The Nectar of Devotion*, Prabhupada's summary of Rupa Goswami's perennial masterpiece on the science of bhakti. Prabhupada said, "An atheist will say, 'Where is God?' Because he has no eyes to see God. But a theist sees God, or Krishna, twenty-four hours. He does not see anything else. The material elements, they are simply Krishna's external energy. So as soon as a devotee sees anything material, he immediately sees the energy of Krishna, and along with the energy of Krishna, he immediately sees Krishna with reference to the context ..."

Krishna, God himself, was in me and outside of me and all around me. Who could fathom such a thing? I was sleeping on God when I lay on my mat, eating God when I ate Malati's *kitchari*, breathing God when I inhaled, touching God when I touched my beads or anything else, stepping on God when I walked the Vrindavan (or any other) streets, seeing God no matter what I saw. It was mind-boggling, mind-exploding. Yet enthralling too. Logically, it made sense—the energy of God is nondifferent from God: God's energy is also God. But how to live a "normal" life with such an understanding?

Prabhupada continued, "If you see God, Krishna, from the Hindu angle of vision, if you see God from the Christian angle of vision, then you cannot see God. That is not seeing God. You have to become freed from all these designations."

Okay, so God is all around me always, but I can't perceive him because my consciousness is covered, because I'm not free of "designations." And, I wondered, when will that fine day come when I no longer identify with my body? Plus, if it isn't happening for me, with all the guidance and opportunities I'm getting, how can I expect it to happen on a larger scale? And Prabhupada wants me to promote this understanding, but how can I effectively promote an understanding that I haven't realized? Doubts bubbled up and dissipated and bubbled up again.

The talk ended, we bowed our heads in respect and gratitude, and a few of us followed Prabhupada into his small room for discussions. Ten people filled up his room, but I'd always squeeze in somewhere, wanting to hear more and to bask in Prabhupada's uplifting aura. One evening I was sitting against the wall to Prabhupada's right when a small monkey darted in from the back door, dashed in front of me, grabbed a bunch of bananas that a guest had put on Prabhupada's low table, and turned to run out the way it had come. As it passed by me holding the bananas, without thinking I raised my arms, which were covered with a chaddar, leaned forward, and placed them down around the monkey. The monkey, suddenly inside the dark tent of my chaddar, crouched low, burst out underneath it, and continued charging for the back door. When I sat back up, I was happy to see that the bunch of bananas remained—only the one banana the monkey had been holding and hadn't let go of was gone. With satisfaction, I put the remaining bananas back on Prabhupada's table.

The astonished guest who'd given the bananas commented, "That was most unusual. *We don't do that with monkeys!*" Prabhupada smiled slightly and cocked his head as if to say, "These Westerners are unusual! It's to be expected," and continued. "Just see how intelligent this monkey is," he said. "This shows that in their own respect all living entities are intelligent. This monkey is so intelligent practically no one even saw him. He just took the bananas and ran out. This is what it's like in the material world. Everyone is very expert in their own sphere. So, we have to become expert devotees, not expert like the monkeys."

A devotee asked Prabhupada about animals like dinosaurs that used to populate the earth but were now considered extinct.

Prabhupada had a scriptural view of extinction. "There are always 8,400,000 species of life in the material world," he said. "Not more and not less. The species that you consider extinct may no longer exist on this planet, but why are you only considering this planet?"

Eight million four hundred thousand species? Life on other planets? I frankly had no idea how many species of life there were and I didn't think anyone knew for sure either. Weren't researchers regularly discovering new species? And I'd been taught that ours is the only planet known that's inhabited.

So, did I believe the scriptural statements Prabhupada was quoting, or did I believe modern scientists?*

Well, at least in Vrindavan, I didn't believe modern scientists.

How was it that I was like a baby bird being borne aloft by some steady thermal of unflinching faith? It was astonishing yet becoming more natural for me to view the world through the lens of the scriptures and to think of Krishna, the master of all mystics, behind everything, to think of myself as a spiritual being unencumbered by the body I inhabited. Prabhupada always seemed to be there with more of the same dynamic knowledge, keeping lofty thoughts unfurled before me, and helping me stay the course. The scriptures, our glorious predecessors, the very soil we walked on, the prayers we offered, the devotion of the Vrindavan residents and their opulence of renunciation, the holy waters, the resonance of temple bells and the deities in those temples, were gusts to bear me and all the rest of us skyward as we stretched and strengthened our tiny wings.

After two hours in his room, Prabhupada said, "Now it's late. We should all rest," and reluctantly I filed out with the others. On the way to returning to my Keshi-ghat room, I sat and watched the goings-on in Loi Bazaar. Mounds of various milk sweets were piled high in sweet shops as chefs, squatting near the mounds, stirred large woks of boiling milk to make more

---

* Later I read in the PLOS Biology journal that scientists now estimate there are 8.7 million species of life.

sweets. Parents bought hot milk for their children and to cool it, the milk sellers poured the boiling milk from one container to another, spreading their arms so the stream of milk became like a four-foot long white, arched elastic band, its steam rising as it cooled in the night air. The din of Hindi haggling and the sweet smells of cooked-down milk hung over everything.

As I watched, I revived the feelings of wholeness and swept-upness I had just experienced in Prabhupada's presence. In my heart, I tried to capture the freshness of his clear-cut certainty and desire to share rare knowledge. His caring was bearing my weight. Prabhupada, I felt, liked me just for myself and welcomed my growing attachment to him, for it meant I'd hear from him about Krishna and become, perhaps, more attached to Krishna. In one way it all felt natural and right, but in another, concerns wouldn't stop niggling at me. What would my atheistic parents and communistic brother think?

And worse, was this path actually mine or was I too weak to find my own path or was I meekly following Yadubara? Since the time I'd been initiated, mine had become a life of attentive listening in order to receive Prabhupada's and Krishna's message. It was by hearing and agreeing with their words that I would supposedly be freed of fear, blindness, hatred, earthly attachments, and the determination to be someone other than my true self (whoever that was); that I'd realize I was known and loved by Krishna; that my destiny was to be in concert with him; that it was more normal for me to act in this way than it was for me to be centered in myself. This change of heart, if and when it ever came, would be the work of Krishna, the work of grace. It would be a divine gift. Or, it would be from being a brainwashed follower—a cult member who was blindly following her husband.

The pressing question for me was, *"What did I think?"* Or, even before that, *"Was I thinking?"*

One night in Keshi-ghat just before I feel asleep, the answer came to me: I was not *just* thinking, I was finally feeling too.

In the year since I'd been initiated I infrequently and remotely thought of the transcendent world. But as the days passed during this singular month, the situation reversed—I was living in the transcendent world and only sporadically remembered the earthly one. Radha and Krishna permeated everything. I was filled with a great, restless, joyful eagerness and expectation. It seemed we were not standing on the sandy surfaces of Vrindavan, but hovering—unfettered by the mundane. Everything, even the dust, was an epiphany of glory filled with the sense of Krishna's immediacy, of another realm where all the pains of this one were unknown, where everything was important—everything was related to Krishna—everything happily mattered. Krishna's presence was so near I could almost see, feel, smell, hear, and taste him everywhere. I was in his place of pleasure pastimes, of heroic deeds, of loving intimacies. He must be by my side walking with me; thus my inexplicable lightness of being, my sense of otherworldliness, of irrepressible gladness, of inexpressible pleasure.

On my Juhu rooftop I'd appreciated Krishna consciousness intellectually. In Vrindavan my skepticism and self-consciousness abated enough that I began to love Krishna. I was swept up by his blissful, all-inclusive, all-attractive divine presence. Everything was laden with meaning, as if a new light had been cast over the world. Not a single moment felt ordinary. The ultimate reality was so overwhelmingly prominent that the relative reality stopped. The whole material world was insignificant; all that had happened in the past was insignificant. I felt as if I was bigger than matter, as if I was beyond history, as if I had everything inside me, and now finally had something to strive for. I brimmed with longing for what was to come.

Prabhupada, humorous and happy, filled with Krishna, was injecting me through his words with the thrill of anticipation and mystery. In recovering my precious self in a precious, welcoming world, I was ablaze with a dizzy feeling of joie de vivre. I was free, completely free, and life was fantastic. For the first time I felt it was truly possible for me to behold and befriend my supreme friend. My thankfulness to Prabhupada and Vrindavan overflowed.

Prabhupada, meanwhile, was trying to extend the Vrindavan atmosphere everywhere. On November 11th, he wrote to Yadubara, who was working hard as the secretary for the Hare Krishna Land in Juhu, that he wasn't interested in big buildings but in engaging everyone in Krishna's service, especially in telling others about Krishna. He encouraged Yadubara to improve in telling people about Krishna and in distributing books about him, for then without a doubt money and buildings for Krishna would come. On reading a copy of this letter not long after he sent it, it seemed to me that Prabhupada's faith, empowered as it was by his own spiritual teacher, was so immovable, so staunch that it was not belief but the substance of things I couldn't see.

One evening two days before we left Vrindavan, Shyamasundar arranged a meeting between Prabhupada and a well-known, blind guru who taught that God is not a person but an all-pervading energy and that we, as part of that energy, were God. I went along to photograph. The four of us—Prabhupada, the guru, Shyamasundar and I—along with two of the guru's followers, sat in a small, bare, yellowish room lit with a single bulb suspended from a two-foot wire. Prabhupada introduced Shyamasundar and me, explaining that I was married and that I photographed for Krishna conscious publications. Prabhupada said, "We must hear and chant and glorify the supreme person, not the void, not the energy of that person." The guru offered no resistance. Prabhupada asked Shyamasundar to sing the Hare Krishna maha-mantra and then me to sing the names of Sri Chaitanya and his associates. Afterwards, back in his Radha Damodar room, Prabhupada told me, "Visakha Prabhu, you sang very nicely." It was the first time anyone had complimented my singing.

November's full moon marked the last night of our stay. Yamuna, Ganga-mayi, and I took our sleeping mats to the roof of the Keshi-ghat palace, basked in the moonlight and talked about Krishna's childhood activities. One of those pastimes, Krishna's confrontation with a malicious horse, had happened at Keshi-ghat, and in the telling it seemed as if it had just occurred. For me, spellbound, this month had been the happiest of my life. I'd never before felt so much joy. In my heart—almost in my hands—incomplete effervescent truths about God, scarcely clear enough to be called realizations, dawned. I couldn't capture these feelings in words, but they led me to more concrete thoughts about my spiritual practices. Divinity had nothing to do with domination or wealth or sex or fame or position or power or drugs. I now understood that if I wanted those dawning realizations to shine forth like the sun, I had to learn to control my mind and senses and put my whole self into my spiritual practices. That was the only way to have something totally transcendent happen to me. From purity, faith would come, and from faith, Krishna. Prabhupada had said so. A baby sparrow could soar.

I was becoming free and strong—free from the constraints empiric reasoning and my former beliefs had put on my experiences, strong from Krishna's presence in fragrance and color and sound and taste and touch. I never expected to receive such abundance. And behind it was the promise of so much more to come if I could only shake off my pesky lingering doubts and reservations—those alien things that hardened my heart.

As I left Vrindavan with my godbrothers and sisters, I contemplated my graceful aristocratic lady friend, faith, who, during my first visit to Vrindavan, had so elusively yet gracefully danced in its many temples and through the lives of its many residents. That charismatic lady was still very much present in Vrindavan, I thought, only now, unexpectedly, she was no longer alone. Now she was with her dearest companion, love.

The two of them were dancing together.

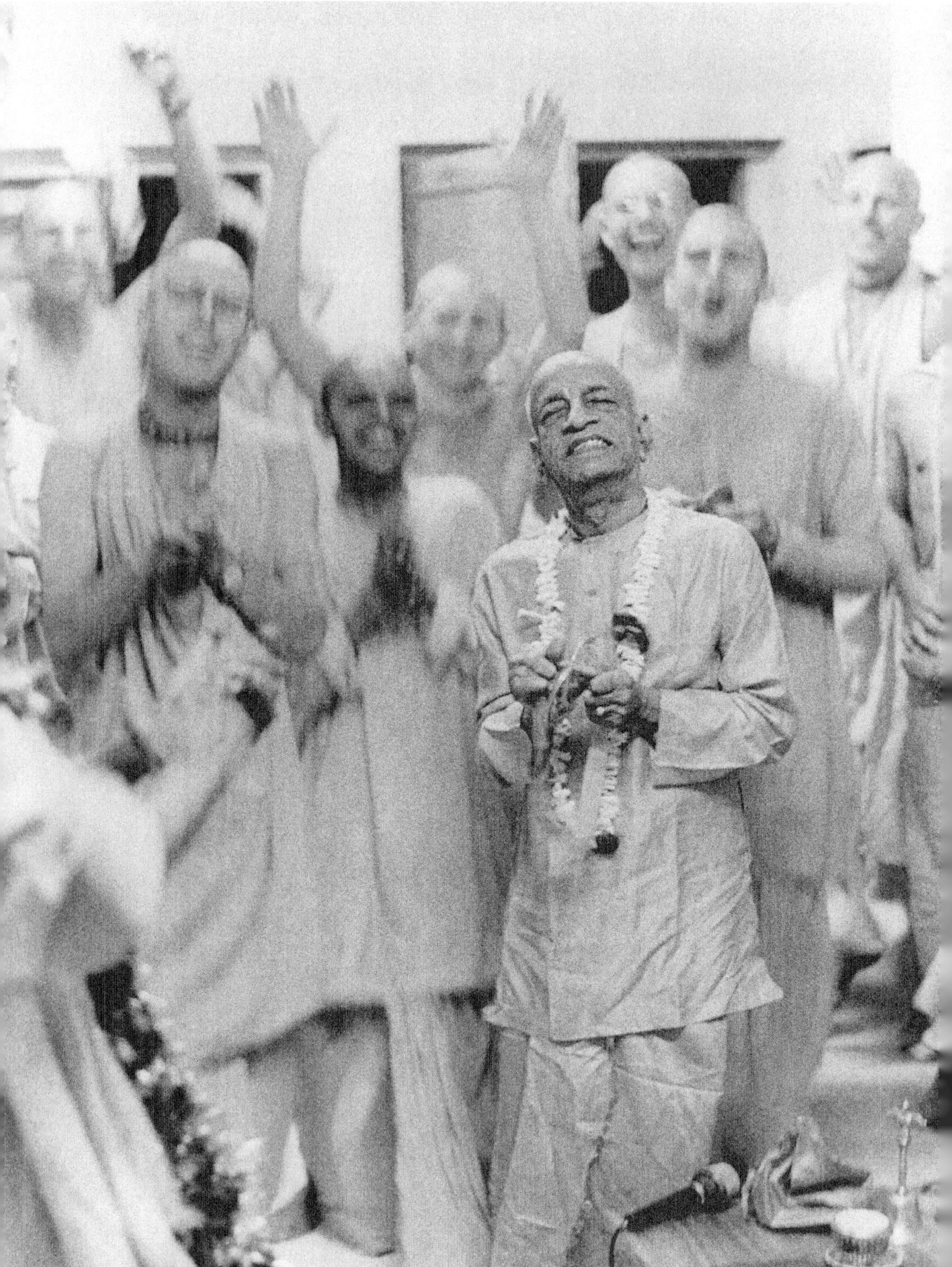

CHAPTER ELEVEN

On Tour with Dichotomy

We traveled south to Hyderabad where Yadubara joined us for a week-long pandal festival near the city center. Just by seeing how supple and energetic he was, I got a sense of how busy he must have been in Juhu, and when we caught up with each other, I found it was so. He'd been on the go there all day, every day since I last saw him. And he was satisfied and even happy with that busyness, which was relieving to hear.

As for me, after the high of Vrindavan, I ached from the formidable black fissure between the person I was and the person I wished I could be. Imagine if I could become aware of the divine presence behind everything and of his goodness? Rooted in that awareness, I could become kind, giving, joyful. But in truth I was absorbed by the pettiness in my life, disturbed by irritations and envies and miserliness, and I longed for comfort and cosseting, prosperity and prestige. How to deal with the chasm between my ideals and my reality? Beating myself up about it didn't seem productive. Neither did ignoring it. Pretending I was something I wasn't left me feeling dismal and others feeling distrustful. Then? I gradually learned that I had to grow up enough to accept and forgive myself without letting myself become defeated and complacent; I had to go on trying without becoming dispirited, trusting that sooner or later, the process of spiritual life would have a positive effect. I foresaw a long, slow journey. I wasn't what I ought to be, but at least I wasn't what I used to be.

I'd given up my bright career path for something exotic and intangible. Sometimes I thought I just might be crazy, as the hecklers in the West claimed we street-chanters were. Maybe I was just deluded, thinking I could come closer to God Almighty by murmuring his names in the wee hours of every morning and photographing gratis for his pleasure. In my effort to move forward spiritually, I'd stopped reading the daily news, hearing popular music, and keeping up with anything that wasn't part of my search for the Absolute Truth. I'd separated myself from that "real" world, which was, I had now learned, a "temporary manifestation of God's external energy," maya, illusion.

In moments of honesty I understood that to an extent greater than I generally wanted to admit, I *was* deluding myself. That in the year since my initiation, although I'd been trying hard, whatever spiritual progress I'd made was fragile and skin-deep. In fact, that "progress" could topple like a Tiffany vase held by a two-year-old. If I toppled, I'd be in shards—I'd find myself nowhere either spiritually or materially.

Profound quandaries invaded my simple life: how was I supposed to feel humble towards and respectful of people who were seriously wasting their lives in futile pursuits? And why weren't most of the devotees, who were supposed to be above worldly matters, happier?

In a very real way, the only solid thing I had to hold onto was Prabhupada. I trusted him.

Daily, using common sense, logic, humor, and knowledge, Prabhupada whittled away at my tethers to and faith in materialistic values and goals. Over and over again he redirected my faith toward bhakti, devotional service to the Supreme Person, Krishna, and everything related to him. Bhakti, I was coming to understand, balanced the soul's intrinsic dignity and power—the soul is, after all, an integral part of the supremely great Person—with the soul's insignificance—it is, after all, only a tiny fragment of that supremely great Person. Finding this balance could unearth my hidden jewels of the enthusiasm to strive for God as my God-given right, and the patience to be contented with a natural progress toward him, because, after all, I am only tiny.

Although I was new to bhakti and still immature, I felt Prabhupada, who was certainly not new and who had a deep connection with Krishna, cared about me. It wasn't that he and I conversed often; in fact, although there were many times when I could have piped up and said something to him, I usually didn't. As a photojournalist, I was trained to intrude on my subjects as little as possible, and I was almost always photographing when I was with him. I was constantly concerned with exposure, lighting, composition, lenses, and film. Aside from that, I wasn't inclined to speak up for fear of looking foolish before Prabhupada. Plus, by nature I was reserved and shy. If all that wasn't enough, Prabhupada was often with jockeying male disciples who didn't want my participation. So, I was (or made myself?) content simply with my service.

Although I occasionally felt uneasy about being so quiet around Prabhupada—did he expect me to speak?—after a while it became the norm. At the same time, since Prabhupada seemed to sense my state of mind, I wanted that state to be one I wasn't ashamed of. I was the silent one scurrying around in the shadows, observing and photographing with what I hoped was a spiritual attitude.

Prabhupada was an enigma to me. He was only five foot four, yet I couldn't think of him as a small person. Sometimes he was a grave philosopher and at other times as full of wonder as a child. I never saw him rush. I almost never saw him use a telephone (there were no computers in those days), yet he ran an institution. He was pessimistic about the value of material life yet lived joyfully in this world, down-to-earth yet otherworldly. And not only did he seem to recognize his own insignificance, but he was also at peace with it. I was in awe of this last one. How did he do that?

As he noticed them, Prabhupada often pointed out and chuckled at life's idiosyncrasies and idiocies, opening me to a new way of seeing things. ("They are smoking Kool cigarettes," he said once, after seeing an ad, "inhaling smoke and thinking they are cool. Do you become cool by inhaling smoke?") I wanted to try to see through his lens, what I came to call "the Prabhupada lens." Perhaps if I could see this way I could become a little more like him—dauntless and convinced.

Looking back to the way I was thinking before I was initiated, I realized how my old convictions were being overturned, how I was suddenly on a new and unforeseen course. There were "head" reasons for this: the logic and breadth of the teachings, the scriptural support for them, the long line of exceptional personalities who represented them, the vibrant culture that embodied them. But still, after two decades of skepticism and atheism coursing through my veins, why was I allowing myself to be subsumed by Prabhupada? I was allowing him to practically swallow me whole. This was an entirely unexpected twist to my life. But instead of feeling constricted by it—domineered by him—I felt stimulated and alive. Another enigma.

Prabhupada was offering me a tantalizing promise of entrance into a world of complete enchantment. And I'd accepted that promise as attainable truth. Not only did I believe what he said, I longed for what he offered. The more that I began to sense the presence of the spiritual dimension, the more I found myself feeling not only sheltered by it but elevated. I was bursting with eagerness to get there.

Prabhupada didn't speak directly to me often, but he made me feel that the possibilities for me, personally, were limitless.

In Hyderabad we stayed at the lavish estate of Mr. Pannalal Pittie, a Life Member. On a walk one morning around the expansive grounds, Prabhupada imitated Guru Maharaji, a charismatic boy who claimed to be God. Someone challenged, "If you're God, then show us your universal form like you showed it to Arjuna."

"I have already shown you, but you did not have the eyes to see it. You need divine eyes to see it," Prabhupada said. "When I see you're qualified, I'll give you divine eyes."

"If you're God, why are you interested in women?" another person said.

"This is my pastime. You cannot understand it. It is inconceivable to you."

"If you're God, why do you get sick and have to see a doctor?"

"That is my mercy on the doctor. I want to give him an opportunity to make advancement by rendering service to me."

One after another, all arguments were quashed until Yadubara said, "If you're God, why did some disenchanted follower throw a pie in your face?" (That incident had been reported in the newspaper headlines the day before.)

"Yes," Prabhupada said, "this is defeat for Guru Maharaji. In all God's pastimes, you will never find him humiliated."

It had never occurred to me that God had never been and would never be humiliated. Of course! Why would the controller of all beings and the giver of all grace allow himself to be disgraced? I don't like to be humiliated, and neither does God. I can't always stop it from happening, but he certainly can. God's a person with unlimited potencies. It was mind-expanding.

Occasionally on our walks, at Prabhupada's request I'd take photographs of something he'd noticed—a cottage made from local building materials, a small island in a lake—and send the pictures to various leaders to give them ideas for developing their projects in West Virginia, West Bengal, and other places.

One afternoon I knocked on Prabhupada's door, heard "Come in," and entered. The curtains were drawn, and it took time for me to adjust to the weak yellow light from the desk lamp on the low table Prabhupada sat behind. Like all the rooms he occupied, this one was pervaded by a youthful verve.

"May I ask a question?" I said.

Prabhupada had his eyes closed. For a moment he didn't answer.

"Yes," he said, slowly, looking at me.

I'd been trying to understand how the modes of material nature—goodness, passion, and ignorance—worked. The Bhagavad-gita explains that a person in the mode of goodness is knowledgeable, moral, and pious, but with a tendency to be self-satisfied. In passion, one is a slave to lust, greed, hard work, and the desire for prestige. And in ignorance, one is a prisoner of laziness, moroseness, and illusion. What I didn't understand was what Prabhupada had written in his introduction to the Bhagavad-gita, namely that "material energies are in the mode of ignorance."

I could have asked Prabhupada about anything in the whole magnificent creation on that sultry afternoon, but I said, "If we take a single material atom, is it in the mode of ignorance, or is it covered by the mode of ignorance?"

Prabhupada responded as if this were the most natural question in the world for a sari-clad young American woman in the middle of India to ask him. "It is covered by ignorance," he said. "All energy comes from Krishna and so all energy is originally spiritual. But when it's separated from Krishna due to our lack of understanding, our forgetfulness, then it appears material."

Prabhupada closed his eyes and broadened the topic.

"We should not be satisfied to remain in a neutral position, simply regarding Krishna with awe and veneration," he said. "Of course, even passive appreciation of Krishna's greatness is good, but better is to actively serve him."

I realized that Prabhupada was not just answering my question but speaking to me, nudging me to go beyond the mind and intellect, for Krishna created those and could not be encompassed by them unless he allowed himself to be. And he allowed himself to be when we reciprocated his love. Krishna wanted my love and my love was expressed through bhakti, through serving him and his creation with devotion.

I'd heard what Prabhupada told me many times, but never spoken by him to me alone. I'd been photographing and studying and, from a safe, neutral place, remaining emotionally distant. Prabhupada was encouraging me to try the richer flavors of devotional service and in that way transcend my introversion, inhibitions, and fears—to be more than a quiet, detached observer. He was urging me to reciprocate with God.

Before Prabhupada I felt vulnerable, receptive, responsive. My mask fell away. I knew he was trying to help me and that I needed his help. I was incredibly sick of having love for Krishna and his creation inside me and being unable to feel or express it. I longed to feel more. Prabhupada was broadly casting vibrant seeds of bhakti and anyone, even a neophyte like me, who came near just one of them was swept up by their potency. Once again, my entrenched skepticism dissolved and Prabhupada's categorical conviction coalesced within me.

And his words also startled me a little. I found myself leaning closer to his desk, as if physical proximity and a careful study of his features would help me grasp his meaning. Prabhupada looked at me, now just four feet away, as I thanked him, grateful for his concern.

I left, torn. On one side, I was disappointed by my stubborn, cautious self. On the other, I felt emboldened by Prabhupada to flourish as an ecstatic devotee of Krishna. If only I could break through the shell of this obstinate mind that covered me, just as the mode of ignorance covered the material atom.

In terms of attendance and favorable response, the Hyderabad pandal was highly successful. G. Pulla Reddy, a wealthy businessman, donated land in the city center for a temple, and newspaper reporters wrote that the yearlong drought had ended due to the sincere chanting of God's holy names at the pandal. Prabhupada gratefully accepted the donation and agreed with the reporters.

Before leaving, Prabhupada wanted to tip two of our host's housekeepers. One had enthusiastically extended himself to make us all feel welcome and comfortable; the other was dutiful. I watched as Prabhupada discreetly gave the first one twice the tip of the second.

After Hyderabad, I rejoined Yadubara in Juhu for a week, and then left to photograph the next pandal, which was near the center of Ahmedabad. By the time I got there, the first day of the pandal was underway and Prabhupada was giving the morning Bhagavad-gita class. Over the loudspeakers I heard him saying, "Our present position is to defy the existence of God. This is our present position in material life. 'There is no God. God is dead. I am God. You are God.' This is defying the supremacy of God. Therefore, to understand God, you have to surrender; otherwise, it is not possible. You cannot defy and at the same time understand God. This is not possible. You cannot understand God by challenging, 'Why God?'"

I paid the rickshaw driver, put my luggage behind the stage and began photographing the huge, attentive crowd. As I photographed, once in a while I glanced at Prabhupada and saw him watching me. During the kirtan following the class, I walked through the audience holding up Gujarati *Back to Godhead* magazines, calling, "*Doh rupia!*" *["Two rupees!"]*. I sold armfuls of them. Again I noticed Prabhupada watching me. Something unusual was going on. A half-hour later, Nanda Kumar told me that Prabhupada wanted to see me.

When I went to his room, Prabhupada was speaking with a couple and their two children. He introduced me as an "expert photographer." Flustered, I knocked over his cane, which was leaning against a dresser. I squatted down and replaced it while Prabhupada continued to speak to the guests. After they left he asked, "Have you eaten breakfast?"

"No, Prabhupada, not yet." I'd been too curious to eat.

Prabhupada said, "Tamal and Shyamasundar are in Juhu, and I suspect they may cancel our sales agreement with Nair. I've tried phoning, but cannot get through; telegrams may not reach them. I'd like you to return to Bombay and tell them that under no circumstances should they cancel the agreement. Actually, this is not a woman's job, but everyone else here is either too new or too needed for the pandal program."

I didn't want to leave Prabhupada, but he'd honored me by giving me a mission. There was no question but to do it. I got my luggage and boarded the next Bombay-bound train. The lurching second-class car was packed with garrulous farmers and their huge baskets of vegetables, crying diaper-less babies carried by frazzled mothers, hawkers, and suspicious-looking loafers. I draped my legs over my luggage, made my camera bag a pillow and, before dozing fitfully on the hard bunk, thought of Prabhupada's words, "Actually, this is not a woman's job."

A couple of months earlier I'd read a letter Prabhupada had written to my friend Himavati, saying,

> In India all the acharyas and their descendants later on acted only from the man's side. Their wives were at home because that is the system from old times that women are not required to go out. But in Bhagavad-gita we find that women are also equally competent like the men in the matter of Krishna Consciousness Movement. Please therefore carry on these missionary activities, and prove it by practical example that there is no bar for anyone in the matter of preaching work for Krishna consciousness.

Although Prabhupada came from a society with orthodox gender roles, if some service for Krishna was required, he saw no reason to prohibit a woman from doing it, in this case to travel alone in a crowded train to be a messenger. Prabhupada was establishing bhakti—Krishna consciousness, freedom from designations—not "the system from old times." I knew that I, for one, could never be attracted to that old-time system. I needed the freedom to expand my interests and use my abilities without superficial social restraints. Prabhupada was giving me and all people a privileged position by prioritizing the universal principle of bhakti: that everybody's divine in themselves and can express bhakti in a myriad of ways.

The next morning, when Tamal Krishna Goswami and Shyamasundar heard Prabhupada's message, they were overwrought: just as Prabhupada had intuited, bamboozled by Nair and the lawyers who were in cahoots with him, they'd already canceled the sales agreement, mistakenly thinking that then our down payment for the property would be refunded. "How could you do that" I said, shaking my head in disbelief, "without Prabhupada's consent?" They seemed to be asking themselves the same question.

When the Ahmedabad pandal ended in mid-December, Prabhupada went to Juhu. Since he hadn't signed the papers canceling the sales agreement, he was able to nullify the documents his students had signed. In

January, Prabhupada and Nair had an angry confrontation in which Prabhupada told Nair that we would leave the Juhu property if he returned our down payment. But Nair no longer had our money. Not long after this meeting, Nair had a severe heart attack. He was in his sixties, with no history of heart trouble, but on February 17, 1973 he was dead. Although I never thought I'd be relieved to hear of someone's death, in this case, I was. Nair's malicious and deceitful attempts to steal large sums of money from Prabhupada, his corruption, and the way he ruthlessly defied all attempts to rectify the situation made me glad he was gone. Now our troubles in taking possession of the property would be over. It had been a year-long, terrible headache for Prabhupada.

In March I was with Prabhupada and his other students once again in Mayapur for the annual festival commemorating Sri Chaitanya's appearance. The tents and pandal were gone, and a four-story building, designed with Prabhupada's guidance, was under construction at the rear of the property, paid for by Western devotees who were daily distributing Prabhupada's books to the public. I was as amazed by the rapid construction as the locals. The Radha Madhava deities were already in the building's ground-floor temple, and the upper floors, not yet complete, had rooms encircled by a wide veranda. I appreciated how the short sides of the building faced east and west to receive the brunt of the sunshine, while its long sides, with their open, marble-floored verandas, received the Ganga's cooling breezes.

I was photographing Prabhupada, who was relaxing in his Mayapur room speaking with some of us, when a devotee entered and announced that Prabhupada's elderly godbrother, Sridhar Maharaj, had arrived. Much to my surprise, Prabhupada sprang up and practically ran down the veranda and a flight of stairs to delightedly greet him on the second-floor landing. Chatting both in English and Bengali, smiling, and laughing, the two of them climbed the stairs together and sauntered back to Prabhupada's room arm in arm.

Once he was comfortably seated, Sridhar Maharaj, who referred to Prabhupada as Swami Maharaj, said, "So, our Swami Maharaja has done a miracle! He has done a miracle. What Bhaktivinode conceived and [Bhaktisiddhanta Saraswati] Prabhupada tried according to his conception to translate into action, we find that through Swami Maharaj in his last days these revelations have been fulfilled. We are happy, we are glad, we are proud of Swami Maharaj, and of you all too."

Prabhupada responded by formally addressing his godbrother, "So we are thinking we are very much fortunate to hear His Divine Grace Om Vishnupad Paramahamsa Parivrajakacharya Bhakti Rakshaka Sridhar Maharaj. He is, by age and experience—in both ways he is senior to me. I am also always fortunate to have his association for a very long time, perhaps since nineteen hundred and thirty or something like that."

In 1930 Prabhupada was a thirty-four-year-old family man who'd accepted Bhaktisiddhanta Saraswati Thakur as his spiritual master but was not yet formally initiated. Eight years before, at their first meeting, Bhaktisiddhanta Saraswati had said to Prabhupada, "You are an educated young man. Why don't you teach Krishna's message to the English speaking people of the world?" It was this instruction, which Bhaktisiddhanta Saraswati had repeated just before he passed away in 1936, that had inspired Prabhupada to go to the United States. The erudite Bhaktisiddhanta Saraswati had galvanized Prabhupada and Sridhar Maharaj—along with thousands of others—with his dynamic, no-nonsense, and scholarly presentation of spiritual science. In his introduction to a small book of hymns, Bhaktisiddhanta Saraswati had written:

> The materialistic demeanor cannot possibly stretch to the transcendental autocrat who is ever inviting the fallen conditioned souls to associate with him through devotion or an eternal serving mood. ... The lines of this booklet will surely help such puzzled souls in their march towards the personality of the immanent lying beyond their sensuous gaze of inspection.

Sridhar Maharaj marveled at the risks and hardships Prabhupada had undergone in going to the West and thrilled in his achievements. And Sridhar Maharaj unreservedly encouraged us.

Knowing that the spiritual vein that went from these two personable and devoted souls—each honestly treating the other as better than himself—also flowed to me, I felt a surge of fortitude. I was part of a lofty lineage. As a child feels secure in her mother's arms, so I felt sheltered as a member of that lineage. I felt I could relax and trust and blossom and delight as nowhere else.

Prabhupada's small room reverberated with his students' kirtan, and everyone, including Prabhupada and Sridhar Maharaj, joyously danced. Later, in the temple room, Prabhupada arranged a dais for two, and he and

Sridhar Maharaj, sitting side by side, addressed us. Toward the end of the program Prabhupada asked Malati to speak. Malati handed four-year-old Saraswati to the person next to her—Tamal Krishna Goswami—stood up, and spoke of Prabhupada's unflagging dedication to his spiritual master's desire and how he had brilliantly fulfilled that desire. She also expressed her debt to Prabhupada for transforming her life.

I shared that debt and, like Malati, instead of feeling burdened by it, felt elated.

Back in Juhu, much to my dismay, Mrs. Nair was carrying on her husband's fight and, on May 18th, a municipal demolition squad paid off by her began tearing down our temporary temple, a simple building of brick, steel tubes, and asbestos sheets at the front of the property. Some frantic phone calls by influential Life Members activated upper-echelon Bombay politicians, who stopped the demolition team just before they dismantled the deities' roof. Then, under the direction of Prabhupada and leading Life Members, Yadubara and I became part of a citywide campaign to inform the press and public of Nair's and the municipality's illegal actions. Within four months the land was finally in our name. Prabhupada said simply, "It was a good fight."

Later, an editor of the monthly *Back to Godhead* magazine suggested I write an article on the protracted battle to acquire Hare Krishna Land. I did some research and wrote three initial pages. After the editor, who was Prabhupada's secretary at the time, read these pages to Prabhupada, Prabhupada said, "To publish this magazine we must spend so much money on paper and printing. And then devotees must take so much trouble to distribute it. If people read about this struggle, how will they benefit?"

In the article I'd explained how Nair had cheated us by taking our down payment while retaining possession of the property, how our lawyer was unethically in cahoots with Nair's lawyer, and how both the lawyers and Nair had been unreasonable with us throughout the transactions. The three pages I'd written were accurate but mundane and, although the Hare Krishna Land battle had absorbed Prabhupada for two years, to him this aspect of it wasn't a noteworthy part of his mission. Prabhupada's focus, I was reminded, was bhakti—the spirit of selfless service to God.

Both the magazine editor and I had thought this article was a good idea. Had I so quickly forgotten Prabhupada's focus on bhakti? Had my spiritual vision so easily blurred? What would happen when Prabhupada wasn't around to clarify things for me—and for all of us? Such thoughts left me in a tizzy.

One morning after a walk along the beachfront in Bombay, I was sitting behind Prabhupada in our Ambassador waiting for Shyamasundar to drive us home when a beggar holding a messy baby and flanked by two messy children came up to Prabhupada's car window with her hand outstretched, asking for money. Prabhupada turned to the three of us in the back seat and requested some paisa, then rolled down his window and gave the woman the coins we'd given him.

I was surprised. I'd been studying chapter 17 in the Bhagavad-gita where Krishna says that indiscriminate charity (that given to persons who may spend it on intoxicants, for example) is not beneficial. After the woman left I sat for a few moments with that scriptural thought lodged in my mind then gathered my courage and said, "Why do we give Krishna's money to beggars?"

Prabhupada was silent. Perhaps he hadn't heard me, as I was sitting behind him. Or had I offended him? More moments passed and he didn't speak.

"Is the money prasad?" I said, thinking that money coming from Prabhupada was actually coming first from Krishna.

"Yes," was all he said.

What could be more natural than a kindhearted person with means giving to someone without means, especially if children were involved? Why was I darkening this simple exchange with dogma? I saw that I had been learning about Krishna by rote, going through religious rituals and routines without even common sense, what to speak of affection for God and his creation. Later I read that Prabhupada's Guru Maharaj told his householder disciples to give to beggars; otherwise their hearts would become hard; they would lack compassion. "Yes," I thought, "Prabhupada was teaching me the same thing in the car that morning."

One afternoon in Juhu, Prabhupada asked Malati, "Where is my kurta from yesterday?"

"It's on the other side of the property, about to be washed," she said. "Do you want it?"

"Yes, please bring it."

Malati jogged across Hare Krishna Land, got Prabhupada's kurta, jogged back, and handed it to Prabhupada. Prabhupada reached into a pocket and pulled out a one-rupee note he'd forgotten. "I've done that very same thing," I thought, "I can relate."

It was Prabhupada's comment, however, that put the incident in a new light. "For Krishna I can spend lakhs of rupees," he said, "but for myself I do not want to waste anything." I had a sudden understanding: Oh, that's what Krishna consciousness is!

In an evening lecture, Prabhupada spoke powerfully about how India—the land of dharma, the land of Krishna—now had slaughterhouses for cows. Then he paused and looked at us gravely through partially closed eyes. In the protracted, charged silence his words resounded in my heart and I glimpsed Prabhupada's depth of feeling for this peaceful animal that was so dear to Krishna. "India has become so fallen," Prabhupada said, "that its government must import powdered milk and brahmins." Again he paused and looked at us, and I, one of the imported brahmins, squirmed under his scrutiny. I'd never had any direct contact with cows, so while from a distance I could appreciate their economic importance and even their role in Krishna's pastimes, I couldn't truly say I had any *feeling* for them.

A middle-aged Indian man dressed in saffron, indicating that he was a renounced sadhu, regularly attended Prabhupada's classes with the rest of us. This man made me uncomfortable because he often eyed me and Prabhupada's other young women students. Then I noticed that Prabhupada also saw him doing this. Prabhupada addressed him, "Do you know this verse, *yad-avadhi mama chetah*?"

The man said, "Oh, you mean *yada yada hi dharmasya*?"

Prabhupada said, "No, no, not that one, this one: *yad-avadhi mama chetah krishna-padaravinde*. Yamunacarya composed this verse. Yamunacarya had formerly been a great king who'd enjoyed sexual happiness in various ways but had gotten a higher taste—a spiritual taste—by engaging in Krishna's service. After that, if sexual thoughts came to him he would spit with disgust. A sincere devotee of Krishna is so absorbed in Krishna's loving service he loses all taste for material sense pleasure."

Sitting cross-legged on the floor before Prabhupada, the man, who was usually talkative and jolly, looked somberly down at his hands. Then he left and never returned.

Every day Prabhupada received letters from disciples around the world, and he began giving the stamps from the envelopes to Kirtan Mahadevia, a Life Member's ten-year-old son. I was happy to see how thrilled Kirtan was with his burgeoning stamp collection.

Through his replies to those letters Prabhupada sometimes had to tackle the tension between his male and female students. Some men, perhaps in their struggle to remain celibate, had taken a handful of statements in the scriptures meant to bolster renunciation, as well as Prabhupada's comments on them, to demean women and to block them from basic ashram facilities and programs. To a disciple in New York Prabhupada wrote,

> Who has introduced these things, that women cannot have chanting japa in the temple, they cannot perform the *arati* [worship of the deities] and so many things? If they become agitated, then let the *brahmacharis* [celibate male students] go to the forest. I have never introduced these things. The *brahmacharis* cannot remain in the presence of women in the temple, then they may go to the forest, not remaining in New York City, because in New York there are so many women, so how they can avoid seeing?

Reading this, I realized that although Prabhupada had made some comments that seemed to fuel this male–female issue, he was balanced about it. His comments had really been meant to decrease his students' distractions so they could more easily focus on spiritual life, and the biggest distraction for anyone trying to give up material consciousness is sex. His frenetic young male disciples, however, with their hormones racing, tended to think Prabhupada's young female students themselves were the distraction. Prabhupada was clear: the actual problem was his male students' uncontrolled minds and senses. They were his beloved disciples, but in their immaturity were protecting themselves by turning attraction into aversion. In Prabhupada's words, "in order to withstand the attack of maya [illusion] and remain strong under all conditions of temptation, young or inexperienced devotees in the neophyte stage of devotional service will sometimes adopt an attitude against those things or persons which may possibly be harmful or threatening to their tender devotional creepers. They may even overindulge in such feelings just to protect themselves … Kindly see the thing in this light and forgive their small mistakes. The big thing is that they have given everything, even their lives, to Krishna—and that is never a mistake."

I certainly didn't have Prabhupada's broad, compassionate vision. At this point, my enthusiasm for Prabhupada's movement was severely dampened by the way some of his male followers related to his female followers. These men's condescending, smug attitude toward the women was ridiculous and obnoxious, I felt. It was the laughable bias of a nine year-old brat who rants, "No girls allowed. I *hate* girls!" If it weren't for Prabhupada and his more mature followers, I would have been back at Rochester Institute of Technology.

Laid up with chronic tonsillitis, I was miserable both from my sore throat and from having to lie in bed while Prabhupada's evening lectures were going on. A doctor recommended a tonsillectomy and Yadubara asked Prabhupada about it. Prabhupada said tonsils help the body function properly, so removing them wasn't recommended. Before he had come to the States, for many years Prabhupada had owned and operated a pharmaceutical business. Without our thinking about it, Prabhupada was not only our guru, but also our father and medical advisor rolled into one. He saved my tonsils.

As we became known around Bombay, Prabhupada and our group were often invited to Life Members' homes for kirtan, a discourse, and a feast. My culture shock from being in India had mostly worn off by this time, but these programs became another sort of culture shock, as I knew nothing about wealthy Indians' opulence. The homes we visited were hidden from street view and usually palatial. Inside, while docile and efficient housekeepers scuttled in the background, our host and hostess treated us like princes and princesses. Also present were the host and hostess' children, brothers, sisters, uncles, aunts, cousins, nephews, nieces, grandparents, and friends. I'd think of my own nuclear family and how I hardly ever saw my few cousins and had never even met some of my aunts and uncles as they were spread across continents. But more marvelous than the sheer number of family members was their attitude. With genuine concern they attended to our every need. I simultaneously felt awed by their wealth and subservient mood, privileged to be present, undeserving, and, by comparison, uncultured. I'd never learned how to make guests feel truly welcomed. And I began to understand why the family bond in India was generally so much stronger than in the West.

At these gatherings, Prabhupada, polite, relaxed and friendly, sometimes asked the hosts their opinion on various matters and explained philosophical points to them. When we were served dinner, Prabhupada would caution us not to take more than we could eat, even though our hosts inevitably tried to give us more. Once, as he left the room after the meal, he noticed the plate next to mine had leftovers on it and quietly asked me, "Whose plate is this?" Before I could answer he continued, "Why hasn't she finished? We do not waste Krishna prasad!" It wasn't my plate, but I was still chastened. Waste displeased him. I would not waste.

In the temporary temple on Hare Krishna Land, the evening programs concluded with Prabhupada distributing dessert prasad to the attending throng, their hands outstretched to receive it. From Prabhupada's long fingers each person got a wad of the sweet pressed into his or her cupped palm. As I was photographing this I saw children sneaking back into the queue for seconds and thirds. Prabhupada noticed them too and, raising a teasing, wagging forefinger at them, grinned and gave them second and third helpings.

I was surprised to see the elite of Bombay patiently standing in the same queue, their palms also outstretched, waiting for a morsel of the blessed food. Later, I heard Prabhupada say how respectable people come to get Krishna prasad because it's not ordinary. These people have ample food in their homes, he said, but they want the privilege of honoring Krishna prasad.

To me it was odd that although a river of piety coursed through these people, making them treasure the prasad they received from Prabhupada's hand, at the same time these same people seemed deeply confused about spiritual life—just as deeply confused as I'd been not long ago. They worshiped a variety of men and gods as if they were supreme. Some of them even thought they could become God. Or they observed rituals with no understanding of their purpose. To me, many of them seemed superstitious.

But Prabhupada seemed at home in this culture, even though his message was, by comparison, so radically monotheistic and single-pointedly based on love of God and freedom from matter. How odd it was that I felt comfortable with Prabhupada's presentation yet at odds with almost everyone else in India—although I couldn't help but appreciate the ardency of their faith.

Yadubara and I were in India when, during one of his world tours, Prabhupada, who was in Los Angeles at the time, met Yadubara's father, Robert Griesser, an American history professor at Orange County College in Southern California, and his stepmother, Marcia Griesser. Prabhupada wrote to us that they were both very nice and that they seemed to respect him. Later, his father also wrote to us about the meeting. "Your spiritual master is a remarkable person. I understand that he is presenting a deep subject, and I will take up studying *Bhagavad-gita As It Is* at once." When Yadubara's open-minded father visited us in Juhu for two weeks—my first meeting with any of Yadubara's family—I hardly got to know him because he got sick from the spicy food. He was also horrified by India's poverty, congestion, filth, and backwardness, and taxed by his son's lifestyle, habits, beliefs, and appearance. Despite all that, when he returned to Los Angeles he wrote to us saying he was pleased to have lost ten pounds on the trip. I remembered feeling similarly after my week-long stay in the Brooklyn ashram—living there was uncomfortable but had proved to be a good weight-loss program.

Meanwhile, in Juhu, I felt inexplicably listless and aloof from everyone and everything—from life itself.

Jaundice.

Semi-conscious, I holed up in a kind neighbor's bedroom for what seemed like ages, pain-free but too weak to move. Hour after hour, day after day, I lay on my back in bed staring through the mosquito net at the ceiling rafters, vaguely aware of distant kitchen smells mingling with street noises, yet feeling as if I were on my own remote island—some floating nether world of indifference to everything living and dead, where nothing was worthy of concern. I lethargically noted the slight rise and fall of my chest as I breathed, the daylight beyond an open window on my right, the smallness and clutter of the room I was in. I'd chant and sleep and eat the tasteless boiled vegetables Yadubara brought for lunch. Staring, chanting, and sleeping through the morning, afternoon, and night, it was as if someone had pulled the plug on my vitality and before I knew what had happened, it had entirely drained away. And I didn't have enough energy to care. As the days piled up, I became convinced this state was my new normal.

Finally I recovered and returned to my rooftop. One morning I was chanting there, enjoying the atmosphere and solitude and planning to skip the temple program, which had come to feel predictable to me, but then I suddenly heard how extra enthusiastic the temple kirtan was. I peered over the roof wall and, although the open-sided temple was on the far edge of the property, I could see devotees there jumping high with their arms raised. "Why such an extra infusion of energy?" I thought, "What's happening?" Then I saw: Prabhupada was sitting on the vyasasan!—he'd unexpectedly returned. Feeling foolish, I rushed down the stairs and ran to the temple, where excitement so filled the air that no one noticed me blustering in from the back.

The Juhu mornings were invigorating, and before the first hint of daylight, Prabhupada would come down the steps of his apartment to go for an hour-long walk along the beach. I always tagged along, camera in hand. My passion, photography, was now my sacred service to Prabhupada and Krishna. I was committed to creating photographs of Prabhupada, his students, and their devotional activities for publication in the monthly *Back to Godhead* magazine, in Prabhupada's books, and wherever else they were useful. Later I'd travel to do this, but now with Prabhupada in Juhu, I was perfectly happy to be where I was.

One morning I was sitting on a landing waiting for him, fingering my japa beads in the dark, when Prabhupada came so gently that I didn't hear him. As he passed by close enough for me to touch him, he said softly, "Thank you very much."

"What's he thanking me for?" I wondered. "For chanting japa?" Since that's all I was doing, that must have been it. It hit me that it really wasn't complicated or difficult for me to please Prabhupada. If I simply chanted, Prabhupada was pleased and grateful. And pleasing God's representative meant pleasing God. Prabhupada had explained, "If you please your guru, that means Krishna is pleased. Just like you have got a small child of your family. Somebody pleases your small child, then automatically you become pleased."

So maybe I could do this thing called spiritual life.

Instead of a kurta, Prabhupada wore his sannyasi cloth draped over his shoulder. Cane in hand, he walked on the firm sand slightly ahead of his disciples with his brisk, confident step, his head held high. On that broad beach, traversing a world he gave uncommon meaning to, his conviction and freshness surcharged everything and entered within me along with the fine sea air I was inhaling. I felt a sweet strength in him, in myself, and in everything around us, and I luxuriated in that strength.

I loved this early hour when the sun was just making its daily appearance, when the world was in a placid pause before humanity's bustle began, when Prabhupada walked and walked beside lapping waves. I could have walked with him forever, photographing, hearing him, speaking up from time to time, feeling as gleeful as a youngster at the beach. Everything in my life seemed just as it should be—wearing a sari, rising at four in the morning, being a teetotaler and a vegetarian, living in an ashram, serving all day without thought of a paycheck. Gamely, I'd let Prabhupada draw me into his world and mold me according to his reality. I was doing what he said to do, following behind him, too enthralled and hopeful to pay attention to whatever lingering uncertainties I had.

Occasionally, Prabhupada stopped and, raising his voice over the breaking waves, challenged us. Once he asked, "What is this ocean?"

"It's the Arabian Sea," someone said.

Prabhupada glanced at him, "Yes, I know that."

"It is Krishna," someone else said.

"How is it Krishna?"

"Because he says, 'Of bodies of water I am the ocean.' The ocean is part of the universal form of the Lord."

"That is not scientific," Prabhupada said. "It is Krishna because it is his energy. Krishna says, 'Earth, water, fire, air, ether—these are my separated energies,' and he is simultaneously different yet nondifferent from his energies."

We continued walking, and I said, "Prabhupada, last night in your lecture I couldn't hear the last point you made. I'm not sure what you were speaking about …"

Prabhupada interrupted, "If you couldn't hear, how can you ask?"

I blushed red from his blunt reply and my head spun—so much so that I veered off and for a few moments was walking toward the ocean instead of alongside it. Later, as my question and his answer played repeatedly in my head, I had to admit that I couldn't recall enough of what I had heard to ask a coherent question about what I hadn't heard. So, as he said, how could I ask? His logic was straightforward and undeniable.

A Dr. Patel and some of his friends usually joined us on these walks. A short, energetic, gentleman in his fifties, always barefoot and in white yogi pants and a white, short-sleeved kurta, Dr. Patel had been raised in a Vaishnav family but influenced by impersonalism—the idea that God is without form, qualities or personality. Prabhupada's mission was to establish God as a person, Krishna, who has a transcendental form, qualities, personality and activities. Sometimes the conversations with Dr. Patel became so fiery that I got angry with the hot-headed doctor.

Regarding impersonalists Prabhupada was forceful with him: "I don't make any compromise with these rascals. No words. No, no. I never made that. Even if I don't get any disciples I'll be satisfied. But I can't make any compromise like these rascals. I cannot make. If I create one moon, that is sufficient. I don't want many stars. That was my Guru Maharaja's principle, and that is my principle. What is the use of having a number of fools and rascals? If one man understands rightly, he can deliver the whole world."

Prabhupada used his cane as he walked, its tip leaving regular impressions in the soft sand just as his words were leaving deep impressions on me.

These walks were exercise for my body as well as a chance to gain spiritual strength—and for me, they were a glorious time to photograph. Sometimes I walked in front of Prabhupada, backpedaling, sometimes on the side so as to make the vast ocean his backdrop. At this early hour, the sky was clear and the sunlight subdued, and when I look now at the photographs from those days, they have a warm, calming tone.

Prabhupada's response to Dr. Patel's cantankerousness was unusual. From time to time he'd ask one of his students to read from Krishna book—his summary of the Srimad-Bhagavatam's descriptions of Krishna's pastimes—as we walked. That always put an end to any conversation. Although Dr. Patel didn't usually walk with us whenever we were reading but took his own walk with others some yards away, over the course of three years, he joined Prabhupada on dozens of morning walks and many years later said that until his talks with Prabhupada on the Juhu sand, he hadn't understood the Gita's teachings. That time with Prabhupada, he said, were his life's most precious moments.

Hearing this soothed my long-lasting frustration with Dr. Patel. His words also reassured me that I and my young Western colleagues weren't the only ones who'd been deeply impacted by Prabhupada: here was a mature doctor, a pious Indian, a lifelong student of the Bhagavad-gita, who'd also been transformed. How was it that Prabhupada made the same points over and over but they remained fresh? How was it that all I wanted was to be with him?

I gave up analyzing and kept photographing.

In the afternoons, Prabhupada would sit on a small dais on the flat rooftop of the building he lived in and devotees, tenants, and guests would join him for informal talks. The light was soft, palm fronds swayed in the background, Prabhupada was jovial and relaxed: it was ideal for photographs. One afternoon, I went a little early and found myself alone with Prabhupada. I sat at his feet, camera ready. Observing me, Prabhupada stopped chanting on his beads and said, "Where shall I look?"

He'd never asked me anything approaching that before, and at first I had no idea he was referring to posing for a photograph. When I'd finally understood his question, my mind raced to think of an answer. Finally I said, "Wherever you like, Prabhupada." Prabhupada turned his head to his right and smiled slightly. I made several photographs that became some devotees' favorites.

A few minutes later, a few devotees joined us, among them a blunt young man named Bhagavat, who had done some traveling in India.

Bhagavat said to Prabhupada, "I have heard so many of these so-called yogis talk about the Bhagavad-gita, but they cannot explain. They have not even an inkling."

Prabhupada said, "No, no, how they can explain? They cannot touch even Bhagavad-gita. They have no qualification. Their speaking of Bhagavad-gita is artificial. They cannot speak, because the real qualification, as it is stated in the Bhagavad-gita, is *bhakto si*. One must be a devotee, then he can touch what is Bhagavad-gita."

"Others cannot explain like you," Bhagavat continued. "When you speak this knowledge, Prabhupada, it immediately enters into the ear and into the heart, and then it is realized."

"Maybe. Visakha, you think also like that?"

I was sitting on Prabhupada's left, recording him while Yadubara filmed, and when Prabhupada addressed me, a thrill went down my spine. But, unprepared for his question, again my mind raced, not knowing how to respond. Truthfully, I questioned Bhagavat's intention and so found his brash praise suspiciously close to flattery—was he going to propose something that he hoped Prabhupada would agree to? I had no way of knowing and anyway, his motivation was not my business. He was talking about Prabhupada and I didn't have to concern myself with anything else.

"Without a doubt," I said.

"Hare Krishna," Prabhupada said, and chuckled.

I wondered, "Was he chuckling at Bhagavat's intent?"

Toward the end of our stay in Juhu, Jagat Purusha organized a drama, "Krishna Lifts Govardhan Hill." Jagat Purusha took the part of Indra, the envious and defiant king of heaven; Bhagavat played Krishna who, in this story, was a child; and I played the transcendental *surabhi* cow who offered prayers to Krishna at the denouement. While everyone else was in the temple room watching the performance, I was behind the altar in a full cow costume, waiting for my part. Before me was a large plate of rich prasad, ready for distribution. Without much thought, I began grazing on this delicious prasad (it was dinner time, after all), and I continued non-

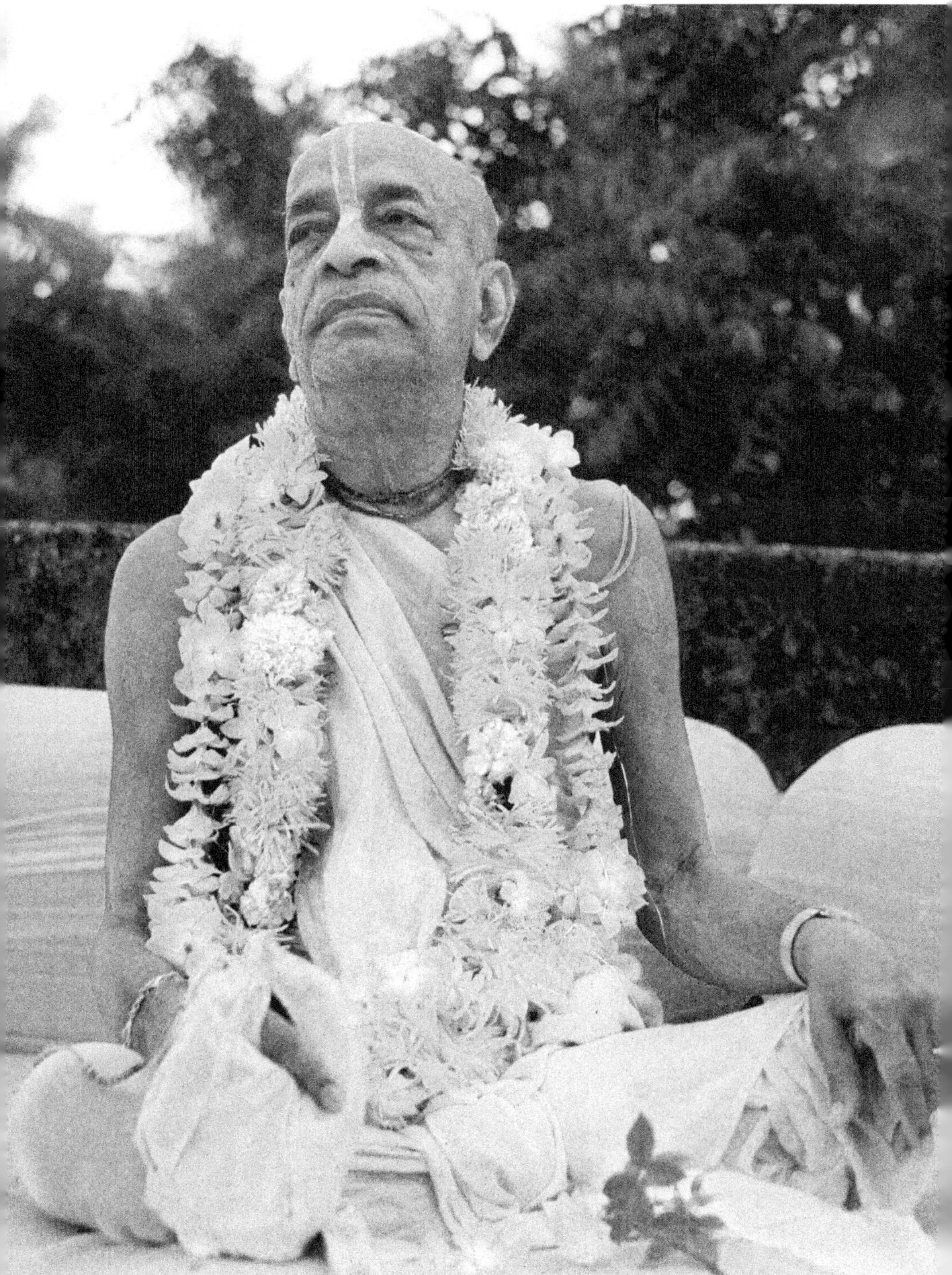

stop until, forty-five minutes later, my cue finally came. Drowsy from the heavy meal, I emerged and stood with folded hands before Bhagavat, who was just to the left of the deities, to say my lines. My eyeglasses were off, my long cow ears hung down, the soft white cow suit around me felt warm and cozy; I shifted my vision to the resplendent but blurry deities to the right of Bhagavat, and tried to stir myself from my semi-sleeping state. Finally, after a too-long pause, I heard myself say slowly but with feeling:

> My dear Krishna, you are the most powerful of all mystic yogis because you are the soul of the complete universe, and only from you has all this cosmic manifestation taken place. Therefore, although Indra tried his best to kill my descendant cows in Vrindavan, they remained under your shelter, and you have protected them all so well. We do not know anyone else as the supreme, nor do we go to any other god or demigod for protection. You are the supreme father of the whole cosmic manifestation, and you are the protector and elevator of all the cows, brahmins, demigods, and others who are pure devotees. O Supersoul of the universe, let us bathe you with our milk. You appear just to diminish the burden of impure activities on the earth.

Somehow or other, my lines had come out more or less coherently. An enormous sense of relief washed over me.

Gentle music began as the narrator said,

> When everything was joyfully settled, the cows over-flooded the surface of the earth with their milk. The water of the rivers began to flow with various tasty liquids and give nourishment to the trees, producing fruits and flowers of different colors and tastes. The trees began to pour drops of honey. The hills and mountains began to produce potent medicinal plants and valuable stones. Because of Krishna's presence, all these things happened very nicely, and the lower animals, who were generally envious of one another, were envious no longer.
>
> This great incident is a powerful example of how Krishna consciousness can benefit the world. Even the lower animals forget their envious nature and become elevated to the qualities of the demigods.

The packed audience gave a rousing applause. Prabhupada beamed. I was woozy and groggy from having eaten too much ghee.

CHAPTER TWELVE

Homecoming Heretic

Wherever we were in India, every six months Yadubara and I spent a day standing in line at a Foreign Registration Office where U.S. citizens applied for visa extensions. As we waited, large overhead fans, their blade edges dark with grime, noisily beat hot air down on us and the paunchy office clerks seated behind desks much too large for them. These desks were inevitably covered with stacks of yellowed papers held in place with hefty paperweights. Thumbed edges of thousands of those papers flapped rhythmically in the fans' breeze, filling the office with a musty, brittle-paper smell. Everything appeared as if it was submerged in inept bureaucracy, but it wasn't. Somewhere among all those papers were ours, with meticulous records of the places we'd visited in India, where and how long we'd stayed in each place, copies of newspaper articles we'd been mentioned in, our excursion to Nepal. After grumbling, paper shuffling, and whispered standing conferences, overworked Foreign Registration authorities would grant us yet another six months.

We had no plans to leave India until Karandhar, a key leader in the U.S. who was in contact with devotees worldwide, suggested Yadubara compile all the existing movies about the Hare Krishna movement into a documentary film on the group's worldwide activities. Yadubara agreed, and Karandhar sent him a one-way ticket from Bombay to New York City.

Although Karandhar knew that Yadubara and I were married and that I was, like Yadubara, trained in photography and actively photographing Prabhupada and his students, he hadn't included me in these plans. I was stunned. I felt like I didn't exist, all that I had done to support my husband's work and to make my own offering was counted as nothing by Karandhar. He considered me unnecessary.

I asked Yadubara, "Why'd Karandhar send only one ticket?"

"He has a small budget for this film, I'm sure," Yadubara said. "He couldn't afford two tickets."

I didn't know what to do with that response. Now I wasn't sure if I'd been left out due to money or because I was just a woman—an easy conclusion to come to given the attitudes of so many of the men in the movement—or if Karandhar didn't think much about our husband-wife partnership.

I never asked Karandhar about it, and mild-mannered Yadubara didn't either, so I never found out. Instead, I swallowed my feelings of being neglected and tried to look at things philosophically, meaning I used the philosophy to sweep aside my emotions. "After all," I thought, "nothing happens by chance. I deserved to be omitted; it was my karma. What's the use of sulking about it? How does sulking help anything? Bear the pain, don't give Karandhar the pleasure of seeing you upset, and go on as if everything's all right. Just think how much you have to be grateful for!"

If that wasn't enough to rationalize away my bad feelings, I'd read a verse in the Bhagavatam that, to me, supported my unreactive nature from another point of view:

> People are not the cause of my distress. Neither are the demigods, my own body, the planets, my past work, or time. Rather, it is the mind alone that causes happiness and distress and perpetuates the rotation of material life.

Karandhar wasn't the problem. It was my mind!

Yadubara wanted me to come with him and asked his sympathetic father for help. His father paid for my ticket with the comment: "Why is this man separating a husband and wife?"

When I showed up unexpectedly, Karandhar hardly took notice. Again a feeling of being unwanted washed over me, and again my husband overlooked my feelings. But, even if I was an appendage, I was glad to be there anyway.

After two and a half years in India, Yadubara and I had returned to our homeland with two suitcases that contained all our possessions. We had no employment or prospects of employment, no income, no home, no car or other assets, and no medical or life insurance. Yet none of that bothered me. I felt not only secure but verifiably rich from all we had: Prabhupada, Krishna, a family of devotees, a path to follow, a cause to live for, a goal to attain.

By this time, Yadubara and I had passed through our romantic college phase, our adventuresome and austere Nepal and India phase, and now, after all of four years since we'd met, were entering a phase of collaborative creativity—which is not to say that our relationship was always smooth. Although we were usually comfortably and effortlessly together, when we argued, I noticed a pattern: after he'd explained and justified his side and negated mine, I'd explain and justify everything I'd said and done. After all, wasn't I a smart, sensitive, stoic, strong-willed person who got things right? Then after a while I'd begin to question what I'd done and wonder if I was actually the cause of the difficulty. I never could quite figure it out for sure. Somehow, though, Yadubara seemed quite sure of his position.

Yadubara and I sat in a small, windowless room in the Brooklyn ashram and viewed footage: kirtan and prasad distribution in African villages, Rath-yatra festivals in London and San Francisco, pandal programs in India—exotic, but not nearly enough for a documentary. We decided that to produce a documentary, we'd have to start filming and recording audio. With money from Prabhupada's Bhaktivedanta Book Trust, we purchased a 16mm camera, a synchronized reel-to-reel tape recorder and two plane tickets to London. During the flight we read the manuals for the equipment, and by the time we disembarked we were a duo: cinematographer Yadubara and sound person/photographer Visakha.

In a breathless month we captured Prabhupada's Paris arrival, the Mayor of Paris officially greeting him at City Hall, his lengthy talk with Catholic Cardinal Danielou, his installing and worshiping the Paris deities, and his many activities at Bhaktivedanta Manor, the property in the London suburbs that George Harrison had donated. I felt excited and privileged not only to be with Prabhupada and able to witness the burgeoning of Krishna consciousness in France and England, but also to be meeting Prabhupada's extraordinary students in these places—especially the women, whom I found earnest, dedicated, affectionate, talented, and intelligent. Sitala, for example, the head pujari (priest) in Paris, was perceptive, clearheaded, very funny, and devoted to Prabhupada. She told me, "Prabhupada's presence makes everything possible and understandable and sure. He isn't just conveying some idea that he's read but he's *experiencing* the things he talks about."

Sitala's friendship and the friendship of many others enriched me and, to my delight, has become lifelong.

On our return to the States, with some trepidation I visited Great Neck, my childhood home. Now wrapped in a colorful sari, bearing sacred lines of tilak on my forehead, abstaining from meat, muttering God's names—how could I possibly explain my metamorphosis to my parents? I needn't have worried—my parents didn't ask a single question. The obscure letters I'd written from India had made it clear enough: I'd become a religious fanatic. Why else would I have changed my name, my dress, my habits, my diet, my friends, my career ambitions, my very life's goals, and be devoting myself to what they saw as bizarre Indian lore? Why else would I, after excelling in college, drop out and abort a lucrative career that had promised travel, prestige, and hobnobbing with the rich and famous?

To me, my parents were plodding stoically through the debris of unexamined conclusions toward death. To them, I was a robot with zeal. My sense of discernment, in their eyes, had left me, and I was obsessively following a possibly demented, if not dangerous, person. We were at an impasse. I didn't want to alienate or disappoint them more than I already had, but I didn't want to be disloyal to my own convictions. I shared the sweets and fruits I'd brought from the Brooklyn ashram; I tried to be pleasant and "normal." Yet our home filled with estrangement and sadness, and we found no common ground. We were separated by a chasm so wide it included a generation gap, a cultural gap, a faith gap, a duty gap, and a trust gap. Even a daughter's love for her parents and theirs for her failed to span it.

I also ran into the young publisher at Amphoto who'd taken a risk by publishing my photomacrography book. He had been banking on my becoming a renowned photographer, writing more books and increasing his book sales, and he was more than disappointed by me—he was disgusted. Seething, he said under his breath, *"How could you do such a thing?"* as if my life choices were a personal affront. It never occurred to me that I'd blemished his career. Unprepared for his outrage, I looked at him blankly—zombielike, in his eyes, probably reinforcing his conviction that I had become a mindless cultist.

If I *hadn't* met Prabhupada and spent time in magical Vrindavan, I'd have been feeling and thinking the same thing he and my parents were. I'd experienced far more than I could convey to them or to anyone. That I couldn't even begin to convey it saddened me.

Yadubara and I had another breathless month filming Prabhupada's West Virginia farm community, the Mexico City ashram, the children's school in Dallas, and Prabhupada's grand Western world headquarters in Los Angeles, home of his Bhaktivedanta Book Trust, *Back to Godhead* magazine's editorial offices, Golden Avatar Recording Studio, Spiritual Sky Incense, a Govinda's restaurant, and a thriving gift shop. More impressive than those things though, at least for me, were Prabhupada's students in each of these places—again, especially the women. Most of them had never conversed or gone on walks with Prabhupada or even been present when he spoke informally. Yet because of Prabhupada's lectures and writings, and because of hearing from those who had met him, these women had thrown themselves into Krishna consciousness with abandon.

On Prabhupada's behest, many of them spent all day every day courageously approaching strangers in airports and malls to persuade them to buy one of Prabhupada's books. I admired these women for their enthusiasm and was astonished at their stamina and brazenness. Gauri, one of the top Los Angeles book distributors, told me that growing up she had been shy and introverted. "I had a heavy, morose, grouchy and intellectual personality," she said. "It was completely wrong for stopping and meeting people. I couldn't even carry on a light conversation or be nonthreatening."

"How did you change?" I asked.

"In the beginning, book distribution was hellish for me," Gauri said. "But I kept at it because I saw that other devotees relished it. Prabhupada said everything comes with practice and I thought, 'If Krsna helps the others distribute books, he'll help me, too.'

"Even though I had a huge false ego and was puffed up, one day Krishna blessed me and I suddenly found it easy to approach people, smile and be free from the clouded personality that I'd had all my life—and I was free from it forever after. I started liking approaching people, giving them books, talking about Krsna and getting donations from them. I found that if I gave my heart and soul to book distribution, more love came from me and Krishna used me more by making me more clever and quick-witted. Krishna can make the dullest, stone-like person into the most brilliant poet and philosopher and joker. It's amazing."

I'd been feeling that selling books to strangers was antithetical to my nature, but after hearing Gauri's story I wondered if I could distribute books too. Book distribution was a glorious service, that much was clear.

But it seemed to me a misunderstanding was emerging about book distribution. Prabhupada's leaders were lauding it as *the* way to please Prabhupada. From their plucky proclamations, these leaders often gave me the impression that those of us who weren't distributing Prabhupada's books weren't pleasing Prabhupada. In the three years I'd been with Prabhupada, however, I'd never once felt that from him. On the contrary, Prabhupada pointed out that *any* service sincerely done for Krishna's pleasure was glorious, including simple services like garland making or cleaning. The essential point was not *what* one did but the consciousness with which one did it.

Similar to the "women's issue," Prabhupada's mood and the mood of some of his followers dramatically diverged. "Those who haven't had Prabhupada's company will get the wrong ideas," I thought. And of course I could do nothing about it. I was a powerless witness.

We edited our footage, Hayagriva helped write the script, and in March '74 we took our thirty-one-minute *The Hare Krishna People* documentary film to Mayapur's Gaura Purnima festival for its world premiere. I was 23.

Beneath Mayapur's humid, open sky, the first building stood complete—a freshly painted monolith surfacing from the lush rice fields, its scalloped archways on the three upper floors running the length and breadth of the building, creating an open, cool, inviting space for the international students who crowded into it. Prabhupada had encouraged all his followers to become spiritually recharged by taking an annual pilgrimage to Mayapur, and a veritable phalanx had responded—and becoming lost in that phalanx did the great service of reminding me just how insignificant I was.

For the premiere, top managers crammed shoulder to shoulder, knee to knee in Prabhupada's small room. As Yadubara set up the projector, I stood at Prabhupada's door, searching for a place to sit. Prabhupada saw me and pointed to a small space by his side. "You sit here," he said. And I did, feeling like a daughter sitting with her dear father. Prabhupada called the film "super-excellent" and said, "You have used good psychology in making it." I smiled at that, as neither Yadubara nor I knew anything about psychology.

Later we showed the film to all the devotees and after that Yadubara submitted it as his master's thesis and was awarded his Master of Fine Arts by Rochester Institute of Technology. Over time, the film was translated into fourteen languages and sent to the Hare Krishna centers worldwide as a major propagation tool.

Toward the end of the festival I was laid up with food poisoning. I got Ayurvedic medicine from a Calcutta doctor and then joined the devotees in Vrindavan for the pilgrimage's final leg. Still weak, I was lying on my back on a straw mat at Fogla Ashram when I heard a POP! I looked in the direction of the sound and saw the brown Ayurvedic medicine bottle had blown its cork. I watched the frothy viscous medicine slowly erupt from the glass bottle, nonchalantly flow down its sides (bubbling all the way), down the shelves and down the wall to create a bubbly brown puddle on the floor by my feet. I propped my head on my hand and contemplated this growing puddle. One never knew what to expect in this country.

Without warning, Karandhar, Prabhupada's right-hand man, resigned. I'd been impressed by Karandhar's efficiency and thoughtfulness (despite that he hadn't sent me a ticket when I'd first left India) and was troubled by his resignation. He seemed to be doing everything right, yet he'd succumbed to temptations. Maybe practicing bhakti-yoga wasn't an effective way to control the mind and senses? Maybe I'd succumb too? I asked Prabhupada about Karandhar's falldown. Prabhupada said, "Sex life. Karandhar was seeing a woman besides his wife. But he is sincere. He thought, 'I am not following my spiritual master's instructions. I must step down.'"

Instead of being angry with or resentful toward Karandhar, in whom he had entrusted so much, Prabhupada appreciated Karandhar's frankness. Hearing Prabhupada's reaction, my critical and confused heart felt suddenly clearer and lighter and even a little more compassionate. And I wondered if Karandhar had ignored me earlier due to his private anguish.

Later, I reflected on how Prabhupada expressed his love for his spiritual master by his consistent effort to offer people spiritual life, for that was his spiritual master's desire. Prabhupada's love seemed greater than any impediment, including whatever we—his often wayward students—did. To me, Prabhupada's efforts appeared sometimes successful and at other times not, as in Karandhar's case, but for Prabhupada, success was simply that he made the effort. The result of his effort was in other hands, and his realization of that fact made him detached not from the person he was dealing with but from the result of his own work. I couldn't really relate to the dimension Prabhupada's detachment and love came from, but I wanted to follow him into that dimension.

In April, a group of us went with Prabhupada to Tirupati, a remote mountaintop temple eighty miles west of Madras, where a deity of Krishna named Balaji, discovered in the second century BCE, resided under a golden dome in a grand, stone-carved temple. Each day, 250 brahmins worked in shifts to serve him.

And each day, 15,000—and on festival days, up to 100,000—pilgrims waited for two to fifteen hours to get a glimpse of him. The temple was encircled by lines in which every type of person in all life's phases was represented: just-married couples in wedding regalia making their first pilgrimage together, renunciants, joint families with their hosts of children, the sophisticated and the unsophisticated, the well-to-do and the paupers, the sickly, the elderly, the crippled, the blind. As they waited for their moment before Balaji, these people snacked, napped, chatted, tended their children, observed those who weren't in line, and occasionally had heated discussions with their neighbors.

Our group was ensconced in three mountainside cottages with panoramic views of farms and villages. Leaving our luggage in our rooms, we walked with Prabhupada on paths that wound through gardens and grassy areas. As we went, Prabhupada referred to a scene in our newly released film, *The Hare Krishna People,* in which some cows ran downhill in slow-motion as Yamuna Devi sang in the background. "Those cows," Prabhupada asked, "why are they floating?" He paused and continued, "Can that be corrected?"

My heart jumped. Not only because I liked that scene and thought it powerful, but also because the film was already released and to change anything in it would be costly. I could feel Yadubara, walking next to me, reacting similarly. With trepidation, Yadubara said, "That's a technique in film called slow motion, Prabhupada." Prabhupada walked on as he responded, "Then it is all right." Yadubara and I gave a sigh of relief.

Our group turned, retraced our steps, and the devotees entered their different cottages. Prabhupada, however, walked on and I stayed with him, camera in hand. After a short time, the path led to a small secluded area surrounded by tall, thick bushes. Inside, Prabhupada sat down on a solitary chair and I sat in the grass at his feet, camera poised to record his gently contoured face as he sat alone on a simple chair surrounded by a rush of greenery. But, clearly tired, Prabhupada glanced at me and quietly said, "Is it necessary?" My thoughts whirled. I realized I was simply thinking about creating photographs, not about the needs of the person I was photographing. I realized that Prabhupada had somehow become less of a person and more of a subject—I'd become callous to his desires and was now subjecting him to mine. My hands dropped to my lap. I peered at the grass, mumbled a regretful, "No, it's not necessary," and scuttled away, leaving him the few serene and solitary minutes he had intended. I regretted my insensitivity, but I also regretted that I couldn't memorialize his peaceful presence in that bucolic whorl.

Well before dawn the day after we arrived we entered the main gate of the temple and passed through its dark inner sanctum toward Balaji's altar. Prabhupada, walking just in front of me, quietly chanted the Sanskrit prayer, *govindam adi-purusam tam aham bhajami:* "I worship Krishna, the primeval person."

This temple's astounding antiquity, vibrancy, and popularity roused me and, now having crossed its shrouded threshold I was agog with anticipation. I felt I was being swept to the sanctified source of life within a metaphysical universal being.

Balaji was awe-inspiring. Solid black, he stood seven feet tall, his lustrous form dimly lit by ghee lamps. The first sight of him was of his prominent tilak—two large, white, vertical, slightly separated rectangles that covered most of his forehead and nose and part of his eyes and cheeks. Moving closer, I saw his jewel-inlaid golden crown, his garland, his jeweled ornaments and, just faintly, my eyes now accustomed to the dimness, his elusive smile. His right palm—open, facing forward, fingers down—beckoned pilgrims to give up irreligion and surrender to him. His left hand, palm facing in and fingers curved toward his knee, indicated that the surrendered need not fear, for he would protect them—for them he reduced the ocean of material tribulation.

I didn't want to leave, yet after just moments, it was time. Thousands were yet to come, and Balaji awaited them also.

We moved on to the *hundi*, a cloth-covered, three-cubic-foot brass vessel where pilgrims placed their offerings to Balaji—money, precious metals, family heirlooms and whatever else they valued. When the *hundi* was full it was replaced with an empty one and carried to a barred and guarded room at the west end of the temple. There, twice each day, *hundis* were emptied and their contents sorted and counted, a five-hour process performed by thirty men picked at random from the Tirupati staff. The counting was observed by two pilgrims, also picked at random, as well as by closed-circuit video cameras. All donations were registered and deposited in a bank. The daily average: U.S. $30,000, or about $11 million a year. I was curious about what became of all that money.

Later, speaking with the government Endowments Commissioner, who helped decide how Balaji's donations were allocated, Prabhupada said, "People are giving their hard-earned money in good faith to Balaji Krishna, and that is wanted. That money should not be utilized for any other purpose except for the pleasure of the Lord. If you have plans to utilize this money for any other purpose, that is not Krishna's mission. That is your mission. So first of all you have to decide whether you are going to execute Krishna's mission or your mission. Krishna's mission is very clearly defined. It is there, everything is declared there in the Bhagavad-gita. It is the government's duty to see that Balaji's money, Krishna's money is, to the farthing, spent for his mission."

As Prabhupada spoke, the Commissioner fidgeted. A portion of Balaji's donations were used for purposes that had nothing to do with Balaji's service. Apologetic, he said his vote was one of many, but he'd inform the others of Prabhupada's directives. In my young heart I thought, Prabhupada just wants God's opulence to be used in God's service. It seemed easy enough, but our multifarious, often opposing desires made it complex. The Commissioner seemed to feel that complexity too.

When, from the veranda outside his Mayapur room, Prabhupada had seen village children competing with dogs for scraps of food left on a pile of discarded leaf plates, he'd said, "No one should go hungry within a ten-mile radius of our temple," and asked some of his students to start a free food relief program, which they did. Yadubara filmed and I photographed Western devotees using flat-ended rods taller than themselves to stir stews of beans and rice and vegetables simmering in eight-foot-diameter woks over smoky cow dung and wood fires. We filmed and photographed the devotees sanctifying this stew by offering it to Krishna, and then the hundreds of families from nearby villages sitting in rows as the devotees ladled generous dollops of this thick steaming stew onto the leaf plates set before them. Yadubara made his film into an eight-minute documentary, I sent my photographs to *Back to Godhead* magazine, and then, in the summer of '74, he and I joined Prabhupada for Prabhupada's U.S. tour.

As Prabhupada's official filmmaking crew, Yadubara and I were now forever draped with bulky gear—he with an imposing movie camera and I with a reel-to-reel tape recorder, microphone, camera and camera bag. By comparison, our years in India seemed so happy-go-lucky. Yet our burden was our good fortune, for it allowed us to be with Prabhupada, touched by the unique aura of his pure intent.

But the technology and the formality that seemed to accompany my old-new service caused a shift in me. Maybe it was the equipment that dangled from my shoulders and neck that turned me into a detached reporter, or maybe what I experienced as the Western ether, thick with cynicism and self-centered consumerism that impacted me. Maybe I just missed the traditional culture that flowed beneath the chaotic and materialistic facade of India. Maybe I was just going through a phase.

Whatever it was, while Yadubara was filming, I'd record the audio and often find myself looking down to monitor the recorder. Gone into the hazy past were my former fleeting epiphanies, my stretching for stars and the stunned moments I'd experienced during those euphoric Vrindavan days. Then, everything had been new. I felt that mysterious world was now slipping away, leaving a quivering emptiness in its wake. I vaguely remembered how I'd felt on the gray morning of November 29, 1971 when Prabhupada had initiated me, remembered how fragile everything had been; and the happiness that had radiated everywhere.

Nothing in my life had prepared me for Prabhupada or for spirituality; I'd had no interest in any aspect of it before. Setbacks were inevitable. Now I was in a holding pattern, circling the spiritual dimension but not actually touching it, despite three years of rising well before dawn to chant God's holy names, attend temple functions, hear holy discourses, and read holy books. I was going through the motions but without feeling. I realized that for me to become truly adept in spiritual life, it would take something more than even Prabhupada's powerful presence, his pristine example, his clear instructions. After all, I already had all that. So why the funk?

What was missing was my intense longing for spiritual life. Why? I had to wonder. Looking around, I could find no one to blame; I could hardly even blame myself. It was a mystery. I'd assimilated so little. I felt waterlogged and dull.

Spiritual life had become an endless rollercoaster ride that I couldn't get off. Sometimes I felt encouraged, as if I were coming closer to being peaceful, content, self-controlled, aware of Krishna. Happy, even.

But other times, I realized, I was in a dither, unsure of myself, ignorant of Krishna and everything related to him. At those times I felt, in truth, not much different from before I'd come in contact with Krishna consciousness. I'd completely changed everything in my life but wouldn't give up my same old suspicious, secretive, selfish, insecure, scathing, seriously scarred, stinky mentality. Deeply anchored to a morass, I was exasperated. And lonely. I had no one to talk to—all the others seemed blissfully busy with their service.

I was ashamed of my sorry state.

Yet I was convinced that just as that state had come, it would also go. I continued with the externals: chanting, reading, attending the temple programs, and photographing, as if everything was all right. And gradually it became all right. I was again relishing Prabhupada's company and feeling eager to be with Krishna. The night had ended.

Soon after he arrived in Chicago, Prabhupada was sitting cross-legged on a cushion on the floor next to the imposing hot-pink, gold-trimmed seat that dominated the room and was meant for him. "Who made *that* thing?" I wondered. The color and size of it seemed all wrong. A reporter asked,

> Some spiritual leaders of various groups live in great richness with a chauffeur and expensive cars and boats.

Prabhupada: Yes.

Reporter: What about you?

Prabhupada [jokingly]: Because I know you are envious, therefore I don't sit here [indicating the enormous seat]. I am sitting here.

Both the reporter and I burst out laughing. Prabhupada had negotiated the sensitive balance between the sincere, if tasteless, offering of his followers and the natural skepticism of nonfollowers.

In early July, tens of thousands attended San Francisco's Rath-yatra parade and festival. Prabhupada addressed them in a sunny meadow in Golden Gate Park, saying that the Bhagavad-gita was the basis of the Krishna consciousness movement. And the Bhagavad-gita reminds us that we are integral parts of God, who is the chief of all living beings. It's God who maintains all living beings. It's he who is the predominator. We are the maintained and predominated.

My heart gladdened to hear Prabhupada explain these basic points. He spoke with conviction, and what he said was based on the authority of scriptures and sages throughout the ages. It was also clear and logical and epically relevant. "Why didn't more people 'get' it?" I thought, completely ignoring the grim fact that only weeks before, for some unknown reason, I'd been missing it myself.

After his talk I started to climb the stage steps to photograph the event when a devotee blocked me, saying, "Women are not allowed on the stage." I explained that I was authorized by Prabhupada to take photos, but this man was adamant. Usually I devised ways to circumvent such obstacles, but this time I found myself disheartened—after all, the fundamental Krishna conscious understanding was that we're not these male or female bodies but spiritual beings, and besides, this person was interfering with my service, and anyway, women as well as men should be on the stage, and so on. Suddenly weary, I meandered to the middle of the field behind the audience and plopped down on an empty chair, thinking, "If I could think of something better to do than Krishna consciousness, I'd surely do it." I wondered what my life would have looked like if Prabhupada hadn't entered it. Through a lens of oversimplification, I suddenly saw myself caught in a web of competition, clambering for photographic assignments, climbing a ladder of prestige while trying to ignore a pervasive stench of

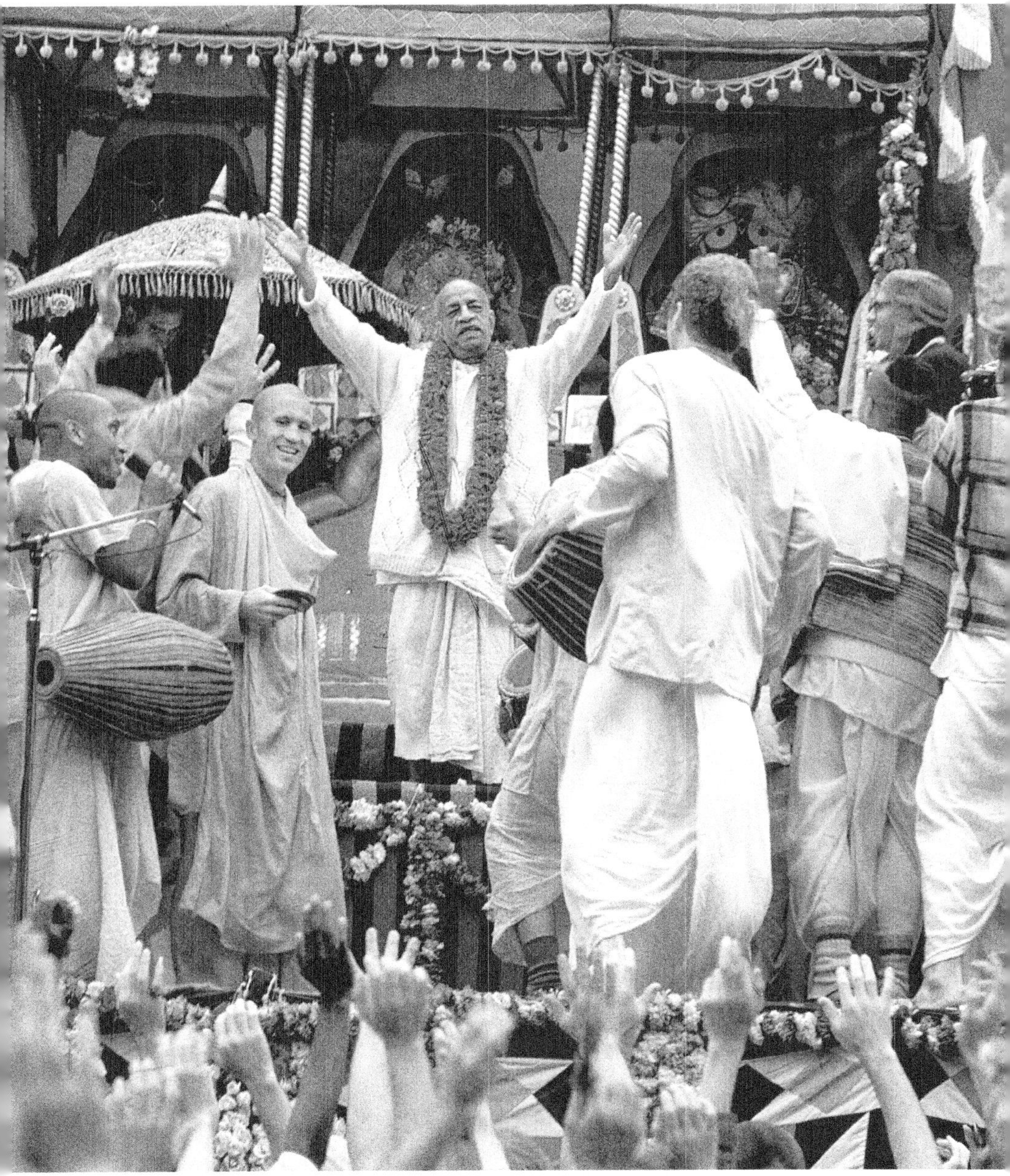

phoniness and meaninglessness. Probably drinking more than wise. Hiding beneath a layer of competence and conviviality. Certainly confused. In summary, miserable.

After a short time the kirtan intensified. I looked up to see Prabhupada getting off his seat. He took a bunch of pink roses and threw them one by one into the huge crowd. Finally, he threw what was left of the bunch and, raising his arms, began to dance. I stood on the chair I'd been sitting on and realized I was in an ideal spot to take photographs: in the lower part of the frame were the audience's upraised hands—black and white, men's and women's, young and old—and in the center was an ecstatic Prabhupada surrounded by his blissful students. Behind him stood the deities.

The experience left me humbled: how easily my consciousness had drooped. How much I needed help with my service, and how ignorant I was of the ways in which that help came. Clearly, awareness of Krishna, which was natural for Prabhupada, was superficial for me. Yet, also clearly, *someone* was trying to help me. I bowed my head in thanks.

The next day we filmed Prabhupada answering questions at a local TV studio. When the reporter asked the reason behind the shaved heads, Prabhupada, perhaps impatient with such superficial questions, began tapping his fingers. Not foreseeing this reaction, I'd placed our microphone next to his hand, which was hidden behind a small ledge. As the questions got better, I noticed that the tapping lessened.

> Reporter: Do you feel that in getting truths from various places like the Bible, the Koran and so forth—don't you run into conflicts at all, or contradictions in those particular philosophies?
>
> Prabhupada: No, I don't find any conflict, because the ultimate goal is God. You have to understand God and try to love him. So you can go through any religious process. If the goal is attained, that you understand what is God and you try to love him, then your life is perfect.

I loved the broad inclusiveness of Krishna consciousness, the equitableness of it. Prabhupada wasn't saying that any group or religion was better or worse than any other. He was saying that I was meant to understand who I am—a spiritual being—and to progress toward where I was meant to go—back to God. I realized that as soon as I felt myself superior or inferior to any other person or group, I'd misunderstood what Prabhupada was teaching. Prabhupada's words, based on Krishna's, snapped me out of my habitual retreat into parochial thinking. I felt opened up, expanded, released from some suffocating and sticky box that I didn't fit in and was never supposed to be in anyway. What Prabhupada was saying was true and beautiful and something I needed to make my own.

During our three-day stay in Dallas, Yadubara and I discussed making a film of Prabhupada's life.

"We could show how traditional and spiritually oriented life was in India when he was a child," I said, thinking of the *National Geographic* style article we'd wanted to do years before.

"Yeah," Yadubara said. "The way Prabhupada grew up is such a contrast to what we experienced growing up in the West!"

Since Prabhupada had celebrated Rath-yatra festivals in his childhood, we decided to ask him what that festival was like, thinking we could reenact it for the film. Prabhupada, sitting on the floor behind his classic small coffee table, heard our question and said, "Yes, my father found one child-sized Rath cart and purchased it for me. I painted it with colors. And I invited all the neighborhood children to come and we had a festival for eight days, just as they do in Jagannath Puri. My mother was cooking. When my father's friends heard about it, they joked with my father, 'Oh, you are having a festival and you didn't invite us?' My father said, 'It is just a children's program.' But his friends said, 'No, no it is a festival! Why didn't you invite us?'

"According to our children's imagination," Prabhupada said, "it was a very gorgeous festival."

When I asked him what his Rath cart looked like, Prabhupada asked for a piece of paper. I tore one out of my notebook and photographed Prabhupada concentrating closely as he drew his small cart. When he handed me the completed drawing, I was startled. It was crude—childlike—yet clear. He'd made a profile of his flag-topped Rath cart and the deity it transported. Near the ground, a horse strained to pull the heavy cart forward, and high above the horse, seated before the deity, a driver sat, holding a long rein that was attached to the horse's neck. Cherishing this notebook page, I practically heard and saw this cart pulled and worshiped through the backstreets of Calcutta by jubilant yelling children.

Later that month I photographed Prabhupada at the Hare Krishna West Virginia farm community, sitting on a grassy knoll and speaking to a small group. He was explaining that no one can become God conscious and at the same time be sinful. "That is impossible." He said sincere persons can understand whether or not they are God conscious by judging their own activities, and he gave an example: if you're hungry and you eat something, you can feel strength and satisfaction. No one has to tell you your hunger has abated. Similarly, if you're God conscious, you'll be free from the inclination to do any sinful activity.

On the grass to Prabhupada's right sat charismatic and eloquent Kirtanananda, the community leader and one of Prabhupada's first students. In years to come, opulence, power, and a host of fawning followers would whittle away his self-control and discernment. Unlike Karandhar's problems, though, when Kirtanananda's began to come to light, they didn't rattle my faith but strangely reinforced it. His fate was a clear life lesson that made Krishna's teachings real. Pride, Krishna explains, was the first and main cause of falldown. Pride would precede Kirtanananda's fall and make sex, money, and power irresistibly alluring to him. Pride would thwart his ability to practice an appealing spiritual process.

Prabhupada prodded me and all his students, "Realization means you should write, every one of you, what is your realization. What is this *Back to Godhead* magazine for? You write your realization, what you have realized about Krishna. That is required. It is not passive. Always you should be active. Whenever you find time, you write. Never mind, two lines, four lines, but you write your realization."

I took Prabhupada at his word and I wrote. The magazine's editor accepted my unexceptional articles and photographs, but he was unsure of the advertisements I created: an orange separated from its peel with the title "Perfectly Packaged by Krishna" and a blurb for one of Prabhupada's books; twenty-five smiling devotees standing on a lawn with the caption "A Return to Normalcy" and an invitation to the ashram; a quote from Henry David Thoreau praising the Bhagavad-gita placed over a forest scene; a father and child looking at each other with the words "If you can't tell him what life is for, you're in trouble" and with information about the Bhagavad-gita; small portraits of thirty devotees and Prabhupada with the caption "The face is the index of the mind" and a Sunday feast invitation.

I sent mock-ups of these ads to Prabhupada and asked his opinion. He responded to them:

> The advertisement proposals are approved by me. Yes, you use your American ingenuity in this way to spread Krishna consciousness.

When Prabhupada came to Brooklyn I had another ad, this one already on the back cover of *Back to Godhead* and ready for print. It showed beautifully bound editions of the Bhagavad-gita, Koran, Bible, and Torah on a bookshelf and said, "If you've read one, you've read them all." Prabhupada disapproved. He didn't want to denigrate any scripture. Hours before the magazine went to press we replaced that ad.

I had so many ideas for the magazine that they kept me up at night; I felt I was part of a mission and had a calling in that mission. But a new editorial staff decided my contributions were substandard. I was sidelined. On one hand, I felt, "Well, they've finally figured out I'm a sham devotee," and on the other, I mutely chafed at their arrogance. "How dare they reject my work!" Prabhupada's words in the recently published Chaitanya-charitamrta solaced me:

> One should not ambitiously think, 'I shall become a great author. I shall be celebrated as a writer.' These are material desires. One should attempt to write for self-purification. It may be published or it may not be published, but that does not matter. If one is actually sincere in writing, all his ambitions will be fulfilled.

I began to think that perhaps my exclusion was for the best. Perhaps pride's tentacles had ventured into my heart, and this hiatus would give them a chance to withdraw. Pride, I was realizing, was a loud sign of ignorance. It was a lack of awareness of God. Whatever abilities or assets I thought I had could be taken from me in a moment. And that meant they weren't really mine to begin with, for something that was actually mine couldn't be taken from me. So on what basis was I proud? What, exactly, did I have to be proud of?

Two and a half years later, the *Back to Godhead* staff was again replaced and, happily, I was again allowed to participate. For one article, "Who's Pulling the Strings?", I made an extensive chart of the modes of nature—goodness, passion, and ignorance—and how those modes affect our faith, diet, charity, duty, knowledge, action, understanding, determination, happiness, and so on. To my delight, Prabhupada showed the chart to his guests to help make the point that Krishna consciousness wasn't simply sentiment but was also a thorough and methodical science that explored the hows and whys behind our functioning in this world.

An iridologist told Yadubara that his severe indigestion was due to aluminum poisoning. Although in India we'd eaten lots of preparations that had been cooked in cheap aluminum pots, I considered iridology bogus and was highly skeptical of this diagnosis. Then, when I heard the prescribed diet, I became alarmed: To rid his body of toxins, Yadubara was to fast from milk and grains. The same doctor gave Jadurani similar advice.

By the time Prabhupada arrived in Los Angeles in July of '74, Yadubara had dropped from 150 to 85 pounds and was too weak to climb stairs. If he got any worse, I thought grimly, I'd become a widow.

But he's only thirty! He's way too young to die! Plus he'd started on his spiritual path only three years before—there was so much farther for him to go, and for us to go together. We didn't even have children yet.

What would my situation be if I was single? Prabhupada welcomed single women, but his leading male followers were less accommodating.

I couldn't even conceive of remarrying.

Everywhere I looked was desolate.

Yadubara, Jadurani, who was similarly emaciated, and I met Prabhupada, who gently touched Jadurani's forehead with the back of his fingers, as if testing for a fever, and said she would be all right. He then told a story: A man's friends decided to play a joke on him. Every time one of his friends saw him, the friend would scream, "A ghost! A ghost!" and run away. At first the man thought it was a prank and ignored it, but after it happened repeatedly, the man started taking it seriously. Finally, after the tenth friend screamed and ran, the man said, "Yes, I'm a ghost."

"Similarly," Prabhupada continued, "since people have been telling you, 'Oh, you're sickly, you're weak,' you've begun to feel sickly and weak."

Prabhupada said the iridologist was speculating and that we shouldn't follow his advice. He told Yadubara to "just take a little prasad," and Yadubara began eating rice, bean, and vegetable stews with extra butter. Jadurani did the same, and they both recovered.

I recovered from my anguish too. I felt like life returned to my body.

From the first time I met him, Prabhupada's consummate practicality had attracted me. This time it saved us.

Toward the end of '74, after seeing the documentary on thousands of Mayapur villagers having full meals at the Hare Krishna food relief program, Prabhupada wrote Yadubara,

> I just saw your film last night and it was very nice. We can collect a lot of money with this film for the food-relief program. But not a single farthing of that money should be used for any other thing …
>
> As far as your future films are concerned I do not think it is possible for the BBT [the Bhaktivedanta Book Trust, the publishing division of the Hare Krishna society] to continue financing these films. BBT is strictly for construction of temples and printing books. My idea is that you can use the original capital that BBT gave you. You don't have to pay that back. You can somehow or another, by business tactics, increase that capital and employ it again to make a new film. Then again use the capital from that film or use the profit from that film to create another film, etc. In this way you can make many films. Generally people enjoy seeing any film. But when a film has something substantial such as our Krishna conscious philosophy to offer, then it becomes a real pleasure. Therefore our films should be the most popular films ever produced. Try to distribute this and your original first film as widely as possible and in this way the finances will be easily obtained for producing further films.
>
> Please continue chanting 16 rounds daily, rising early, attending mangal arati and classes, and following the 4 regulative principles. By following this simple formula as I have given from the very beginning, your life will be completely free from anxiety.
>
> I hope this meets you in good health.
>
> Your ever well-wisher,
> A. C. Bhaktivedanta Swami

Filmmaking was to become a lifelong service for both of us.

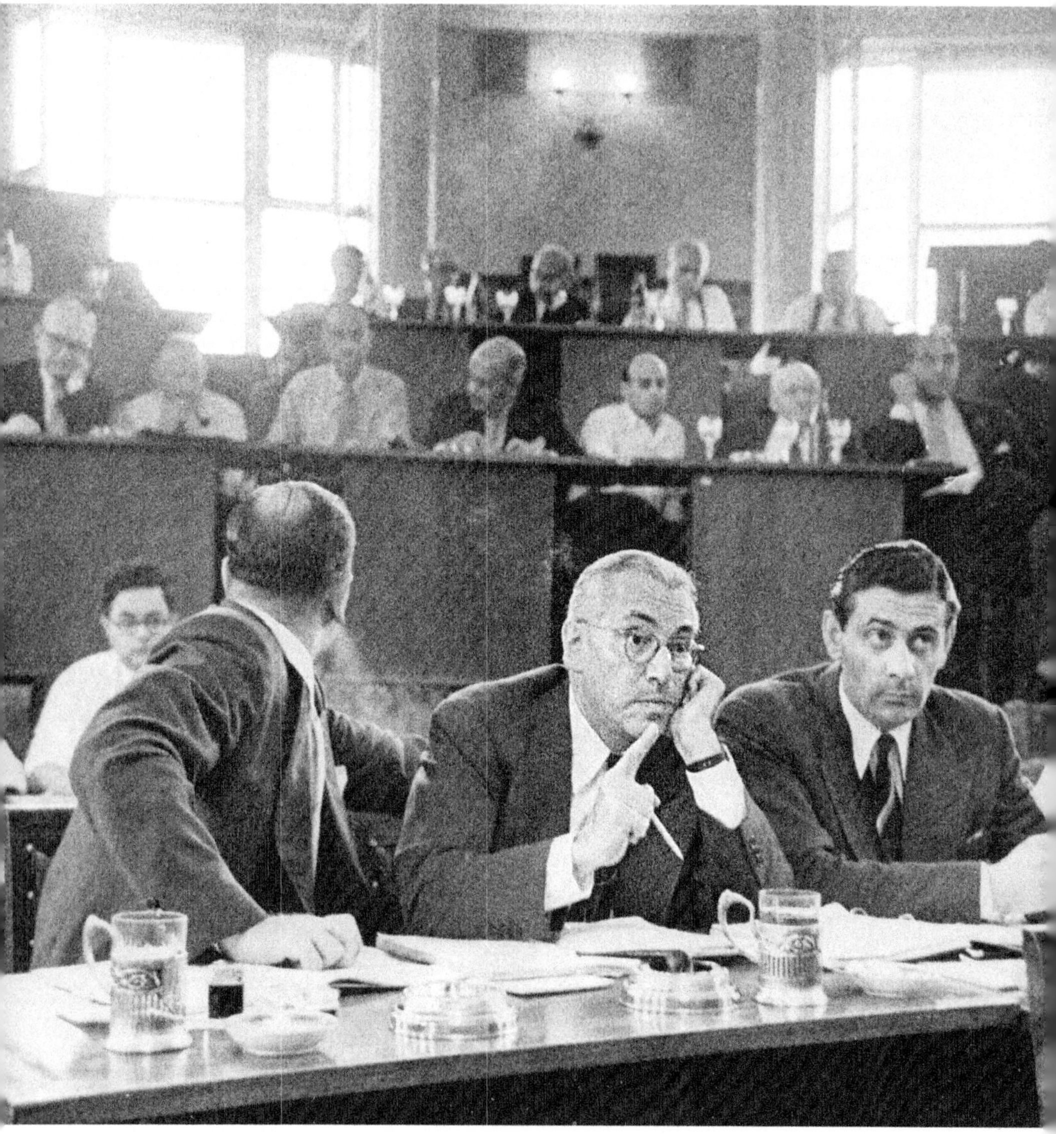

CHAPTER THIRTEEN

A Brown Bottle

One night my brother called. With a resigned and tired voice he said, "I've been trying to reach you all day. I have bad news. Dad came home from work feeling unusually tired from the flu, went to bed and passed away."

"Oh, no! How's Mom taking it?"

"She's really upset. There was no warning. She heard his breathing stop, went in the bedroom and that was it. He was gone."

"I'll be there as soon as I can." I was a welter of anxiety and moroseness.

I flew from Los Angeles and arrived in Great Neck to an empty apartment—my mother was with my brother in Manhattan. Our home was exactly the way I remembered it, especially my father's room: his next day's shoes, suit and matching tie waited on a free-standing, shiny, pinewood rack; his books about World War II, Adolph Hitler, the Third Reich, Abraham Lincoln, and the Civil War lined two shelves; the TV was ready for hours of weekend football; his pipe rested on its diamond-shaped, thick glass ashtray waiting to be stuffed with his favorite tobacco, lying next to it; wine glasses and red wine awaited guests.

But there was also something new. On the top of his bookshelf was a quart-size brown glass jar with a black plastic screw-on lid. I picked it up and read the label: Reuben Papert 2/14/75 and the name of a crematorium.

My brother hadn't told me that Dad had already been cremated.

Every nerve in my body tensed. I recoiled, hastily put the bottle back, left the room almost running and dropped onto the living room couch, my mind empty from the shock. Then thoughts rushed in.

So great was my father's presence just moments before that he had all but ambled into his room and, in his mild way, given me a half-grin and asked about my day while he sat on his bed, loosened his tie and took off his shoes. I could hear his genial voice, feel his concern for me, smell his infernal pipe, see him lift his knee and use both hands to untie the shoelace on his shiny brown leather shoe. Practically he was there. And then that bottle.

A small part of me dimly rationalized that that brown bottle contained only remnants of the body that contained my father—a soul—for this one lifetime. The ashes were those of a vehicle whose driver had gone. That driver, my father, was still present—not just in my memory, but also as a tangible, spiritual fact I could not observe.

But theory wasn't enough; that damned bottle was still loathsome and I was still alone. Tears flowed. Losing my father was unexpected and I missed him. From him I had gotten a deep overall optimism about the future that, although it sometimes seemed to defy reason, made me just as he was—lighthearted despite everything. My father had also gifted me with a sense of humor, an ability to see the absurd and the ironic and to laugh well about it. Even my permanent sense of financial insecurity, a result of growing up under his care, was a blessing, for it now balanced Yadubara's sometimes too liberal ways. But mostly I was indebted to my father for sincerely caring about me and for his example of tireless hope. My dear Dad never quit. My Dad always kept trying.

Later, as the bottle's eerie brown pall dissipated, something else was there. When he was alive, Dad must have sensed Prabhupada was like a father to me and that, in addition to my long absence, must have pained him. I was sorry. In truth, however, it was Prabhupada's knowledge—shining knowledge that established the soul's eternality and glorious qualities, God's beautiful personality and his love and justice—that gradually and gently assuaged me in this solitary, needy time.

Darkness settled in. Our home was quiet as the grave.

CHAPTER FOURTEEN

Hobbled Holy Times

Although recovering from the milk and grain fast that had emaciated him, Yadubara had been too weak to come with me to deal with my father's passing and was also too weak to attend Mayapur's annual Gaura Purnima festival in March. With his encouragement, I went with our 16mm Bolex movie camera, lights, and my still cameras. I was elated to once again be in the holy land with Prabhupada.

Thrilled devotees crowded around Prabhupada's white Ambassador as it pulled up to Mayapur's scaffolded main gate, and accompanied the car as it passed under the ponderous archway and down the narrow road through the center of the property to the temple-guest building in the rear.

But beneath this gleeful welcome, tension brewed. For the past year, sannyasis and their celibate assistants had been traveling in buses throughout North America selling Prabhupada's books and recruiting people to move into their ashrams. Many of these young men refused to preach to women, because "Whenever you make a woman a devotee, you lose one man"—meaning women would eventually want to marry, and that meant their husbands would become absorbed in household life and diverted from preaching. Although Prabhupada had yet to comment on this attitude, to me it was an alarming misunderstanding that fostered anti-women/ male superiority sentiments. It made me silently brazen. I wasn't about to allow the men's mentality to inhibit me as I moved around to photograph Prabhupada. I would—politely—go where I wanted when I wanted and they would live with it. I was stoic. I was doing my sacred service. Why should I let these men's disagreeable attitude interfere? Not only was Prabhupada fine with what I was doing, he encouraged me. A few of his followers would not affect or inhibit me.

The next morning, as the sun sent brilliant shafts over acres of rice paddies, I joined Prabhupada and the small group walking with him. When Prabhupada saw me a wave of concern crossed his face. Due to my father's passing and my empathy with Yadubara, I'd lost weight. Prabhupada didn't say anything, but studied me and with concern still on his face looked down thoughtfully. Within myself I assured him, "I'll get better in this beautiful land of Mayapur."

Cane in hand, Prabhupada traversed the narrow raised ridges between the cultivated fields that bordered our property as he replied to mock challenges posed by his students:

Pusta Krishna: They think that we are limiting God by saying that he's a person or that he has form.

Prabhupada: That is their foolishness. They are thinking that God is a person like them. They cannot conceive that a person can be so much more powerful than they are. That is the defect. A person has inconceivable power—just like you are a person. You cut your hair. It is growing. Do you know how it is growing?

Pusta Krishna: No.

Prabhupada: Then? That means within you there is an inconceivable power. So if an ordinary human being has so much inconceivable power, how much inconceivable power God has. That is God.

I enjoyed this bantering, for the materialistic arguments devotees put forward were often the same ones I harbored, and Prabhupada's retorts revealed how logical his conviction was. I sometimes wished I could express atheistic challenges to Krishna consciousness and hear Prabhupada's replies, but I never thought the arguments through enough to actually do it.

The group of us continued on to the bank of the Ganges where Prabhupada squatted, Indian-style, next to the sacred water, reached out, cupped a few drops in his right hand and put them on the top of his head, saying, "Three drops on the head has the same purifying effect as bathing." I buried my camera in the folds of my sari as the rest of the entourage followed suit and holy drops started flying everywhere.

Noticing an unusual plant growing nearby, Prabhupada asked Kanva, our energetic and eccentric Mayapur gardener who was standing next to me, what it was.

"I've seen it before," Kanva said. "I can't remember what it's called but it doesn't have any use."

"It has a use," Prabhupada said. "Everything in God's creation has a use. You just don't know what it is."

A light lit up inside me. "Of course!" I thought. "The Creator has some purpose in mind when he creates something. *Everything has a use. Nothing is useless!*" It was like a long missing puzzle piece had finally been put in place, suddenly making the puzzle more intelligible. I saw everything with a little more appreciation.

Walking back toward the temple, we came upon a steep embankment and to traverse it, Prabhupada took hold of one of his disciple's arms. Once on top, he brusquely pushed the arm away. I was surprised—it was uncharacteristic for Prabhupada.

"This is what impersonalists do," Prabhupada said.

I didn't understand.

"They take help from their guru," he went on, "and when they feel they've achieved their goal, they reject their guru."

"Oh lord!" I thought. "What an ungrateful mentality!"

We approached the temple entrance and, my brazenness reaching new heights, I elbowed my way among the sannyasis to a spot just behind Prabhupada. Due to their current sexist mood, for me to break through the ranks of these saffron-robed men was a courageous act of defiance. But I was on assignment and their opinions—they surely thought I was a pushy and uncultured woman—would not deter me. It wasn't that I didn't care what they thought, it was that my service came first. Walking directly behind Prabhupada, I filmed his students greeting him from his vantage point.

Then Prabhupada lectured before the sweeping, packed temple room, explaining that anyone can become advanced in spiritual life. Advanced, he said, means that one understands that Krishna is the Supreme Personality of Godhead. It wasn't difficult to be advanced. All the Vedic literature was written for us to come to this understanding.

Afterwards, Prabhupada circumambulated the deities. Two large bells hung high from the ceiling on both sides of the temple room, and with each round Prabhupada rang them. Tall, affable Vishnugada held my light and stood behind me as I filmed Prabhupada walking up to the bell's long rope, grasping its knotted end and jerking it firmly to make crisp rings as his students joyfully jumped, danced, and sang the maha-mantra in his wake. After several rings, each one timed to the beat of the kirtan (a musical feat due to the long rope), Prabhupada, smiling, let go of the rope and continued his circumambulation. Vishnugada and I walked backwards in front of him, the light glaring, the students ecstatic.

For these glorious minutes—while chanting God's names after hearing his philosophy—it seemed to me that different genders, races, nationalities, and cultures united in an enchanted harmony. The feeling was uplifting, rapturous. I wished it could continue throughout all the hours of all the years to come.

And in some ways, in Mayapur it did continue. The exhilarating days and nights included pilgrimages on fleets of boats down the Ganga, chanting en masse on Bhaktisiddhanta Road, crowding Sri Chaitanya's birthplace and the home of the great teacher Bhaktivinode Thakur, and touring the new pavilion on our property, where 1,200 people at a time could sit for prasad. Yet, when I stepped back from the buzz and simply observed, I saw Prabhupada's rambunctious young followers, myself included, bursting with passion for spiritual life, ceaselessly jockeying to be noticed by Prabhupada, and cocky. We were, after all, special—*we were devotees of Krishna, we were dear to God himself.* I thought, "We are—*I am*—too full of myself. There's a collective pride going around here that's unhealthy." I remembered a passage I'd read from *Conjectures of a Guilty Bystander* by Thomas Merton, an American Trappist monk:

> We belong to God. Yet everybody else belongs to God. We just happen to be conscious of it, and to make a profession out of this consciousness. But does that entitle us to consider ourselves different, or even better, than others? The whole idea is preposterous.

In his final lecture Prabhupada said,

> Krishna is explaining himself in the Bhagavad-gita, Krishna is sending his representative acharya to teach you, and Krishna is within yourself trying to teach you if you are actually serious. Then where is the difficulty? Inside, outside, always, books, knowledge—he is prepared. So where is the difficulty to make yourself perfect in Krishna consciousness? There is no difficulty at all. Provided you are serious, you can become fully Krishna conscious in this very life. You are all young men.* You are not old man like me. I have no opportunity …

Suddenly Prabhupada stopped speaking. We waited in utter stillness. It was like he'd left us and gone somewhere else by the strength of his meditation. Then, after long moments, someone began to sing—jarringly—and Prabhupada regained his external consciousness and softly chanted along.

The next evening, the lustrous full moon rose, marking the end of the festival and 489 years since the appearance of Sri Chaitanya. It was the boldest moon I'd ever seen, and as it lingered in the Mayapur sky, its placid light illumined everything.

---

* In those days, the word "men" was understood to include women.

Sitting in those moon rays, I started to acknowledge that spiritual life was an ongoing cauldron of contradictions. On one side, Prabhupada said there was no difficulty at all in becoming fully God conscious. *I could do it—and I could do it in my lifetime.* On the other side, knowing myself, it was hard for me to believe that statement, especially when I compared my consciousness to Prabhupada's. Plus, the very organization Prabhupada founded and was guiding was clearly beset with a lack of God consciousness, the foremost example this year being the men's misogyny. "I'm not serious enough about spiritual life," I surmised, "and as a group, I guess we're all not serious enough."

But, I thought, what would it look like if I and others *were* serious?

I remembered reading a letter Prabhupada had written in the winter of 1965 to a leading godbrother of his. Prabhupada, then 70 years old, had recently arrived in New York City and was supporting himself by selling volumes of his Srimad-Bhagavatams to booksellers. He was alone and had no other source of income, no backers, no students. Through letters he'd suggested to his godbrothers in India that they could cooperate to raise funds for a Radha Krishna temple in Manhattan, but his godbrothers said they were unable to help him in any way. In response, Prabhupada had written, "I am not a man to be discouraged." Given the circumstances, an amazing statement.

Success is not determined by the result of an effort, I was reminded, because the result of any effort is in another's hand. Success is the consciousness with which the effort is made. And happiness lies waiting in the same place: the consciousness with which an effort is made. That consciousness was up to me, it was my free choice. I remembered one of Victor Frankl's sentences,

> Everything can be taken from a man but one thing: the last of human freedoms—to choose one's attitude in any given set of circumstances, to choose one's own way.

I didn't have to be affected by hubris or by the pathetic but mushrooming misogyny among the male students. I was sheltered by Prabhupada's teachings and example and acceptance and encouragement and love for me, which I was immersed in every day all day. I could follow his precedent and try to feel his mood within myself, that "I am not a woman to be discouraged."

But then what to do with my dismay with the men? When I was busy photographing, which was most of the time, I buried that feeling. Burial, however, didn't seem like a beneficial way to deal with feelings. What I would have *liked* to do was to grab these men—my godbrothers—by the shoulders and shake them into knowing how far they'd veered from Prabhupada's example, how much they'd misinterpreted some of his writings, how deeply and needlessly discouraging and hurtful they were being to us women. What I actually did though, in my typical, taciturn, timid, detached, distant, neutral style, was absolutely nothing. I continued mutely photographing, just as I always had.

If the truth be told, some of these men really didn't care about Prabhupada's example or the women's reactions to what they did. They wanted to dominate and were using some of Prabhupada's statements to justify doing so. And they labeled those who defied them with what they considered a pejorative: "feminists!"

I marveled at how something as beautiful and profound as Krishna consciousness could be made so ugly and twisted. And I wondered, Why didn't Prabhupada put an end to this mood?

Of course, Prabhupada didn't have a magic wand to turn immature people into mature ones. He couldn't force anyone. He gave his teachings. He gave his example. He strongly corrected, too. (He'd removed the leader of the touring bus party and asked him to introduce Krishna consciousness in China.) But, after growing up with licentious habits in a licentious society, some of his male students, who were mostly in their early twenties, were now attempting celibacy. Their endeavor was laudable, as sense control was necessary for spiritual progress. But, for such passionate, overbearing, ambitious young men, an unfavorable outcome shouldn't have been surprising. They'd perverted their attraction for women into aversion for them.

What we did with what Prabhupada gave us, I thought, was up to us. *And what I did with it was up to me.* I appreciated how by his example Prabhupada was modeling Krishna: he wasn't being authoritarian; he was allowing all of us our free will.

Mayapur's pure air and wide open space cleared my head and revived my appetite and health. I'd brought a big bag of granola with me, and eating that along with regular meals helped me regain much of the weight I'd lost. I felt strong.

After years of delays and consternation, in April '75, Vrindavan's grand Krishna-Balaram Temple opened amid a hub of activity: Indian brahmins chanted complex Sanskrit mantras and performed elaborate Vedic rituals, the Governor of the Indian State of Uttar Pradesh and leaders from the other Vrindavan temples observed the ceremonies, and devotees from around the world, some of whom chanted the maha-mantra in shifts throughout the day and night, attended. Prabhupada said the continuous chanting of the holy names was the proper way to inaugurate the temple and honor the deities. In his discourse he explained that the purpose of installing the deity was so we could see and think of him. The deity was not different from Krishna; for the devotee, the deity was Krishna himself. "God is Absolute," Prabhupada explained. "That means he is nondifferent from his name and from his form. We are spending so much money, lakhs, not for worshiping a statue. When we worship the deity we are directly worshiping God."

Prabhupada performed the first arati ceremony for Krishna and Balaram before a jammed temple room. I struggled through the crowd toward the altar with my camera, thinking that the battalions who had been in Mayapur and the throngs around me now indicated that Prabhupada's movement had emerged from obscurity and was cresting on a surge of acceptance. In time, I thought, it would be a major voice among world ideologies.

After bumping, shoving and squirming, finally only one person stood between me and a clear view of Prabhupada: Tripurari, the world's number one seller of Prabhupada's books, whose hefty contributions had helped build the temple and who was so mesmerized by this moment that he refused to acknowledge my repeated taps on his shoulder. Camera in hand, I extended my arm over his shoulder so he could see my camera and surmise my intent to photograph. No response. I turned the camera lens toward him, indicating he was the obstruction. No response. In desperation, I leaned over and put my mouth next to his ear. Over the blaring kirtan I yelled, "If you stand there, you can see Prabhupada offering *arati*. If you let me stand there, the *whole world* will see Prabhupada offering *arati!*" If this statement didn't move him, I wasn't sure what I would do next, but I was not about to give up. I'd be making another attempt after this one. Then another. Tripurari didn't look at me. He took one long last look at Prabhupada, now offering incense to Krishna and Balaram, and stepped aside. Later, when I related this story, people cheered on hearing of my stubbornness and Tripurari's sacrifice. Our cooperation struck a chord in people's hearts.

A few days later I was on a morning walk photographing Prabhupada as he spoke about the moon. Prabhupada's understanding of astronomy, which, like all his understandings, was based on scriptural statements, differed from what I'd learned. Hearing him that arid morning, I thought how I'd already found that his teachings about the soul and the goal of life were pragmatic and logical, and how I'd benefited from the process of bhakti he promoted. Besides that, I trusted Prabhupada. "Why should I place more faith in astronomers and their evolving theories than in the writings Prabhupada refers to?" I thought. Walking briskly next to Prabhupada and the group of twenty men surrounding him on that darkened road, my usual preoccupation with lighting and composition, expressions and exposure lessened as I recalled a passage from the Bhagavad-gita, a book I was becoming more and more fond of.

In his commentary to one of Krishna's statements in the Gita, Prabhupada had written that due to the moon's influence, vegetables become delicious and that without moonshine they would neither grow nor taste succulent. Moonlight's effect was totally unfamiliar to me. Ordinarily, part of my photojournalistic role, which was also part of my character, was to remain as invisible as possible. Attracting attention was an anathema to me and if there was risk of embarrassment it was even worse. While taking the initiative to talk to Prabhupada about something I'd experienced or thought was beyond me, asking a question I really wanted to know the answer to was not. Nervous but filled with a kind of righteous determination—knowing that no one could deny me this moment, that I was claiming my right as a student to inquire from my teacher—I said to Prabhupada, "In the Bhagavad-gita, Krishna says the moon nourishes vegetables. How is that?" I expected a technical answer akin to photosynthesis.

Prabhupada stopped walking. The whole group and I stopped walking too. Forty intrigued eyes rested on Prabhupada and me as he turned toward me, leaned slightly on his cane and seriously regarded me, now standing three feet to his left. His eyes looked straight into mine and filled me with expectancy. His eyes—all that I saw for those short seconds—shone with his virtue, with who he was inside. They filled me with energy. To find myself on a gloomy Vrindavan street, flanked by a cadre of men, gazing into Prabhupada's eyes as he gazed deeply into mine, was uniquely discomforting. But I didn't flinch. What was the answer?

A couple of beats passed. Then Prabhupada said, "Why don't you ask him?"

So unforeseen was his statement that as he turned and continued walking with his retinue, I remained standing for a couple more seconds, startled. Dumbfounded. And feeling some deep, foggy sense surface within me: The universe was populated with powerful sentient beings, beings beyond my comprehension, beings who controlled forces that affected me from moment to moment. Prabhupada had popped the bubble of my dead mechanistic universe to reveal a universe teeming with personality. With fresh eagerness to access that life-filled place, I jogged to catch up with the group.

Before I left for this much-anticipated month-long pilgrimage to India, from Los Angeles (where Yadubara and I were staying), I repeatedly called my mother, who was still in Great Neck, Long Island. But she never answered the phone. She was a regulated and dutiful person, punctual and predictable so, worried, I asked my brother, Tony, to stay in touch with her. As soon as I returned, I again repeatedly tried to call her, but she never picked up.

Days later, Tony called. Just hearing his voice on the phone made me stiffen with foreboding.

"Mom's depressed."

"About Dad?"

"Yeah, about Dad, but not just about Dad. She's also depressed about me being such an active socialist and about you being a Hare Krishna."

I knew that my brother's and my life choices disturbed Mom—Tony had been part of the student uprising at Columbia University—but I hadn't realized how much. I began trying to call her daily, and then several times a day, and finally, the day I was going to buy another ticket for Great Neck, Tony called again. Again I stiffened.

"The doctor told Mom she had cancer that metastasized. He said he thought she wouldn't live much longer."

"No!"

"I went to see her yesterday. She had taken a bottle of aspirin and cut both her wrists with a razor blade. She was dead in her bed."

I was devastated.

I flew to Great Neck and entered the apartment. Tony wasn't there. I walked through the still rooms, cautiously, and was grateful there was no brown bottle and no blood. But some vast emptiness had taken over this place where nothing ever seemed to change—an emptiness so pervasive it made everything completely different.

"For years and years together," I thought, "Mom had been there for me when I needed her. But now, when she needed me, I was nowhere to be found. I was traipsing the world doing my thing while my mom was suffering alone. What a wretch I am! What an ingrate!" A huge, hollow feeling welled up inside me—an emptiness big enough to swallow me whole. In a vital way I had dismally failed.

Before long I was reading my mother's diary, which I had not known she kept until this day. On one page she wrote with her usual, steady flourish:

> I have brought two children into this world and I don't know why. There is no meaning to this thing called life, and there is nothing here to live for. It is all purposeless, a waste of effort and very, very painful.

The most agonizing thing was that, caught up in my own life, I'd made little effort to cross the gulf—if that gulf was crossable—between my Mom and me. I hadn't tried hard enough. I had neglected my parents, especially my mother. Along with an abiding sense of dutifulness, from her I had inherited a helpful dose of skepticism. Over the years that skepticism had obliged me to question motives, actions, and words—no matter how big or prestigious the persons they came from—and it repeatedly saved me from being cheated and hurt.

Beyond that, both my parents had inadvertently shown me the alarming, irrefutable futility of worldly life. And both of them loved me. I felt grateful to them both. Yet at the same time I could not ignore the desolate, persistent wind of disbelief that had blown through me all through my formative years from the dark horizon of their lives, and which, if I allowed it, would have leveled my attempt for something more than the mundane. Perhaps that was why I had kept my distance. But it was not reason enough.

Sadness invaded me, a sadness so profound it seemed to seep in from the stagnant air, from the whole star-studded universe in which I was less than a speck, a sadness that was the awareness of my vast insufficiency and incapability.

Amid these seething, sorrowful feelings, others came. Prabhupada had given me a new understanding of the body and the life it housed. At this desolate moment, I treasured his gift. Life did not die.

Looking out our living room window toward Grace Avenue Park—once my entire world—a whole new generation played. My children wouldn't have reason to play there, for my father and mother had moved on. They would never know their grandchildren.

After the funeral, I returned to Yadubara who, absorbed in filming and editing, had remained in Los Angeles, where he and I now shared an apartment across the street from the temple. I would have liked to have had Yadubara's comforting presence in Great Neck during this trying time, but I was glad the film was progressing. As I rejoined him and became absorbed with him, the ache in my heart slowly subsided.

CHAPTER FIFTEEN

Platonic Love and (In)Equality

Yadubara and I were living together for the first time since our stay in Vrindavan three years earlier. Since he and I had shared space as college students and while traveling, living together was comfortable for us. But there was a huge difference between our former, more wild days and now: astonishingly, due to Prabhupada's potency, our relationship was, for the time being, platonic. Of the five vows we'd taken at the time of our initiation, one was "no illicit sex," which had two meanings: the stricter one was sex was only between married couples and only for procreation. The other, more relaxed meaning was no sex outside of marriage. Although many would call it unnatural, without really discussing or thinking (!) about it, Yadubara, who was 32, and I, 25, were following the first course. Prabhupada had convinced us we would not be long in this world and we had best use our short time in it to strive for something sublime. With that as our goal, and with faith in our relatively new-found spiritual path, our relationship, which had begun with romance, evolved to abstinence. Some newcomers (who often didn't stay) felt this restriction denied life's prime necessity, but somehow we'd accepted abstinence as an aid to spiritual focus.

Living in the midst of a culture that didn't treat sex as sacred and that took abstinence as a shockingly unhealthy perversion, I contemplated how common social exchanges in the West often led to sex, which in turn often led to enormous emotional and life-altering upheaval and pain. In the non-Western world, though—the world Yadubara and I had recently been living in—men and women mixed less freely and intimacy was between husband and wife. In that world, fidelity and abstinence were more valued. Living in Los Angeles, a hub of sensuality, I felt the self-ownership of fidelity and abstinence help settle my ever-roaming mind; they simplified my life. Our marriage, Yadubara and I hoped, would be gratifying and fruitful through our common striving in bhakti-yoga.

And to some extent it was.

Like an ocean liner creating a massive wake as it plies through water, so Prabhupada had created waves of spiritual urgency that continually lapped on the shores of his students' lives. Each of us, almost without exception, felt an urgent need to become Krishna conscious ourselves and to help others do the same. It's hard to imagine, but Yadubara and I, sitting in our Los Angeles apartment, hundreds or thousands of miles away from Prabhupada, who continued traveling the world, felt this urgency daily. We were rising at 4 a.m., attending temple programs until 9 a.m., making documentary films throughout the day, attending evening temple programs, and going to bed at 10 p.m. We were idealistic. We had a sacred mission. We wanted to please Prabhupada. He was with us all day every day and his presence brought with it a strong feeling of being rightly situated—a feeling that made me happy.

In Dallas some months back, Yadubara had said to Prabhupada, "We would like to make a film biography of your life."

"Why do you want to do this?" Prabhupada had said.

"We want to show who started the Hare Krishna movement. People have heard the Hare Krishna mantra and they've seen the devotees, but they're curious to know about the person who started it and spread it in the West in such a short time."

Prabhupada had thought it over and said, "When I was a boy, I would take twenty-five paisa from my mother and go see the movies. I was very keen to see the movies. Then talking pictures came and I was even keener to see them."

He agreed to our idea, and when he arrived in Los Angeles on June 20, 1975, Yadubara filmed and I recorded his arrival address in the crowded temple room. Sitting behind and just to the right of his seat, through my headphones I heard Prabhupada say, "we are receiving transcendental knowledge through a succession: from spiritual master to disciple."

That one step of becoming Prabhupada's disciple, I thought, had been a huge one for me. My faith in the knowledge he gave, a faith that had gamboled into my existence from nowhere, had changed my life trajectory. It was due to that faith that I was in this seemingly bizarre situation.

Prabhupada continued,

> So we have to simply take instruction from guru, and if we execute that with our heart and soul, that is success.

Prabhupada made success seem so attainable! … but then again, had I ever in my life executed *any* instruction with heart and soul? Prabhupada's most basic instruction was to "always remember Krishna and never forget him." I'd been trying to do that for years with only sporadic success. For me, that singular, simple, foundational instruction was challenging.

Sigh.

Prabhupada illustrated his point by giving himself as an example:

> That is practical. I have no personal qualification, but I simply tried to satisfy my guru. That's all. My Guru Maharaja asked me that, "If you get some money, you print books."

Prabhupada's secret to success lay in satisfying his spiritual master and my success would be in satisfying Prabhupada. In Prabhupada's case, success meant writing, printing, and distributing Krishna conscious books. For me it meant creating Krishna conscious movies, photographs, and writings. Those, at least, were things I'd been doing and could continue to do.

At two o'clock the next morning Yadubara filmed and I photographed Prabhupada in his room sitting crosslegged on a cushion on the floor before his low desk using a dictaphone to record his translations and commentaries of Srimad-Bhagavatam verses. As he spoke, his brow furrowed in concentration, he leaned over and scrutinized a thick book of Sanskrit commentaries by previous spiritual luminaries. After saying a few words into the dictaphone, he'd pause it (the control buttons were on his handheld microphone) to study the book some more, and then start the dictaphone again to say a few more words. His writings, he once commented, were his devotional ecstasies.

I was in awe of the sacrosanct ambiance of devoted determination that pervaded his room. And I was nervous.

At daybreak four hours later, we filmed and photographed Prabhupada walking on Venice Beach with some of his students and Dr. J. Stillson Judah of the Graduate Theological Union in Berkeley, California. Prabhupada asked Dr. Judah, "If we are offering, 'Here is God,' why not accept it? What is the objection?"

> Dr. Judah: There isn't any objection. I think the great problem in the West, of course, is that the Western world has always been involved in materialism.
>
> Prabhupada: That means they don't want to know God. So this is a very horrible condition.
>
> Dr. Judah: That's true.
>
> Prabhupada: In human society, either he is Hindu or Muslim or Christian, there is some arrangement for understanding God. Now they are also neglecting that, everyone, all over the world.

Krishna consciousness was automatic for Prabhupada. His father had been devoted to Krishna, he'd grown up in a devotional culture, and his childhood was replete with devotional activities. But for me, coming from atheistic parents and a culture that stressed money-making and acquiring comforts and prestige, Krishna consciousness was an uphill effort. The problem wasn't the four rules and regulations—I accepted and followed those as part of a healthy, sane lifestyle. And it wasn't the japa meditation—I'd pleasurably incorporated that into my days and never skipped. The problem was that true awareness of Krishna would come to me, by Krishna's grace, only when I loved him selflessly. But I didn't. He was too elusive, too hidden, too distant, too theoretical, too bewildering, too overwhelmingly incomprehensible for me to love selflessly.

After being around someone who *did* love Krishna, my lacking was blatant. I could feel that love nearby but it was outside me, not in me. I was unqualified to access it—a moth in the night endlessly beating its wings against a light bulb.

And yet I did have *some* sense of God. I did think of him at odd times, like when I saw a bird-of-paradise flower on my daily neighborhood walks and when I got a whiff of the night-blooming jasmines in the temple garden and when I heard a melodious kirtan. Flickers of awareness and love were within me.

After his walk, Prabhupada entered the temple room just before 7 and, when the deity doors opened promptly at 7, offered his prostrated obeisances before each of the three elaborately decorated altars. Behind him, hundreds of devotees in the packed temple room likewise offered their obeisances. I photographed Prabhupada as he gazed appreciatively at the forms of Krishna on the altars and then followed him as he walked to and sat on his raised seat to lecture on a verse from the Srimad-Bhagavatam.

A few days before, the head of the Bhaktivedanta Book Trust had told me that he only wanted portraits of Prabhupada with his eyes open; he felt it was inappropriate to publish photographs of Prabhupada with his eyes closed. Although normally I would have disagreed with him and tried to convince him otherwise, at this point I took him as my boss and agreed.

With that directive fresh in my mind, I was sitting on the floor beneath Prabhupada's seat as he sang *Jaya Radha Madhava*, his eyes closed in weighty meditation. I waited, glancing hopefully at the three dedicated flashes I'd attached high up on nearby pillars to compensate for the dimly lit temple room. Prabhupada sang on, his eyes closed. I waited. And waited. Suddenly I felt a sharp hit on my backside. Startled, "What in the world could that have been?" I turned around. A Swami sitting behind me had decided I'd been sitting in the midst of the swamis doing nothing long enough—it was time for me to move on, and to make his point he'd hit me with his *danda*—a stick swamis carried as a symbol of their renunciation. I looked from him back to Prabhupada, who had opened his eyes in time to see this unusual interaction. Through the dark slits of his eyes Prabhupada looked at this Swami as his face, which had been softened with immersion in his transcendent song, turned flinty.

Relieved that I hadn't been the recipient of the sternness of that look, I thought, "Oy vey! What a contrast between Prabhupada's meditations and our activities! What could he be thinking of us?"

Prabhupada continued singing, now with his eyes open. I made many photographs, all my flashes obediently popping, and then before he began to lecture, left to take distant photographs of the devotees listening. I took the Swami's hit as an occupational hazard. Prabhupada never brought it up.

In the course of his Los Angeles talks, Prabhupada wove the frayed, traumatized threads of my recent life into a vibrant tapestry with a harmonious and venerable design. That afternoon in his garden, he said to Dr. Wolfe-Rottkay, a linguistics professor,

> Those who do not believe in God, to them God will come one day as death, "Now believe me. Get out!" Finished. All your pride finished. Your pride, your property, your family, your bank balance, your skyscraper building—all taken away. "Finished. Get out." This is God. Now understand God? You believe or not believe, God will come one day. He will take you, take everything, and "Get out!" That is God. You may believe or not believe—it doesn't matter. The same example: the tenant may not believe the landlord, but when the landlord comes with the court order, "Get out," then you have to go. That's all. That is stated in the Bhagavad-gita: "Those who do not believe in God, to them I come as death and take away everything, finished." That one has to believe, "Yes, as sure as death." Then God is sure. You may challenge as long you have got a little life for a few years, but God will come and drive you away from your present pride, from your prestigious position, "Get out." So unless one is madman, he cannot say, "There is no God." Anyone who denies the existence of God, he is a madman.
>
> Dr. Wolfe: Prabhupada, wouldn't it be better to say he is blind, he is stupid?
>
> Prabhupada: Yes, the same thing. Mad is the sum total of all stupidity. When I say mad, it is the sum total of all kinds of stupidity.

My father had been evicted; my mother had evicted herself. Both had met their Landlord, as would I. If I kept death before my eyes, then God would be before my eyes. And if I could just realize his many aspects, he'd be more present in my life. I wanted to *feel* this knowledge, to allow it to enter and relax in the innermost chamber of my being, and from there radiate throughout me. But right now my understanding was only cerebral. I'd recently lost both my parents, and I missed them dearly.

Remembering my father and mother, I thought how they were good and caring people. Sadly, I'd never really told them how grateful I was for their presence in my life and all they'd done for me. I'd never really told them how much I loved them. Their passing left me with a despair made deeper by their and my recent and sudden estrangement over my spiritual path. They'd passed on before I could explain my choice to them or introduce them to Prabhupada. Would they have found any beauty and validity in my new life? Would they have appreciated anything I was doing? I'd never know the answer to those questions; we'd had no time for reconciliation. I felt I'd broken their trust in me.

Deep regret and sorrow seeped through my being, obliterating my thoughts. Never before had I experienced such brutal loss, made all the more so by my inexcusable incommunicado. Living with myself became painful.

Fortunately I was busy from morning to night filming and photographing Prabhupada. I had so much to learn from him about karma, responsibility, desire, self-forgiveness, tolerance. And about unconditional love—love's most unexpected and brilliant aspect.

The next afternoon we filmed and photographed Prabhupada meditatively chanting japa as he walked back and forth in his small upstairs rooms. One of these rooms—his study—was painted sky blue and, well-lit by a skylight, boasted a large, prominent portrait of Gaur Kishore das Babaji, the spiritual master of Prabhupada's spiritual master, who looked about eighty-five years old. He was depicted wearing only a loincloth and seated on a large rock in a wooded area, fingering his japa beads. Yadubara was in the next room changing film when Prabhupada briefly stopped walking, indicated the painting and said to me, "Such an old man and still he is chanting."

When he'd initiated me, I'd promised Prabhupada I'd chant a minimum of sixteen rounds of japa daily. This day, Prabhupada was indicating that my vow would not end with my old age. I looked from the painting to Prabhupada and imagined a future day when I was old and Prabhupada could proudly say of me, "Such an old lady and still she is chanting."

Yadubara rejoined us, camera reloaded. Before we resumed filming Prabhupada said, "Husband and wife working together, this is very nice."

"Prabhupada," Yadubara said, "I heard you said that married life without children is zero." The day before Prabhupada had made this comment to Yamuna Devi and her friend Dinatarine who, both formerly married but childless, had given up married life to fully dedicate themselves to Krishna's service. Prabhupada was encouraging them in their renunciation.

"That is for ordinary people," Prabhupada said to Yadubara. "You have Krishna as your child."

At first, this surprised me. Prabhupada had initially made the statement, "Married life without children is zero," to two extraordinary students—talented, serious, sincere, and unflinching. Yamuna and Dinatarine were far from ordinary, so why did Prabhupada say something to them that was meant for ordinary people?

Then I laughed, treasuring Prabhupada's mood. As he had encouraged Yamuna and Dinatarine in their renunciation, so he was now encouraging Yadubara and me in our film service by putting a different twist on the same statement. I was also relieved that, for the time being, Yadubara and I had "Krishna as our child." At this point, I didn't want a child, as it would have interrupted our service. Children, I thought, could come later when I could give them the time and attention they require.

I'd written a simple article for *Back to Godhead* magazine about how the soul and the body were different. The editors thought my text was fine but questioned my illustration for it—in trying to point out how we are different from the body, I'd shown a person recalling his younger days and thinking of his future ones. Since Prabhupada was in Los Angeles, the editors suggested that I ask him his opinion. So, one bright afternoon I went to Prabhupada's room, showed him a mock-up of the illustration and explained my concept. Yadubara filmed the exchange.

"This is a proposal for *Back to Godhead* magazine, an article to show how I am not this body, to illustrate it graphically," I said, feeling foolish.

"What is that?" Prabhupada asked, referring to the illustration.

"This is a person who's thinking that, 'I can remember I was a baby sitting on the lap of my mother and now I am in the middle of my life and I know I will become old and die, but who am I? I'm not this body which is changing so much.' We're trying to put these concepts into visual terms so people can easily understand them," I said, thinking how odd it was that I, who was known for not speaking, was doing more talking than Prabhupada.

"So I'll have to read it," Prabhupada said.

"If you like, I can leave the written matter. I have it with me."

"Yes."

Prabhupada hadn't given me the yea or nay answer I expected, but something far more valuable.

Although at this time he had shouldered responsibility for thousands of students and dozens of centers all over the world, he gave his undivided attention to me, one tiny student and her four-page article, as if nothing else existed. Fully present and unhurried, Prabhupada was simply not going to make a snap judgement. He pondered the illustrations and in the end said he couldn't make a decision about the graphics without also reading the accompanying text, even though that text had already been okayed by the editors. His mindfulness and presence and focus and thoroughness about even a small question was a lesson for me in God conscious decision-making.

The article was later published in the September 1975 issue of *Back to Godhead* and illustrated with a devotee's painting of a thoughtful-looking person (the editor's decision).

After a week in Los Angeles, Yadubara and I accompanied Prabhupada to Denver. There, during a morning walk through a park, devotees discussed special diets with Prabhupada. Prabhupada had always encouraged (and was still encouraging) all his students to take prasad to their full satisfaction, but some of his students had special dietary needs. Yadubara said: "I'm a good example that these diets are not very good. I can testify. I tried for one year to alter my diet in so many ways, and it never worked. It was useless."

Prabhupada said, "The diet is useless or you are useless?"

"Ouch!" I thought. "A person is useless for accepting a certain diet?"

Yadubara was speechless.

But on reflection, Prabhupada's point was clear and typically practical: The concocted diet wasn't the problem. The problem was the person who'd chosen to accept the concoction.

We are responsible for our choices. The choices aren't the problem; the choosers are.

In his Denver room, Prabhupada sparred with a student:

Brahmananda: You say that you are presenting the Absolute Truth and that the Absolute Truth is God, Krishna. But I think your position is dogmatic. There are many truths; there are many gods.

Prabhupada: The Absolute Truth is one; God is one. God cannot be many. If God has competition, He cannot be God. If you don't admit Krishna is God, then you present who God is. But if you don't know who or what God is, then you cannot say that Krishna is not God. If you speak in that way, then *you* are being dogmatic. You do not know what God is, yet dogmatically you are saying that Krishna is not God. God, Krishna, comes before us and says, "There is no truth superior to me," and his words are confirmed by great teachers.

Prabhupada was completely fixed in his reality. And his words repeatedly reawakened me to that reality.

Yadubara and I set up bright lights on either side of Prabhupada's temple room seat to film his morning lecture, but their intensity hurt Prabhupada's eyes. He had us turn them off and later said, "They were filming me in Los Angeles, now they are filming me here. Why are they doing it again? Whether I am sitting here or in Los Angeles, what's the difference?

"This film biography is not very important," he concluded.

Our project came to an abrupt, unexpected halt.

Besides being the sound person for our films, I was also photographing for the monthly magazine and for Prabhupada's books, so my service with Prabhupada on the tour would continue. I joined Upendra, Brahmananda, and Pradyumna as part of Prabhupada's entourage. But Prabhupada's statement had ended Yadubara's service of compiling footage for a film biography on Prabhupada. Prabhupada, concerned, asked "What will Yadubara do?"

We decided that Yadubara would return to Los Angeles to begin work on a script for the documentary—*The Spiritual Frontier*—about life in the West Virginia farm community Prabhupada had established.

The morning before we left Denver, Prabhupada said, "Your guru has said that 'You chant Hare Krishna, observe these rules.' Do that, don't speculate, and you will understand everything."

I was doing those things, but I still wasn't understanding everything. Okay, okay, it would take time, but *how much* time? Would it get easier as I went along? And what would I feel as my understanding grew? Would I ever be bold and inclusive and loving? I didn't think so. I was too far from those qualities. I was negotiating between unrealistic optimism and depressing realism.

For the two and a half years Yadubara and I had lived in India we had moved as if to some alluring, complex, Krishna conscious waltz; now touring the U.S. and Canada with Prabhupada during the summers of '74, '75, and '76, for me the tempo was more like a Krishna conscious marching band. In all three countries the holy names were with us, along with Prabhupada and his realizations about Krishna and Krishna's majestic, awesome, intricate energies. But in India Prabhupada had spent weeks in one place; in the U.S. and Canada he spent only days. In India we had relaxed, regular access to Prabhupada; in the U.S. and Canada hundreds of disciples wanted his company, and access was restricted. In India Prabhupada had made managerial decisions; in the U.S. and Canada he gave guidance and then left the management to his students. In India a few years back, I surely would have discussed my mother's suicide with Prabhupada and received the warmth of his understanding. In the hubbub of the U.S.–Canada tour, it didn't even occur to me to discuss it with him.

More in the U.S. and Canada than in India, I began pulsating with the excitement and energy that Prabhupada's followers in the West exuded. Prabhupada's high expectations of us—me and all his followers—were a thermal of hope that propelled us to meet those expectations, that is, to become more aware of God and to act accordingly. The soaring nature of my ambitions and how far I was from realizing them regularly eluded me. Along with the others, I overflowed with vibrant possibilities that felt at once strange yet natural.

But really, what did Prabhupada actually *do* when he came to a temple on these summer tours? In the early morning, he'd translate and comment on the scriptures. At sunrise he'd go for a walk with a small cadre, he'd return to have darshan of the deities, he'd sing *Jaya Radha Madhava* and give a short philosophical talk in the temple room, he'd write letters and meet with guests and devotees in his room. Not glamorous activities, yet we followers were beside ourselves. What was happening was what Yamuna Devi had years ago termed "Krishna magic": the forceful inner glow of the supremely better life available to us propelled us toward ecstasy.

Swept up in Prabhupada's bright sea of possibility, my heart filled with a song of delight. I pared down my camera equipment to what fit in a small case that forever draped from my right shoulder and, in a black canvas shoulder bag that hung from my left shoulder, I kept a straw sleeping mat, pajamas, toiletries, a towel, and a change of clothes. This left me free of baggage check-ins and claims and allowed me to stay with Prabhupada throughout his airport departures and arrivals—the most emotional parts of his tour—where, despite the monolithic glass-and-steel confines, the devotees' faces shone with an otherworldly love, the awakened energy of their souls. (In these years prior to terrorist attacks, we were allowed to go all the way to the departure and arrival gates.) To the astonishment of onlookers, terminals in major American cities were backdrops for the boundless exhilaration of meetings and separations, and all worldly power and glory did not equal the devotees' exuberance within these modern-day gateways.

Similarly, the ashrams and temples were vital reservoirs of spiritual life, crescendos of joy, success, fulfillment, doing, making, following, sharing. To record events in these places a part of me had to be constantly in motion, considering angles and composition, lighting and exposure, lenses and film, timing and the poignancy of the moment. Another part of me—a small part—was absorbed in Prabhupada, whose entire orientation was to make "a cultural presentation for the respiritualization of the entire human society." Unceasingly, Prabhupada injected whoever was around him with the germ of that respiritualization. The wonder was that, injected and re-injected, as I and the other students were, we wanted only more of the same.

It wasn't that Prabhupada didn't repeat himself. He would make the same point in slightly different ways dozens and dozens (hundreds?) of times. (He would sometimes charm us by saying, "As I have several times explained …" and make the same point yet again.) Yet, there was a quality to his words that made them so potent that, if they weren't always able to alter my thought patterns, they at least altered my orientation—*I was an aspiring devotee.* Prabhupada's repeatedly-made points never felt the same. They were fresh and challenging and of vital importance. I needed to hear them.

On these summer tours Prabhupada wasn't stressed or hurried or preoccupied, and whenever possible he related current events to scriptural statements, turning the scriptures into relevant guides. In Chicago, however, our next stop, he met resistance.

During the two and a half hour flight from Denver to Chicago, Prabhupada felt tired. Upendra and Brahmananda, who were sitting next to him, found other seats so Prabhupada had three seats to himself. He lay across them for a nap and before closing his eyes I noticed that he glanced at his watch. When he awoke a half hour later, the first thing he did was to again look at his watch. He was marking how long he'd slept. I'd heard him mention how sleep took time away from his writing and speaking about Krishna, and now I saw him noting just how much time sleep had taken away. Time, he'd said, was another aspect of Krishna and not to be wasted.

On the flight Prabhupada also noted Time magazine's June 30, 1975 cover article, "Crime: Why and What To Do?" The article began,

> America has been far from successful in dealing with the sort of crime that obsesses Americans day and night—I mean street crime, crime that invades our neighborhoods and our homes—murders, robberies, rapes, muggings, holdups, break-ins—the kind of brutal violence that makes us fearful of strangers and afraid to go out at night.
>
> So said President Gerald Ford last week as he sent a special message to Congress on a subject that has long plagued the nation and frustrated several Administrations: the nation's continuing crime wave.
>
> Ford's characterization of anti-crime efforts as being "far from successful" is a major understatement …

The nation's crime wave became the opening theme of Prabhupada's Chicago visit. I photographed as he spoke about spiritual practices as an effective method of crime control in his Chicago airport press conference and later at televised interviews, as well as talks with the mayor of Evanston, a representative from the Chicago police department, a city councilman, and the state senator.

But some reporters had another topic in mind for Prabhupada. The pungent issue of patriarchy in Prabhupada's movement had come to their attention and a few days after Prabhupada arrived a woman television interviewer asked him, "What should we do in the United States? We're trying to make women equal with men." Prabhupada said,

> You are already not equal with the man because in so many respects your functions are different and man's function are different. Why do you say artificially they are equal? The wife has to become pregnant, not the husband.

How you can change this, both the husband and wife will be pregnant? Is it possible?

Woman reporter: No, it is not.

Prabhupada: Then by nature one has to function differently from the other.

To the reporter, "equality" meant women's wages and opportunities were the same as men's. To Prabhupada though, "equality" meant women and men having the same functions, which in some ways they clearly didn't. Prabhupada explained to the reporter that the husband was duty-bound to support his wife and children. He and the reporter were speaking of different realities—the reporter of what was going on in modern Western society, Prabhupada of a culture carried on over millennia. The reporter, trying to express her version of reality to Prabhupada, said,

Many women have children and have no support from husbands. They have no husband.

Prabhupada: Then they have to take support from others. You cannot deny that.

I thought of women I knew who stayed at their jobs through their pregnancy and who went back to work shortly after childbirth. Although that didn't seem like the best situation for the mother or her child, these women weren't taking support from others. Prabhupada, though, was speaking of traditional relationships that benefited the mother, the child, and the father too.

Yet, by promoting a woman's economic dependence—she's supported by her husband—I worried that Prabhupada would be seen as confining women to a narrow, stultifying role. I certainly didn't want my abilities throttled in the name of dependence; I wasn't about to force myself into some preconceived social role. Did Prabhupada want me to put my camera down, stop writing and filmmaking, and instead devote myself to being a housewife and mother?

The answer, I thought, was clearly no. Prabhupada's Bhaktivedanta Book Trust had paid for my camera, film, and airline tickets. Prabhupada himself had agreed to my being on his traveling party while my husband stayed in Los Angeles. I was doing what the Chicago woman interviewer was doing and Prabhupada liked it. Hardly a woman's traditional role.

In Chicago, Prabhupada addressed me directly:

Prabhupada: Where is the independence? Where is the independence of woman that she has to carry the weight of the pregnancy and the man is free? What is the answer to this question? Hmm? Answer, Visakha.

Visakha: A woman is trapped by her body. She has no choice. By her body she must.

Pregnancy, I knew, was a joy for many women. But whether a woman took it as a joy or not, either way the experience was for women and not men.

Later, I reflected that "I"—the person called "Visakha"—was connected to a deep truth, namely, that I was a spiritual being who was temporarily inhabiting a woman's body. By its constitution, that body (and mind and intelligence) could do certain things and couldn't do others. But whatever my bodily and mental gifts and limitations, I was everlastingly a servant of God who was meant to end all bodily identification and enter his company. The whole focus of the ideal Prabhupada upheld was single-minded: for me and for each and every individual to understand our deepest identity and to function in that capacity.

Gradually it became evident to me that for Prabhupada, the purpose of tradition, of society, and of life itself was to make progress in bhakti, devotional service to Krishna. When tradition helped that progress, he promoted it unreservedly, and when tradition didn't lead to progress in bhakti, Prabhupada disregarded it. So there I was, away from my husband and around Prabhupada constantly for months, using my camera in devotional service.

Prabhupada's promotion of tradition baffled this reporter, but I could see that when tradition was illumined by bhakti, it was beautiful; it didn't fit into a hackneyed stereotype but was dynamic and unbinding. (Earlier in Chicago, when asked if a woman could be temple president, Prabhupada had immediately replied, "Yes, why not?") For Prabhupada, bhakti, not gender, was the issue. The whole idea was to keep the goal, bhakti, clearly in view and to steadily move toward it. That made complete sense.

Prabhupada was the maestro conducting a full orchestra in a complex classical composition. To my ears, some of the sounds were discordant, but the overall effect was beautiful. And the way that music flowed in Prabhupada's character was irresistible. From the moment I'd met him, all I'd experienced—and was still experiencing—was his encouragement. He aroused in me a spirit of voluntary, enthusiastic service. He generated an atmosphere of fresh challenge and I enthusiastically agreed to rise and meet it. He drew out my spontaneous loving spirit of sacrificing my energy for Krishna. He appreciated my efforts. He wanted me to be all I could be for Krishna. I never sensed a smidgen of male chauvinism or misogyny, superiority or self-righteousness, hubris or haughtiness in him. Neither a whiff of desire to exploit, oppress or repress women or anyone else.

Prabhupada was prying open gates to allow the holiness of natural feminine softness and courage and confident devotion to flow. He was putting me in touch with my uniqueness; he was speaking of a graceful, harmonious, spiritual dynamic between Yadubara and me in which both of us benefited and were deeply fulfilled. He spoke of things that were difficult to relate to, given my and most people's background. I couldn't say that I'd deeply experienced the potency of dependence and vulnerability, but I did appreciate his vision.

The joy of this path of devotional service to Krishna was lucid for Prabhupada. He said,

> These boys and these girls, they are no longer thinking that they are American or European or Canadian or Australian or Indian. They are equal. So if you want equality, fraternity, friendship, love and perfection, solution of problems, all problems, economic, political, social, religious, then come to Krishna consciousness. Come to this platform. Then all your ambitions will be fulfilled and you will be perfect.

Prabhupada's ambition was to help me realize that I was not my body, mind, or intelligence. His method—Krishna's method—was bhakti, which was for everyone equally. Whether man or woman, bhakti, devotional service to Krishna, took precedence. He said:

> My only concern is that people shall not waste their valuable human form of life. After so much struggle they have got this human form, and I do not want that they should miss the opportunity. As for me, I cannot discriminate—man, woman, child, rich, poor, educated or foolish. Let them all come, and let them take Krishna consciousness, so that they will not waste their human life. It is not an artificial thing. It is not a material thing. Chant and follow the four rules and pray to Krishna in helplessness.

Prabhupada's teachings were a continual out-of-body experience and his position was for social practicality, not chauvinistic oppression. But how easy it was for me to lose my grip on these subtleties and become insulted, resentful, and outraged when some of his male students interpreted Krishna consciousness as sexism, when they had an imperious attitude toward women. That made my hackles rise and made me identify with what became the bristling indignation of the Chicago reporter. These students used Prabhupada's teachings to bolster their superiority complex and to manipulate and exploit the women. Before them, I was as rancorous as the reporter. Although in the orchestra, these men had somehow missed the essence of the composition and when they tried conducting, the noise was cacophonous, strident. Theirs was an intolerable and blatant misunderstanding of Prabhupada's example and teachings. And yet, to my astonishment and dismay, it was an all too common undertow among his male followers.

Occasionally Prabhupada tried to correct this misunderstanding that hurt devotees and threatened the well-being and development of his teaching efforts. As early as 1968, he'd said,

> The girls who come, you should treat them nicely, at least. I heard that Gargamuni, after his wife left him, he became a woman-hater like that. That is not good. You see? Yes. After all, anyone who is coming to Krishna consciousness, man or woman, boys or girls, they are welcome. They are very fortunate.

Too often his male followers overlooked such directives.

This blindness, I felt, made Prabhupada's chauvinistic male followers violent not only to women but to themselves also, for it meant their faith in the inconceivable potency of bhakti and the holy names of God was lacking. In Prabhupada's words,

> By the grace of the Supreme Personality of Godhead, anyone can do anything, for the Lord is present in everything, all things being his parts and parcels and increasing or decreasing by his supreme will.

Opaque to such transcendentally powerful truths, these men's innate spiritual sensitivity was covered by mundane considerations. What a travesty to Prabhupada's legacy! I chaffed with frustration that I could do nothing about it and resolved to always keep my experience of Prabhupada—how he impartially urged all of us toward transcendent realities—alive within me. But despite my resolve, these men's behavior damaged me. Each undermining act, each belittling comment piled up on the others to create a scar within me.

I feared the effect of these men's mentality on me and on Prabhupada's mission and that it could unfairly cast Prabhupada in a negative fashion.

Spiritual seekers could be turned away by narrow-mindedness, and rightly so.

Sometime later, on a morning walk on Los Angeles's Venice Beach, Prabhupada put this male–female issue to rest for me. Draped with cameras and recording equipment, I was thirty feet in front of him, who, as twenty men clustered behind and to the sides of him, was walking with assured, brisk steps and commenting on gender differences. Then with a glimmer in his eye, Prabhupada looked at me and said, "Don't you mind!" while continuing to look at me curiously, as if waiting to see my reaction. I looked at him, smiled, and in my mind yelled, *"Aham brahmasmi!* You've taught me that I'm a spiritual being and I believe you. And you've taught me to appreciate and utilize my female nature, to see it as an asset for me and for society, and to see that it's a favorable platform for devotional growth. So I don't mind!" Later, Yamuna Devi assured me that Prabhupada had heard me.

Prabhupada had tirelessly and repeatedly taught me that I was not my body, mind, or intelligence but a transcendent spiritual being. His reference to "women" was not a reference to me—a soul—but a reference to something external to me—my physical and subtle (mind, intelligence) body. Prabhupada was describing something that I was wearing and using, much as an airline steward explains how to wear and use a life jacket. Gender differences were details. A few months before, Prabhupada had written in a letter,

> We are not concerned with male or female position in life. That is simply bodily concept of life. It is not spiritual. Whether one is male or female, it doesn't matter, simply chant Hare Krishna and follow the four regulative principles and your life will be perfect.

In the Chicago temple room I photographed Prabhupada as he initiated a hundred people. When one of them came before him, Prabhupada noted his torn dhoti. Turning to a nearby leader, I heard him say, "You must take proper care of all these men and women. They must be fully cared for. They are giving their lives to Krishna."

CHAPTER SIXTEEN

Bedrock and Evil

In the course of this '75 summer tour it became more and more apparent to me that humility and faith were spiritual bedrocks. From Chicago Prabhupada wrote to one of his godbrothers, "I have no other asset except [my guru's] causeless mercy." And to a disciple:

> This feeling of insufficiency is good for progress. No one should think that now I am complete. It is good to think that I am incomplete and useless. Actually Krishna is unlimited, and our energy is limited. Actually we cannot serve the unlimited, but Krishna's unlimited mercy induces us to serve, and he accepts. Actually we are unworthy. He is so kind that he accepts our little service as if it were very big and great.

At the conclusion of a morning walk: "Unless [my guru] is pleased, what I am worth? It is due to his pleasure. Otherwise, what I am worth? Everyone said, 'You have done wonderful.' What can I do wonderful? It is by his pleasure it is going on."

Prabhupada was self-effacing, I thought, because he was certain of his own insignificance and had complete confidence in his guru and Krishna. I considered myself also self-effacing but for quite different reasons. One, because I was aware of my many shortcomings. Another, because throughout my formative years, I'd been overshadowed by my brilliant brother and outclassed by my peers in my snobby upscale Long Island hometown. But whatever the reasons, my self-effacing mentality placed my ego squarely in the center of my concerns. Prabhupada's mentality placed his guru in the center of his concerns.

Of course, part of me wanted to please Prabhupada any way I could, just as he had given his all to please his guru. But another part held me back. That part whispered in my ear, "Stay safe. Don't go outside your comfort zone. It won't work. You'll fail and be miserable." That part wouldn't be quiet.

The word "humility," I discovered, came from the Latin *humus*, meaning "earth," "ground," and "lowly." But humus, I thought, is much more than lowly earth: it's the richest of all earth; it's organic, dark, friable soil that's poised to support life. Seeds thrive in humus, and so from humus the food that sustains earthly life is produced. Such a vital yet neglected substance is appropriately connected to the word humility for, from what I was understanding, humility was the attitude that sustains spiritual life. Humility was the foundation of the skyscraper of spiritual aspiration. Humility made holiness possible: It was an expression of knowledge, the root of trustworthy intelligence, and had the lofty by-products of tolerance, gratitude, and a love for all that is genuine.

I was lacking something vital.

My shyness and reticence, I thought, were another side of someone else's (like the Brooklyn charging rhino ashram president's) blustering arrogance. Both were karmically acquired personality traits that had nothing to do with Krishna's devotional service. If necessary for that service, I reasoned, I should be able to be outgoing, charismatic, even lioness-like.

Occasionally for making photographs I could be bold for Krishna. But mostly I was lamb-like, which wasn't humility. It was just me with my hang-ups.

At our next stop, Philadelphia, Prabhupada spoke on a myriad of topics and continued his theme:

> No addition, alteration. You have to approach guru—guru means the faithful servant of God, Krishna—and take his word how to serve him. Then you are successful. If you concoct, "I am more intelligent than my guru, and I can make addition or alteration," then you are finished. If you want to make real

progress, then you must be firmly faithful at the lotus feet of guru. This is the instruction of the whole Vaishnav philosophy.

My faith, I realized, rested in Prabhupada. That aristocratic lady—faith—whom I'd first glimpsed in Vrindavan, had danced into my heart on the symphony of Prabhupada's earnestness. Now she pirouetted on words that revealed beauty and completeness, words that were validated by sacred texts and by the statements of sadhus past and present. Those words fixed me on my path: Krishna, God, is my well-wisher and most dear friend and I am his servant. Happiness and fulfillment are mine when I serve him with unmotivated devotion. Prabhupada's trust in this knowledge was contagious. It was the basis of my faith and my hope that, despite all my shortcomings, I'd progress spiritually. When those distant cries of my inner skeptic said, "Hah! What spiritual? It's all phantasmagoria. What you see is what you get. Get real!" I could at least emphatically answer, "Enough. Shut up already!"

En route from Philadelphia to Berkeley the captain of our nearly empty United Airlines plane came out of the cockpit, sat down next to Prabhupada and had an animated conversation with him. I stood in the aisle filming with our 16mm Bolex movie camera, all the while wondering what they were talking about. The plane was too noisy for me to hear anything and I was too shy to ask Prabhupada later what had been said. I resigned myself to never knowing. But then, during his arrival address in Berkeley a few hours later, Prabhupada mentioned the conversation. He said the captain had asked, "If everything is created by God, then what is evil?"

Prabhupada told the captain that evil is also God's creation. For God there is no good or evil; everything is good. Prabhupada explained that goodness, or piety, was God's chest, and evil was God's back. "The chest and the back of my body are equal. It is not that when there is some pain on the back side I don't care for it; I simply take care when there is pain in the chest. No. Although it is back side, it is as important as the front side."

"Then evil and good are of the same importance?" the captain had asked.

But Prabhupada said again, "For God, nothing is evil."

Then the captain had asked a question that has confounded philosophers for centuries. "If, from God's point of view, everything is good, then how can there be evil?"

To explain, Prabhupada gave an analogy. He said on the sun there's no darkness, but we experience darkness and light. When we turn away from the sun we find darkness—our shadow. And when we face the sun, we see only light and no darkness. "So it is my business: I create darkness," Prabhupada said. "As soon as I change my position—instead of remaining in front of God, I keep God back side—then there's darkness. Otherwise there is no question of darkness. But in the sun as it is there is no such darkness. Therefore God is all good. And for us, when we forget God, that is evil. And when we are in God consciousness always, everything is good."

Prabhupada's point was so confoundingly easy at first it eluded me. If evil was the result of my turning away from God, I later realized, then I was responsible for whatever evil was in my life. Yuck! Surely there was someone to blame besides me? This simple proposition is the crux of the principle of karma.

Anyway, I was delighted that this graying captain had chosen to have this deep, philosophical inflight conversation with Prabhupada. That he had taken Prabhupada's words seriously meant others could, too—even people like my parents and brother, had they cared to listen, could have begun to see the world differently and, perhaps, more wholesomely. After all, I thought, who benefits when God is shut out of the world?

The day after Prabhupada arrived in Berkeley, representatives from major newspapers and television stations came for a press conference. Under the glare of TV lights in the large Berkeley temple room, a reporter asked, "What will happen to the Movement when you die?"

"That's a good, practical question," I thought. "A question I'd never considered asking."

I couldn't foresee a world in which Prabhupada was not present somewhere, untiringly piercing the material masquerade and smashing its illusion of happiness, yet possessing a healthy love for the world as a gift from God. Prabhupada, who was completely his own person yet unswervingly loyal to the tradition he lived; who was steeped in that tradition yet whose vision was always fresh, never hackneyed or stereotyped; Prabhupada, who marked vast social, political, and historical degenerative cycles—and daily confronted his followers' failures—yet remained positive and ever patiently revamped our spoiled dispositions. Prabhupada, who insisted that we, his students, know who God was, know who we were, know how the material energy operates, and know the consequences of our acts—karma. Prabhupada, who unceasingly, untiringly, repeatedly inundated us with Krishna's philosophy. What would I do without him? I refused to go there. The idea of Prabhupada dying was as inconceivable to me as Krishna's presence in me.

Prabhupada took the reporter's question in stride. "I will never die," he said. Devotees cheered. He continued, "I shall live from my books, and you will utilize."

I had something of a sinking feeling inside. "Your books aren't the same as you, Prabhupada," I thought. "I'd take you over your books any day!"

We traveled on to San Francisco, and as on his other stops, Prabhupada met with professors and religious and political leaders. He also participated in a hugely successful Rath-yatra.

On a walk the day after Rath-yatra, the topic of faith came up. Without faith in guru and God, Prabhupada said, we couldn't make advancement. Faith came from purity. As we became purer, our faith became firmer—we then trusted the spiritual master, mixed with the faithful, and found our faith still stronger.

"What are the symptoms of purity?" someone asked.

"Just like 'Don't do this. Don't do this. Don't do this.' So if you have faith, you will not do it. But because you have no faith, you will do it, and therefore you will go to ruin," Prabhupada said. Whether or not we had knowledge, he said, if we simply followed the regulative principles, our faith would increase. "If you have no faith, then Krishna will not give you instruction. When one is faithless, he will not make progress.

> As you become purified, then your faith becomes fixed up with knowledge. That is stated in the Bhagavad-gita, 'One who has finished his sinful life, he can become a devotee.' Otherwise one cannot. First of all, the beginning is faith. Then, by following the process, one becomes completely sinless. Then full knowledge.

This was counterintuitive for me. Prabhupada was saying that I didn't have to have knowledge of the self to have faith, but I had to have faith to have knowledge. Yet thinking it over, I saw that this was my actual experience. On my first trip to Vrindavan I had no knowledge, yet somehow faith had come. Later on, Prabhupada said, as my faith strengthened, knowledge would come automatically. That hadn't happened to me, at least not yet, but

I recognized it as the promise Krishna makes in the Bhagavad-gita: "When a devotee is faithful, I help that person get knowledge."

Prabhupada was asking me to do something great: to be what I was—small. Faith was not extraneous to me but was an innate, indigenous quality of the soul—of me. By patiently hearing from him, from sages, and from the scriptures, faith and then knowledge would come. If instead I remained ambitious for things of this world, what future did that hold? All those things were like sandcastles—however spectacular, time's tide would wash them away forever.

Our traveling party returned to Los Angeles, where Prabhupada encouraged his students and continued his theme. At the end of a walk on the Pacific shore, the rising sun glittering on countless ripples, he said, "Remain humble and meek. You will understand God."

From time to time I wondered how much of these compelling concepts I'd ingested. Had I made Prabhupada's teachings my own? Was my knowledge rote or had it touched me in the innermost core of my being? If it had, then I'd surely love Krishna and his creation. Did I? I was afraid to answer.

But I *did* love the way Prabhupada presented Krishna, the wide embrace of Krishna's philosophy, the way it challenged standard understandings, how it made me stretch and push and break through assumptions and boundaries I didn't know I had. The philosophy was convincing, Prabhupada's integrity was unimpeachable. The beautiful Person I worshiped along with all the other devotees was attractive. And material endeavors were, in the long view, transitory.

My chosen path was a good one. But my pace was impossibly slow. Was I moving, even?

I was one of three photographers who alternated traveling with Prabhupada, and when my shift ended Prabhupada continued his world tour without me. I rejoined Yadubara and together we continued making documentaries. In the fall of '75 we filmed the West Virginia farm community, and that winter completed *Brilliant as the Sun*—about the writing, publication, and distribution of Prabhupada's books. In February '76 we left for Mayapur's Gaura Purnima festival to premiere this twenty-four minute documentary.

After two days of travel, we finally saw bullock carts lumbering along Bhaktisiddhanta Road, their drivers' wizened faces surveying us with accepting astonishment. Already I felt at home and at peace with the world; our stressful, urban lives amid glass and concrete became a vapid memory next to this virtuous, rhythmic life where simple labor was sustained by eons of tradition, where people depended on the earth and the animals who plied it for life's necessities.

Every morning in Mayapur Prabhupada gave a class, and his theme continued: "You should remain very humble. That is required. And you should hear from the realized soul in humbleness. Then Krishna, the great, he will be conquered by you."

Five years earlier—in October of 1971—in Calcutta, Prabhupada's words had raised me from pettiness to the challenge of using my life for a cause greater than myself. Now he spoke further, saying that whatever happened in my life, I was to humbly accept it. But this degree of rampant humility frightened me. Wouldn't it make me weak and vulnerable, open to exploitation? However healthy and scripturally sound this mindset, wouldn't it encourage injustice?

This aspect of the philosophy was so exalted I shied from it. My American training was to boldly defy discrimination, to fight unfairness, to demand God-given rights. Yet, I could see that if I was confident of God's mindfulness of me, if I accepted that whatever happened to me was not accidental but my karmic due, then I could continue to oppose injustice while at the same time allowing it to evoke my tolerance, patience, and God consciousness. Genuine humility could be a vital expression of my acceptance of God's mysterious ways.

Two contrary mentalities vied within me. On one side, my human response to injustice: justified rage and rebellion. On the other, knowing of a great plan behind apparent injustice that was, in the final analysis, for my benefit. If I failed to humble myself before this great and transcendent plan, I would remain bound by my false ego and its mundane effects—ambition and envy, greed and anger—in confusion and loneliness.

I could see that far from subjecting Prabhupada to injustice, humility had made him stronger than it—humility had unshackled him from resentment and wrath, hatred and revenge. Prabhupada had entered a whole new breadth of existence where the unimaginable greatness and incomparable perfection of God, although unknown to me, were in some way known to him. God's presence in Prabhupada's consciousness allowed him to move in this world untouched by it and fearless; it allowed him to be in and to relish the beauty of each moment. Far from exploiting him, humility had made him powerful. And free.

Humility was not self-effacement and passive submission. Krishna spoke the Bhagavad-gita so Arjuna would stop being passive—so he'd risk his life to fight injustice. When Prabhupada said, "You should remain very humble," he was speaking of a natural, dynamic spiritual response to whatever happened, for any other response would only create more difficulty.

Acting like a wimp, I realized, could be as artificial as acting brashly. It was with humility that I could serve Krishna with the personality that fit the circumstances (as soft as a rose, as hard as a thunderbolt); with humility I could so align myself with Krishna's natural order that no one and nothing could change my course. Humility meant opening myself to—being accepting of—Krishna's ways. It meant coming under his shelter. It meant becoming impervious to mundane miseries.

Humility was enticing, but well beyond me.

A couple of days later, Prabhupada saw *Brilliant as the Sun* in his room and liked it. He began showing it regularly to his many Mayapur visitors.

After the festivities, Yadubara and I, along with a group of thirty other devotee pilgrims, returned to the States in full regalia—with flowing saris or dhotis, prominent white tilak lines on our foreheads, bead bags, braids, sikhas, and holy books or boxes of prasad in the shoulder bags that draped from us. By the time we disembarked at the Los Angeles International Airport we'd been traveling nonstop for 24 hours and I was giddy and giggly from exhaustion and relief at having finally arrived. Around midnight I found myself face to face with the airport customs agent, a carefully coiffed 40-ish woman, who surprised me by leaning over my open suitcase on the conveyor belt and with a challenging and piercingly expectant look, asking in a clear undertone, *"What's an intelligent person like you doing with people like this?"*

My light mood vanished. Encircled by the devotees while entering this familiar Western world of gleaming efficiency and modernity, I'd been feeling myself an enthusiastic member of Prabhupada's revolutionary mission. Now I gazed at this woman with what must have been the same solemn look my parents had seen me with.

"Where do I begin?" I yelled inside. My Himalayan emptiness, my Vrindavan epiphanies, my encounters with Prabhupada, my enthusiasm for Krishna, all whisked before me. Where were the words to convey such transformations next to a conveyor belt at LAX in the middle of an exhausted night?

"Yeah, we look kooky," I wanted to say to her. "Yeah, we've stepped out of mainstream society. And we've come upon something substantial, something life-altering.

"Should I not follow my chosen path because it varies from the norm? Should I not follow because you don't understand or approve? Do I have to look and act like you to be acceptable?

"No, I'm sorry. I will continue to allow myself to be molded by my Guru Maharaja, someone expert in the art of spiritual molding. His guidance is bringing me closer to who I am. I'm becoming happier."

The woman, quickly satisfied with her inspection, waved me on and called the next person to come forward. Closing up my suitcase, I considered how much there was to say, how little time there was to say it, and how inept I was at even trying. And also, maybe her question had been rhetorical?

Settled in Los Angeles again, Yadubara and I edited our farm community documentary while Prabhupada traveled from India to Australia, Fiji, and Hawaii. On the first of June 1976, seven hundred exuberant devotees from all over the States, Canada, and Mexico greeted him as he triumphantly arrived at the Los Angeles International Airport. (I wondered if my customs agent was in the airport at the time.)

When Prabhupada had come to Los Angeles two years earlier, I'd craved his attention, thinking myself a special, older disciple. At that time he'd overlooked me. Now in the midst of this torrent of exuberance, I was overwhelmed and would have happily disappeared into the crowd. The ashram leaders, however, wanted Prabhupada's arrival photographed and had announced that all devotees must facilitate me and the two other photographers assigned to cover the event. So when Prabhupada disembarked he was directly in front of me with a sea of saffron-clad devotees next to and behind him. Prabhupada walked toward me, looked directly at me and smiled broadly.

I didn't believe what I saw. Thinking my wide-angle lens was deceiving me, I took my camera from my eye. Prabhupada was looking at me, smiling. Later I found Prabhupada had reciprocated with others as he had with me. At first, I was dismayed—again, I was thinking I was special—but Prabhupada was seeing everyone as special. Then I loved him for the broadness of his love. No one was outside it.

What was Prabhupada's magnetism? It lay, I thought, in his ethos of giving and in the solid substance of what he gave. And that he gave that substance to everyone, including me. He gave me knowledge and spiritual focus, and even more he gave me what he lived, which was, finally, faith and love—faith and love that continued no matter what the beloved did. Sri Chaitanya expressed the quality of this love by saying, "Even if Krishna handles me roughly by his embrace or makes me brokenhearted by not being present before me, still I love him." That was Prabhupada's faith in and love for Krishna. And Prabhupada loved me—us—his students, unconditionally as well. I could feel it and see it and almost taste its sweetness.

In his travels, Prabhupada's underlying intention was not to make new students or open new centers or discuss with reporters and distinguished guests. Although he did all that and more, his intention was to spiritually strengthen us, his students. He said, "I'm traveling all over the world twice, thrice, in a year. My duty is to see that my disciples who have accepted me as guru, they may not fall down. That is my anxiety." To defy the force of our faithlessness was part of Prabhupada's lifelong commitment to his spiritual master, and he did it as naturally as the surf wears rocks or as green shoots push up from dark soil. Prabhupada did not simply fortify our tottering spiritual life; he infused it with a happiness that was alive and tinged with the radiant hope of success. He assured us that we could do it. And in his presence, we were sure we could.

When he translated and ate prasad and chanted japa, Prabhupada would be alone in his room, but otherwise (which was most of the time) he was continuously engaging people in Krishna's philosophy and its application. His was nonstop energy and focus on extending the reach of Krishna consciousness.

Once, after being with him for a good length of time, I started to feel overextended—that I was a simple artist who, having spent too much time with an advanced soul, was out of her league. I felt like I was trying to be the person I was supposed to be but wasn't, that I was trying to fit into some mold that I didn't fit into, that I wasn't ready for. I needed my own space to relax and to spend time in my own way. Plus, I was taking in so much knowledge, but what was I doing with it? Where was my self expression?

What Prabhupada was offering was exalted and irresistible. Yet I was so far from it! My capacity was limited and I had no ability or qualification to attain what he was offering. For me to keep trying was exhausting. I was reaching and reaching for something that seemed close yet, no matter how hard I tried, was beyond my grasp. At the same time, though, Prabhupada regularly reassured me that Krishna consciousness was natural—that I could do it, that *I could become pure in my motives and acts and I could love and be with Krishna*. Part of me believed him and craved what he offered. Part of me continued to scoff at myself: given my disqualifications it simply wasn't going to happen. No way *I* was going to get there.

On one morning walk on Venice beach, someone said, "In some Western theological literature, Srila Prabhupada, it refers to 'God is love.' In what sense …"

> Prabhupada: No, I have already explained. What is not God? That is already explained. Anything you bring, God is there. Without God, nothing can exist. So why this or that? Anything, that is God. But he's absolute. His love and his enmity, that is the same thing. We distinguish, here in this material world, "This is love and this is animosity." But God's animosity and God's love—the same thing. That is achintya. Here in the relative world we cannot adjust how animosity and love can be the same, one and the same … In our relative world, we can see so many differences in the dealings of God, but he is absolute, one. That is conception of God.

Such explanations affected me deeply. They opened me to a world of stunning, joyful, simple complexities, a world that had been unknown to me before Prabhupada had entered my life.

In Los Angeles, a group of Prabhupada's followers had confined their reading of his books to sections concerning the confidential activities of Krishna and the *gopis*, Krishna's cowherd girlfriends. Years ago in India, when Mr. Balu had approached Prabhupada about Krishna and the *gopis' rasa-lila*—their dance of divine love— Prabhupada's reaction had been firm but restrained. With his students, however, he was like a thunderbolt:

> If they at once go to *rasa-lila*, because they are not trained up neither they are liberated, they'll think this *rasa-lila* is just like our young boys, young girls mix together, have sex like that. Thinking of Radha-Krishna *lila*, that is in liberated stage, not in the conditioned stage. How have you understood Krishna so easily, within two years? What you have understood about Krishna is materially understood. You do not know what is Krishna.

Throughout India I'd seen that this sort of misunderstanding was rampant, and hearing Prabhupada speak so strongly made me scared that I could also easily misunderstand Krishna and spoil everything sacred in my life. Prabhupada saw this tendency as coming from pseudo-devotees in Vrindavan and wrote to a disciple at the Krishna-Balaram Temple,

> I have received information that some of our devotees are mixing with the *babajis* in Vrindavan. This has produced so many problems amongst our men and women who visit Vrindavan. Here in Los Angeles, we have found that there is a group of about forty devotees who privately meet to discuss the intimate pastimes, artificially thinking that they can enter into the understanding of the *gopis* prematurely. This will create havoc in our society, and the result will be that if this is allowed to go on, our preaching work will be greatly hampered. This premature desire to understand the *lila* [transcendental pastimes] of Krishna is due to mundane sex life desire.

Some of his students were turning their backs to the sun and creating a shadow.

In a completely packed temple room, Prabhupada viewed *The Spiritual Frontier* film on the West Virginia farm community. When he saw a close-up of puris cooking, I heard him chuckle and say, "Give me one," which made me want to scoop up a couple of those hot, fresh puris, put them on a plate and give them to him right then and there.

In his last Los Angeles lecture, Prabhupada said,

> If you want to cheat Krishna, Krishna is the greatest cheater. Then you'll be cheated. Don't be cheater. Simply, fervently, very honestly, obey the orders of Krishna and without any doubt, you'll go back to Krishna. What more do you want? Take the instruction of Krishna and be happy.

It's so easy! I can do this! Nothing to it!

Prabhupada's whirlwind tour took him to Detroit for a few days and then Toronto, where he had a long conversation with Professor Joseph O'Connell, a noted scholar of world religions. Professor O'Connell taught at St. Michael's College, University of Toronto, and he'd brought a couple of his colleagues with him to meet Prabhupada. I expected to hear a scholarly discussion about Chaitanya's teachings, but Prabhupada opened the conversation by pointing out that what's normally taken as advancement of civilization is not actual advancement.

With a laugh, Prabhupada said, "The dog is running on legs, and they are running on cars. So, actually what's the difference? This is advancement of civilization, that the dog is running for nothing, here and there, on legs, and human being is running on nice car. Does it mean there is advancement in civilization?"

Professor O'Connell was listening respectfully and I was wondering how he was taking this. Probably, I thought, from a scholarly viewpoint, not a personal one. But for me it was personal. Prabhupada's words were yet again realigning my values and perspectives, yet again disengaging me from the entire thrust of the modern world. Actual advancement meant to fathom my spirituality, my relationship with Krishna and his energies.

Everyone, it seemed, had a need to advance, but people mostly confused material advancement with actual advancement. That's why they strove for power and fame, why they so actively created things and made and spent money. But all mundane positions in this world and all worldly possessions were fleeting. The temporary vs the timeless: ongoing vying perspectives within me. Okay, the former was ephemeral, *but at least it was here now!*

As the discussion continued, Professor O'Connell asked, "Is it possible, Swamiji, for a woman to be a guru in the line of disciplic succession?"

Prabhupada said, "Yes," and gave the example of Jahnava, a woman who'd become a guru in the disciplic line. He went on to say that not many women took that role, but "The qualification of guru is that he must be fully cognizant of the science of Krishna. Then he or she can become guru. In our material world, is it any prohibition that woman cannot become professor? If she is qualified, she can become professor. What is the wrong there? She must be qualified. That is the position. So similarly, if the woman understands Krishna consciousness perfectly, she can become guru."

Prabhupada's was an equal opportunity program. In his eyes, all of us who sincerely tried could go past the haze and chimeras of this fleeting world to enter and be active in the imperishable one, just as a dreaming person awakens and has breakfast. This opportunity was for men and women both. If it had been any other way, I'd have long ago said, "Forget about it!" But clearly the concept that "we are not this body," indicated that the body's gender is not so relevant. This basic logic, however, eluded too many.

A few days later, I was sitting with Prabhupada on the grass on a tranquil hillside in the West Virginia farm community where local devotees were working toward self-sufficiency. Prabhupada commented,

> Clear sky, sun, this is life. We get rejuvenation in this atmosphere. What is this nonsense, all skyscraper building, no air, no light? The mind becomes crippled, the health becomes deteriorated, children cannot see even the sky, everything is spoiled ... Improve this mode of life. Live in open place, produce your food grains, produce your milk, save time, chant Hare Krishna. Plain living, high thinking, ideal life.

Having grown up in a Long Island suburb, for eighteen years I'd regularly visited Manhattan and, after at first being overwhelmed by it, I'd become fascinated and stimulated by it. But I wouldn't have chosen Manhattan or any city to raise children. Or to live a stress-free life. Years later, Yadubara and I would move to an off-the-grid community in the British Columbia wilds where our younger daughter would grow up.

After so much traveling, Prabhupada, now 80, was in poor health. He missed several morning walks due to heart palpitations, uremia caused his legs and feet to swell, and sometimes he felt weak. Although he continued giving morning classes, answering letters and, in the afternoon, receiving guests and devotees, more and more during discussions he'd ask someone to read a relevant verse and purport and then say, "Now you all discuss this point from different angles."

I was dismayed. No one could field questions as Prabhupada did and no one could make the knowledge as fresh and dynamic as he did. And I was worried. I needed Prabhupada. He resuscitated my spirituality and kept it vibrant. Around him, I felt thrilled by glimpses of mystical prospects. Now, as he stepped back from actively teaching, there was a different flavor. Not that his students didn't try or weren't sincere, but they hadn't yet *felt* what they were saying as Prabhupada had. There was a superficiality to their words, a stiff crust like stale icing. While his disciples discussed the philosophy, Prabhupada listened with some inner ear that seemed to hear more than what was being said. He trained us to counter atheism and impersonalism, and when someone failed to do so properly, he reproved, "You do not know how to answer. That means you do not read." That way, he encouraged more reading and learning.

At night, before he chanted and wrote his purports in the wee hours of the morning, Prabhupada rested for two hours, and after lunch he rested for another two hours. After one of his midday rests I entered his room with a glass of fresh coconut juice and a wildflower garland. For once my camera was not with me. I placed the glass on the low desk near Prabhupada and bowed down, holding the delicate garland in both hands as I put my forehead to the floor. Prabhupada, sitting cross-legged on a cushion, looked simple and timeless, regal and relaxed. Who could imagine this one individual, so small and unassuming, could make such a difference to so many people, could transform so many lives, could become the cynosure of my life? He was lifting me into surprising air—air that thrilled with faith. I put the splendid multi-colored garland, with its varieties of fragile, quick-to-wilt flowers, on his neck (I missed my camera!). He looked down at it, held it to better see it and appreciated its wild beauty.

"Oh, they are from here, these flowers?"

"Yes, they are wild and were just picked for your garland."

"Very nice."

I wanted to express my gratitude to Prabhupada, but finding no words to do so, within myself offered him my love and engraved this quiet moment in the innermost recesses of my heart.

The last Srimad-Bhagavatam verse we read at the farm was, "God is the father of all living entities. Consequently there are no impediments to pleasing him or worshiping him under any conditions, whether one is a child or an old person. The relationship between the living entities and God is always a fact, and therefore there is no difficulty in pleasing him."

I could do it, I could do it, I could do it! How wonderful.

From a young age, I'd fully accepted Darwin's theory that life evolved from matter. Prabhupada, however, didn't accept this theory at all. During our first evening in Washington, D.C., he spoke at length with students of his who held doctorates in chemistry and mathematics and who, under his guidance, had established the Bhaktivedanta Institute to promote the scientific basis of Krishna consciousness, beginning with an understanding of the difference between life and matter. Life, according to Prabhupada, comes from life.

Prabhupada wanted these students to challenge Darwin's theory that life evolved from matter as well as the commonly understood cosmology. I wasn't sure how I felt about this. Darwin's idea was not only ingrained in me, but it was ingrained in Western society too. To challenge it could drive away otherwise sympathetic people. Prabhupada, however, had no qualms about going against the grain of modern thinking—in fact, he rose to the occasion. He wasn't about to pander to me or to anyone. The prevailing winds of fashionable theories didn't sway him. He wasn't interested in concessions or faithless followers. With conviction, he presented scriptural teachings, evoked our faith, and urged us to also boldly present those teachings.

In the class the next morning, instead of continuing to speak from Srimad-Bhagavatam, Prabhupada switched to a section of the Chaitanya-charitamrita describing how Sanatan Goswami, a highly qualified minister in the government of the Muslim magistrate, gave up his post to humbly approach Sri Chaitanya. Sanatan Goswami said to Sri Chaitanya that he was considered learned by the people in general and he also thought himself as such. But in fact he didn't know his own identity, or why he was suffering, or what his duty was. Even more, he didn't know the goal of life or how to attain it. "Being merciful upon me," he said, "please explain all these truths."

I looked from Prabhupada to the audience, which had many devotees with doctorates. Such qualified students could easily become proud of their learning, I thought. They could easily feel themselves better than Prabhupada, who didn't have their degrees or titles. In his own humble way, Prabhupada was evoking humility by highlighting it in the exalted person of Sanatan Goswami.

Within myself, when I admitted that I didn't know much about transcendence and that I hadn't progressed much on the transcendental path, I felt comfortable in that frankness. My longing for admiration waned. My disease, I realized, was a desire for that which was material; even while advancing in spiritual life, I wanted material acclaim. A travesty!

Pride, I thought, came with the weighty price tag of stress: "What about *me*—my pleasure, my position, my prestige?" If I worshiped this altar of self-importance, ambition, and control, I'd sacrifice my happiness and blockade myself spiritually. I needed to focus on others more than myself, to be more eager to give than to receive.

> Pride is the root of all evil … pride is the beginning of all sin. Seven principal vices spring doubtless from this poisonous root, namely, vainglory, envy, anger, melancholy, avarice, gluttony and lust.
>
> — St. Gregory the Great

Krishna consciousness made perfect sense of this world, of the futility of living only for materialistic ends, of the proper use of my intelligence, of why I wasn't satisfied simply making and spending money on comforts and enjoyments. The soul's eternal presence, the concepts of karma and reincarnation, of God's greatness and goodness, filled my need to see past the obvious, to be imbued with joy, to care about all creatures. Considering its antiquity, its modern practicality, how it answered my deepest calling, the exacting Sanskrit language it was conveyed in, its thoroughness, sweetness and purity, I wanted Krishna consciousness, not skepticism and not Darwin consciousness. I didn't want a dark wall of doubt within me due to scriptural statements concerning truths I could not see, statements that defied my practical and sensory knowledge. Without that wall, I could relax into the metaphysics of bhakti like sinking into a comfortable couch.

In Prabhupada's words, "Our position is that if some portion we cannot understand, it is our incapability." The core of God consciousness was humility, which meant in part to accept scriptural statements I could not fathom, statements that sometimes seemed contrary to modern science. A heart steely with pride made me skeptical and distant. A heart softened by humility left me enchanted and open to the possibility of other realities.

For faith to remain an aristocratic presence within me, humility was essential. If I thought I knew God's limitations, that pride would lock me out of his company. Krishna's world was beyond the range of my intellect, reasoning, logic, arguments, and perception. "Unless one accepts the inconceivable nature of God, one does not accept God," Prabhupada said. I didn't want to scoff at God's activities but to savor them. And I was with the first and only person I'd ever met who opened me up enough to begin to do that.

On the evening of July 4th, 1976, I crowded into one of many overflowing vans and joined a lively kirtan with the van doors open as we crawled along congested highways to the center of the nation's capital. Prabhupada sat on a lawn chair on the grass to watch the fireworks of the century commemorating the 200th anniversary of American independence. A few days later we commemorated the tenth anniversary of the founding of ISKCON, the International Society for Krishna Consciousness. I photographed as Prabhupada took a long-bladed knife and cut the celebratory cake.

I continued photographing Prabhupada in New York City where, eleven years before, he'd arrived alone ("just like a vagabond," he'd said), with no help and no money to execute the order of his Guru Maharaja. At first he'd been "loitering in the streets." I saw his former rented office on 72nd Street at Columbus Avenue where he lived without facilities to bathe or cook his meals. At that time (November 1965), he'd written that he was experiencing "night starvation." He ate so infrequently that he became quite hungry at night. A few months after he wrote that, someone broke into that office and stole his typewriter and tape recorder, his only valuables. Now Prabhupada had a society that owned, among many other valuable properties, an eleven-story building on 55th Street. And this center, like his others, was filled with devoted and energetic students.

On July 14th I was in Prabhupada's room on the tenth floor of that building photographing as Kevin Layhart of *Newsday* newspaper interviewed Prabhupada. When Layhart asked on what basis Prabhupada chose leaders within his organization, Prabhupada said, "Basis, just to see whether he's qualified, that's all. Just like ordinarily one manager is appointed by the superior authority on the merit, on his qualification. That's all."

Layhart: Okay. Is it a mediated choice or is it a direct communication from Krishna? That's my question.

Prabhupada: Yes, God speaks to you when you are qualified. You cannot expect God as order supplier. When He sees that you are qualified, He will speak to you ... God is situated in everyone's heart. As soon as He sees that "Here is a qualified person," then He gives him instruction.

Layhart: But in the same way that Krishna says he'll provide for all your needs, you still must work to achieve whatever Krishna is giving you.

Prabhupada: Yes. You work for Krishna. You have to work to get your necessities.

Layhart: In the same way I'm curious with respect to the way Krishna communicates with you, whether it's in a similar kind of way that he gives you your necessities ... Or do you, by judging him, say this person is qualified?

Prabhupada: Yes, because a devotee always consults Krishna, and he gives order.

Layhart: It's a more direct communication.

Prabhupada: Yes. And he gives order.

Then Ramesvar, one of Prabhupada's appointed BBT Trustees, interjected saying, "Our philosophy is that intelligence comes from Krishna. So suppose my intelligence sees that this person is qualified, that means Krishna has told me."

At this point Prabhupada gave me and the few other students in his room a jolt. He said, "No, not necessarily. Krishna will tell directly. A devotee always consults Krishna, and Krishna tells him, 'Do like this.' Not figuratively; practically."

Ramesvar gazed at Prabhupada with his mouth open, suspended in surprise. I could almost hear Ramesvar's synapses popping as they absorbed Prabhupada's statement. My synapses were doing likewise.

Prabhupada had just said that God the Almighty directly spoke to him. Did I believe him? Could I take his statement at face value?

All that I knew about Prabhupada and all the impressions that I'd had of him for the past five years flashed before my mind.

I found no reason not to believe him.

Seemingly nonplussed by Prabhupada's answer, Layhart continued his questioning:

Layhart: Does that apply then to other kinds of decisions and other kinds of activities as well?"

BEDROCK AND EVIL 245

Prabhupada: Everything. Because a devotee does not do anything without consulting Krishna.

Here was a petite, unassuming person, Prabhupada, saying without apology or conditions, that he consulted God before doing anything. And here I was, believing him. Did I believe him because I loved him? Was love making me blind to some egregious or not so egregious flaw in him? But what? He was abiding by the same regulative principles he asked his students to follow, he wasn't extorting money or taking sexual advantage of his students, he was constantly promoting pure bhakti. What was I overlooking?

Of all the people God could directly commune with, why shouldn't he choose Prabhupada? But—how was it possible for me, a former atheist and a inveterate skeptic, to believe this? And how was it that I'd continue to believe it for the remaining decades of my life? But isn't the goal of bhakti yoga to commune with God? Then why would he not reciprocate? Many religious traditions include God speaking directly to the adherent. Others falsely claim that God speaks to them. How can we tell who speaks the truth?

It's a miracle for God to commune with someone, and when I tried to decipher it I came to the shining, deep, potent but invisible bedrocks of humility and faith. I knew that if I chose not to humble myself before what was greater than me—Prabhupada and all he represented—I'd be captured by what was less than me—pride and its mundane effects. And then, inevitably, I'd be disappointed and dissatisfied. Innately I, a spirit soul, was humble for I was tiny. Pride, being artificial, created inner violence for it was an attitude that contradicted who I was. To be humble, I thought, was as natural as walking on the ground.

I was attracted to the qualities of a humble heart: how it extended itself to others and dealt modestly with them. How it was jubilant, friendly, forgiving, and caring. Instead of fantasizing about personal perfection—a self-indulgent and hollow line of thinking—the humble were pleased to voice others' good qualities. As Prabhupada's godbrother, Sridhar Maharaj said, "If I do not like to give honor to others, then my self-seeking is present and can be traced. But when I can give honor without wanting honor for myself, I will be qualified to search for Krishna, the Absolute."

The truly humble had abandoned every attempt at being humble and instead had entered into a whole new dimension of existence, where the unimaginable greatness and incomparable perfection of God overshadowed their own smallness and faults. Such persons were less and less subject to their fickle mind and the dictates of society. Grounded in an authentic spiritual tradition, daily spiritual practice, and ordinary tasks, the humble responded to people and events with empathy and grace. They were spiritually alive and happy in their own situation. The vulnerability of humility fructified in this strength and freedom.

From what I understood from Prabhupada, humility was the cause of proportionate spiritual realization, by which one could ultimately meet God in person, as a person met another person face to face—just as Prabhupada dialoged with Krishna. As a gardener joyfully shared the bounty of the rich soil, so God graciously made his bounty accessible to the humble. It was the humble who did not harm the earth or the beings on it, for they avoided waste and were satisfied without extravagance. In reciprocation, God provided the most necessary thing of all: the rich inner harvest of genuine meaning and love.

Historian and social critic Arthur Schlesinger, Jr. writes, "There is no greater human presumption than to read the mind of the Almighty, and no more dangerous individual than the one who has convinced himself that he is executing the Almighty's will."

But that person who'd met God was protected from impertinence by humility.

During Prabhupada's stay in Manhattan we celebrated a magnificent Rath-yatra down Fifth Avenue that drew many thousands. The parade ended in a packed Washington Square Park where Dr. Thomas Hopkins, Chairman of the Department of Religious Studies at Franklin and Marshall College, spoke to the crowd:

> It's an astonishing story. If someone told you a story like this, you wouldn't believe it. Here's this person, he's seventy years old, he goes to a country where he's never been before, he doesn't know anybody there, he has no money, he has no contacts. He has none of the things, you would say, that would make for success. He's going to recruit people not on any systematic basis, but just picking up whomever he comes across … he was an old man in a strange society dealing with people whose backgrounds were totally different from his own … Bhaktivedanta Swami's achievement then, must be seen as unique.

The festival was favorably covered by NBC, ABC, CBS and Channel 5 television stations, as well as the *New York Times, Newsday, Newsweek* and the Associated Press. *The Daily News,* with a circulation of millions, devoted its center section to photographs of the festival with a headline Prabhupada appreciated: Fifth Avenue, Where East Meets West.

Sitting in the airport lounge waiting for his flight to London, Prabhupada had a heavy cold. Senior students had asked him to delay his trip and recuperate, but he'd refused; he wanted to continue his service to his spiritual master. I stood nearby, camera in hand, angst in heart. I wasn't going and I didn't know when I'd see him again. Or if I'd see him again.

By seemingly pure happenstance my life and Prabhupada's had crossed paths. I'd been touched by a great, genuine saint. Now he was leaving me on a spiritual threshold with vast beckoning lands stretching before me. Having had a glimpse of the richness of spirituality, I was eager to travel those beautiful lands with their promise of a happy, illimitable life. It was up to me. In a letter to a disciple written from New York, Prabhupada had said, "Do everything conscientiously and my blessings are always with you."

As he was faithfully following, he expected me to do the same. Even in his absence. But I didn't want to be in his absence. Ever.

I remembered that not long after Prabhupada initiated me, in November of 1971, I was walking alone on Juhu Beach one morning when I thought, "I'll try Krishna consciousness for five years and if I'm disappointed, I'll return to my photojournalism career." Five years had passed now and although I was disappointed in my own spiritual progress, I wasn't disappointed in the bhakti process or in Prabhupada, its deliverer. He'd cracked opened the door of my heart enough to allow a gust of his weather to sweep in. That gust was irresistible. Over the years, I'd been tugging and tugging at that obdurate door to open it further. And I was tugging yet.

I was part of a big and growing family of godbrothers and sisters daily worshiping, singing, chanting, serving, and celebrating together. But I sometimes felt alone and lonely, pained by my blatant spiritual failings. Who could I open up to? Who could I reveal my disappointments and doubts to? We each were in our own blur of busyness. I was stuck in mine.

CHAPTER SEVENTEEN

Krishna's Cuisine and a Calamitous Cloud

April 1977: Yadubara was on his way to Hare Krishna Land in Juhu to show Prabhupada our latest film, *A Spark of Life,* a docu-drama about the spirit soul, but I wasn't accompanying him. I'd received a phone call from my dear friend Yamuna Devi, who was living with Dinatarine in a quiet, rented ashram in Grants Pass, Oregon.

"I'm finally working seriously on my cookbook—the one that's been on the back burner for ten years," Yamuna told me. "Would you like to come here to photograph dishes to illustrate it?"

"Sure," I said. "I'd love to!" although I had little idea what awaited me and no idea I'd be contributing to what would become Yamuna's classic *Lord Krishna's Cuisine,* which would later become the first vegetarian cookbook to win the IACP/Seagram Award for best cookbook of the year.

When I arrived at Dinatarine's and Yamuna's ashram, a doublewide trailer in a tiny cleared opening in the Siskiyou Forest, I first noticed that due to their enthusiastic gardening the area enclosed a riot of vegetables, hyacinths, and miniature roses. Smiling, laughing and, calling me by the nickname Yamuna had given me, "Vish," Yamuna and Dinatarine welcomed me with hugs and, arm in arm, the three of us went inside.

The interior was simple and immaculate and the small bedroom they gave me had everything I needed to be comfortable.

The first morning of my visit and every morning thereafter, as the spring sun streamed in, the two of them would sit in a circle of golden sunlight in their flower-bedecked temple room singing songs by great Vaishnav teachers. Our days passed peacefully as we absorbed ourselves in basic bhakti practices—chanting Hare Krishna on our beads, reading and discussing Prabhupada's books, maintaining the ashram, and gearing up for a photography marathon. Here, tucked away in the southern corner of Oregon, Krishna consciousness was personal and sweet.

Two weeks after I'd arrived, I received the first of many letters from Yadubara, this one dated April 17th. He wrote that when he saw Prabhupada in Juhu, Prabhupada said that he looked good and he also asked about me. Yadubara told him where I was and what I was doing and then showed Prabhupada our new film. Prabhupada enjoyed it, saying we'd done a great service and it should be distributed in schools and colleges. He also gave Yadubara directions for our next film, namely to elaborate on evolution, or how the soul evolves through different species of life up to the human form, at which point it has a chance to understand God. Yadubara thought that film could also include an understanding of transmigration and reincarnation. "We can be bold," he wrote, "and show how the subtle body desires in a certain way and one gets a corresponding body." As their meeting concluded, Prabhupada had said to Yadubara, "Go on trying your best."

Reading this I hankered for Prabhupada's company. I realized that even though I'd spent so much time with him, in his absence I retained little of his potent ambiance. Now I was left only with a distant memory of his potency. What was wrong with me? Why did I so dismally fail in this way?

Sure, I didn't have Prabhupada's knowledge and, more significantly, his wisdom. Neither did I have his lifelong devotional background. But ultimately these were excuses. It was my heart that fell short. There was something in my heart that was hard and unyielding and that stopped me from saturating myself in Prabhupada's mood and allowing it to permeate me so I could take it with me always. What was that iron-like ingredient? Its usual, default components were some combination of lust, anger, greed, envy, illusion. I could glibly and lackadaisically say I had all of those, but in truth my failing was something even more. I was firmly in the grip of false ego. While I loved the concept of my being a spiritual entity, I did not/ could not/ would not realize I actually was one. I'd left my heart, which should have been as soft and pliable as moist clay, in the hot kiln of illusion for so long that it had become baked into something brittle and unforgiving and impenetrable. In short, something ugly. Something I'd had no intention of creating. But there it was.

While those feelings churned within me, I also started wondering how Yadubara and I could make a convincing film on the soul's passage from lower to higher species. What a daunting assignment!

Just five days later a second letter arrived. "I feel Prabhupada wants all of us to carry on as we best see fit," Yadubara wrote. "To take off the burden from him. Prabhupada seems to be retiring more and more and indicates he wants us to decide our own course of action."

Prabhupada retiring? Us deciding our own course of action? WHAT?

But Prabhupada himself had said Krishna's devotee doesn't retire. He'd said that he himself wanted to die on the battlefield, preaching against illusion for Krishna's pleasure. And I wanted him to decide my course of action! I loved his decisions.

As Yamuna, Dinatarine, and I discussed Prabhupada's new mood, trepidation filled the air.

A third letter arrived, dated May 7th. Prabhupada had decided to go to Hrishikesh in the Himalayas to try to regain his health and Yadubara had been assigned to be Prabhupada's driver. "Krishna is so kind to fulfill my desires," he wrote. "I wanted to be able to do some little personal service for Prabhupada in a quiet atmosphere."

"How wonderful!" I thought, with some envy mixed in. "To travel with Prabhupada to Hrishikesh and stay there with him, what an opportunity!"

But—Prabhupada was going there to regain his health. How bad was his health? Yadubara had given no indication. Instead, he wrote about the diary Prabhupada had kept when he was on a ship coming from India to the U.S. for the first time. During that thirty-six day crossing, Prabhupada had suffered from seasickness, headache, and then two heart attacks that were so painful he said, "If a third one comes, surely I will die." He had been on a cargo ship and without any medical assistance.

Somehow Prabhupada recovered, Yadubara wrote, and on September 10, 1965, his diary entry was "Today the ship is plying very smoothly. I feel today better. But I am feeling separation of Sri Vrindavan. I have left Bharat

Bhumi [India] just to execute the order of Sri Bhaktisiddhanta Saraswati in pursuance of Lord Chaitanya's order. I have no qualification but I have taken up the risk to carry out the order of His Divine Grace. I depend fully on Their mercy so far away from Vrindavan."

"Prabhupada has not given up the struggle," Yadubara concluded. "Somehow, we have to follow in his footsteps. I'll write from Hrishikesh and keep a full record of events."

Three days later, another letter arrived with mention of some of those events. "Today, on the invitation of the Hrishikesh townspeople, Prabhupada will start giving evening lectures in the town assembly hall. In the last two darshans he was very forcefully denouncing the bogus gurus and politicians who change the Gita."

That sounded like the Prabhupada we knew. The three of us breathed a little easier.

Meanwhile, in this tiny ashram, for Prabhupada's pleasure we applied ourselves to our devotional service, which included milking the agreeable cow Bimala Prasad morning and evening (we had more milk than we knew what to do with), gardening, serving the deities, and especially photographing dishes to illustrate the encyclopedic cookbook. Unfortunately, Dinatarine's health was not good at this time and she spent much of her day in her room reading and resting while Yamuna and I, with some trepidation, approached the cookbook illustrations.

Yamuna and I had known each other for over six years, but now for the first time we started working closely together. We'd decide what preparations we wanted to portray, drive to stores to ponder and purchase suitable dishes, silverware, serving ware, placemats, and other props, create and photograph the preparations. Yamuna had learned Krishna conscious cooking, a refined culinary art passed down through centuries, directly from Prabhupada and she'd also studied it in India under expert cooks. The exotic dishes she made looked, smelled, and tasted superb.

I was confident of her ability to make exquisite and diverse dishes, and Yamuna had more faith than I did in my ability to execute this demanding and specialized type of photography. Collaborating to create strikingly attractive illustrations, we struggled and were frustrated and challenged and exhausted and delighted and distressed. Our mutual absorption brought me to an unexpectedly enchanting, convivial realm of devotional service with camaraderie. Yamuna and I bonded through our shared, intense devotional service. With her—a witty and insightful and giving and disarmingly honest friend—I discovered that doing something I loved with someone I loved and for someone I loved was nothing less than ecstatic. A life of shared service for Krishna is a sublime life.

Yamuna had such a presence that when she simply walked into a room, heads turned to acknowledge her. When she spoke, everyone was riveted on whatever she said, even if it was something they had no particular interest in, like how to make great ice cream. When people spoke to her, she heard more than what they said and responded in a way that brought them to unexpected conclusions. Her laugh was so heartily carefree, so spontaneous and genuine, it was contagious. When she and I talked, I felt her deep attachment to Prabhupada and how that attachment survived the disappointments and long trials she'd had with some of his followers. Her openness and kindness and thoughtful probing beneath the surface drew me out. Yamuna would ask "why" questions that opened me to new life perspectives.

In the mornings, before our photography started, Yamuna and Dinatarine taught me some of the many arts involved in caring for the beautiful deities they worshiped, and with their urging, I even sang devotional songs. In Grants Pass, Krishna consciousness was fresh and attainable.

As the days went by, I realized that spiritual progress takes its own seemingly meandering path. That instead of bemoaning my lack of progress, as I was wont to do, I could instead happily serve Krishna. The essential point was to go on trying.

After long hours of intensive photography sessions we finally completed the illustrative photographs and then, although Yamuna had already tested all 500 recipes, she decided an inexperienced cook—me—should try testing the recipes.

I felt like a freshman chemistry student on her first day in the lab as I struggled to distinguish mustard from cumin seeds, urad from mung dal, garam masala from asafetida. I didn't know how to mix spices, knead dough, or use any of the kitchen machinery. Nonetheless I tested, and Yamuna was always somewhere in the vicinity, ready to instruct, correct, encourage, and cajole, and sometimes to reprove for careless mistakes.

Another letter arrived from Yadubara, this one undated. "Last night I massaged Prabhupada when he was in his bed," he wrote. "His hands and feet are very swollen and he must be in great pain. Prabhupada asked again where you were when I went in—he said you were very qualified. Then he mentioned my parents—how they were very nice and came to see him in L.A. I asked Prabhupada if he felt any better after coming to Hrishikesh and he said 'No, not much.'

"After being trained yesterday, today I made prasadam for the devotees (about 9 of us) and Prabhupada. I served Prabhupada and sat with him as he tasted each preparation. He said everything was nice—3 veggies, rice, dal, chapatis, *shukta,* and tomato chutney—especially the chapatis. The devotees really liked it. Prabhupada said we should all take turns but I should continue for the next few days to really learn well. Then someone else could take over. He said make this the standard and you will enjoy eating!

"I serve him every night now from 9:30–11:30. Sometimes he will sit for 20 or 30 minutes after translating one verse with his eyes closed. I am awed by the whole experience. I can only try to serve as best as I can. Krishna fulfilled my desire to be with Prabhupada and I can try to serve him in my awkward way while I am here …

"I hope you are making good progress on the cookbook."

Hearing of Prabhupada's physical condition, our ashram filled with nervous portent.

Yet at the same time, it was inconceivable: Halfway around the world, Prabhupada, despite serious health issues, was preaching strongly, translating the Srimad-Bhagavatam, and teaching Yadubara and others how to cook. Yadubara was personally cooking for and directly offering Prabhupada his lunch, and in the remote place where I was, I was doing the same thing.

After breakfast each morning I went into the kitchen armed with some of Yamuna's recipes, took a deep breath, prayed to Prabhupada and Lord Krishna, and began cooking for their pleasure. As it turned out, the recipes weren't the only things tested.

I quickly learned turmeric was a bright yellow powder that stained everything and mustard seeds were small, round, and black and dashed everywhere when spilled. Other lessons took more time.

I studied the jars of urad and mung dal intensely, trying to tell one from the other—too embarrassed to ask Yamuna again which was which. Was cumin brownish-gray and fennel greenish, or was it the other way around? And then there were measurements. How many teaspoons in a tablespoon, tablespoons in a quarter cup, ounces in a pound? Toward the end of the morning I was so dazed by the mental exertion that I'd forgotten if I'd salted a dish or not. By twelve o'clock the dishes were finished and the cook kaput.

We'd offer the meal to the deities and then sit down together for lunch, our talks quickly turning to the news in Yadubara's letters. Another one arrived, dated May 16th and the most ominous of all:

> We spent about 8 days in Hrishikesh. It was very nice until the end, when the weather started getting bad. Prabhupada was not improving so much. His hands and feet were still swollen and he was still weak and unable to walk without help … The night before last, the wind was blowing fiercely and doors and windows were banging and the electricity was out. I fixed up a kerosene lantern on Prabhupada's desk, and he sat down to translate and then found that the battery in the dictaphone was not charged. Prabhupada just sat there and then said, "What can be done?" I apologized and wished there was something I could do. He said, "There's nothing to be done. It's Krishna's desire."
>
> I can understand that Prabhupada's translating work is his life and soul. This was the second night he could not translate. About 2:00 am that second night TKG [Tamal Krishna Goswami] woke me up and said we were leaving. Prabhupada was saying that his condition wasn't good and if he was going to die, he wanted to die in Vrindavan. So, we all packed up and left by 10:00 a.m. that morning. Even though Prabhupada spoke of dying, all the devotees with him couldn't foresee this. He is still preaching every day … P.S. We're in Delhi and devotees just arrived from Vrindavan. Upon his arrival, Prabhupada called devotees into his room and said he had given everything in his books and there was no need for any more questions. This material body is meant for dying—it is not the important thing. Most important is the service, which is eternal.

There it was, staring up at us from a floppy, blue Indian aerogramme: the "d" word.

The sweetness of the company I was in, of the place, of our blissful service together all became tinged with an intractable despair. It hung over everything.

What to do except to go on doing what we were doing? Would Prabhupada want anything else?

After testing more than two hundred recipes, I could indeed tell urad from mung and cumin from fennel (fennel is greenish). I was far from expert, but the clear, comprehensive recipes enabled me to cook dishes that were, Yamuna told me, pleasing to Prabhupada and Krishna.

Of course, real cooks could make tasty meals without recipes; real cooks applied the principles and procedures of a tradition to make innovative dishes that were still in keeping with that tradition; the real cooks' art was dynamic—they applied their expertise in unexpected and pleasing ways— and no matter how much they knew they were keen to learn more. Yamuna was the maestro, I the novice; but the beauty of spiritual life was that even a novice's service, if done in the proper mood, could be accepted by guru and God.

Stretching beyond Yamuna and Dinatarine's property were miles of woodlands, and after lunch I'd take long walks on narrow forest paths that curved beneath fir and pine, maple and myrtle. Chanting the maha-mantra on my beads, accompanied by the songs of red-winged blackbirds, wood thrushes, and starlings, even as I felt a dark cloud of separation from Prabhupada hanging over our future and ached for it to dissipate, I also felt fortunate and sheltered to be with two good friends and to have such sublime service.

After losing myself in Krishna's forest artistry for an hour or two, I returned to the ashram rejuvenated.

Yadubara's next letter was dated May 19th:

> It is now 1:15 a.m. the first night with Prabhupada in Vrindavan. He is sitting translating and resting every night on the roof above his rooms. It is a very beautiful scene to see him sitting at his translating table with one table lamp on, surrounded by black except for the temple domes looming up nearby. Prabhupada told TKG that Vrindavan is his home—his residence. Bombay

is his office and Mayapur is for worshiping the Supreme Lord Sri Chaitanya Mahaprabhu.

Prabhupada had been seriously ill several times before this, Yamuna told us. She'd been in San Francisco when he'd had a heart attack in 1967. At that time he'd asked all his students to pray to Lord Krishna, "My dear Lord, my spiritual master has not yet completed his work. Please protect him." Yamuna and everyone else in the San Francisco temple had stayed up all night praying and chanting. Later, when he'd recovered, Prabhupada had written to them,

> My dear boys and girls,
> I am so much obliged to you for your prayers to Krishna to save my life. Due to your sincere and ardent prayer, Krishna has saved my life. I was to die on Tuesday certainly but because you prayed sincerely I am saved. Now I am improving gradually and coming to my original condition. Now I can hope to meet you again and chant with you Hare Krishna. I am so glad to receive the report of your progressive march and hope there will be no difficulty in your understanding Krishna consciousness. My blessings are always with you and with confidence you go on with your chanting Hare Krishna Hare Krishna Krishna Krishna Hare Hare Hare Rama Hare Rama Rama Rama Hare Hare.

After this heart attack, when he had recuperated enough to travel, Prabhupada had returned to India for five months to regain his health fully. Once restored, he preached so vigorously and traveled so extensively that his young disciples could hardly keep up with him. Seven years later, in Vrindavan in 1974, he again became seriously ill, this time, he said, due to the looseness of the leaders of his movement, eighty percent of whom were not strictly following the rules and regulations. As in 1967, his students throughout the world held continuous kirtan and prayed to Krishna for his recovery. Two weeks later Prabhupada's fever finally broke, he resumed his normal schedule, and his students resumed theirs.

Prabhupada's illnesses, Yamuna said, were not from ordinary causes and were not cured by ordinary methods. Now, caught in the throes of Prabhupada's current health crisis, the three of us chanted Hare Krishna feeling distraught and helpless. The next letter intensified our feelings.

May 21, 1977:

Today Prabhupada told TKG that there were two courses at this time in regards to his health—one is to fight for survival and the other to prepare for departure. Prabhupada said we must prepare for the latter. Prabhupada is not getting better ... It is amazing to see how Prabhupada pushes on his translation even at this time. It is a great lesson for all of us—to push on preaching no matter what obstacles are there. Prabhupada said today that the Vaishnavs' only concern is to alleviate the difficulties of others. Then he said kirtan and Bhagavatam are very pleasing to the ear and mind (pointing to his ear and heart respectively) and that this is the real medicine. Again he said that we should not worry.

As I was reading from the introduction 1st volume Bhagavatam to Prabhupada I could understand that Prabhupada will never die—that he lives on in his books—just like he so gloriously and emphatically stated at the news conference in San Francisco. Simply we have to take his teachings very seriously, become Krishna conscious ourselves and make others Krishna conscious. That will please Prabhupada, Krishna, and everyone.

What I'd felt at that news conference I again felt, but more emphatically: I'd take Prabhupada over his books any day. It was like the difference between studying incredible recipes and eating an incredible meal.

Yadubara's last letter to me in Grants Pass, dated May 30th, didn't offer hope. He quoted Prabhupada saying,

> "Everyone has to die so we should die gloriously by hearing and chanting. Just keep up this sound vibration. That is why I have brought all of you here. Please do not leave me."
>
> The chanting is going on very nicely from 7–10 a.m., 3–9 p.m. and 1–5 a.m. with 6 devotees chanting for 1½ hours. Only a very small pair of kartals is played, and the kirtan is very simple and sweet. Prabhupada hears most of the time, and nods his head in time and sometimes claps softly. ... Prabhupada said that this hearing and chanting "cure" is so nice that effective or not, it is still glorious.

In their spotless temple room, Yamuna, Dinatarine, and I had a long, soulful kirtan. There was nothing else to do.

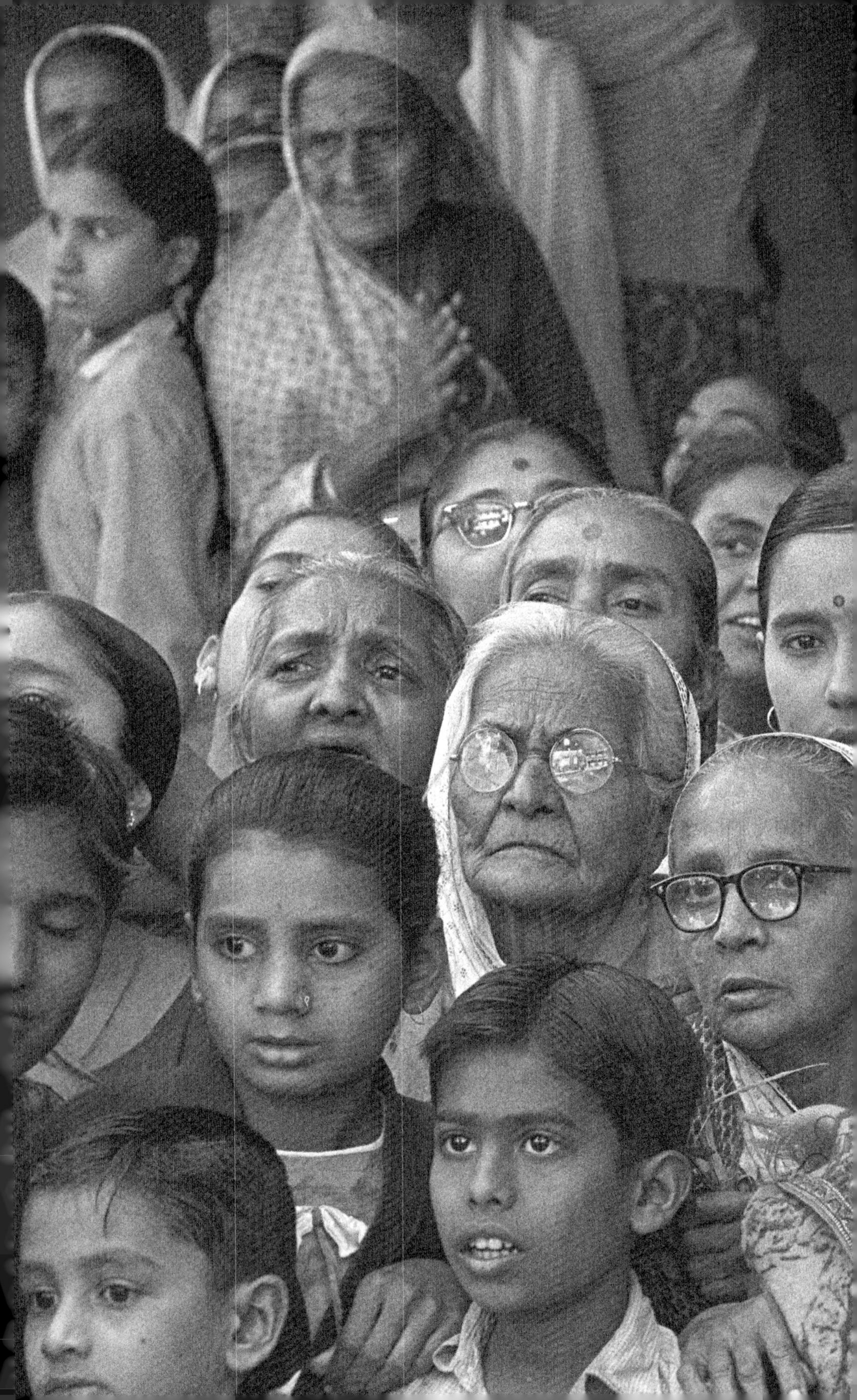

CHAPTER EIGHTEEN

Five Years, Eleven Months, Sixteen Days

In June, Yadubara returned to the U.S., and in September he and I went to Juhu where the entire front part of Hare Krishna Land, formerly a jungle-cum-dump, had become a construction zone where a graceful, white-marble dome—flanked on each side by matching smaller domes—dominated the south end of the property. A magnificent white-marble temple room beckoned in the center, and six-story-twin circular guesthouses towered over the north end.

Prabhupada had just completed a taxing yet joyous trip to one of his ashrams in England, Bhaktivedanta Manor. Now, despite the constant noise from the hundreds of onsite construction workers, Prabhupada had chosen to stay in his rooms on the top floor of one of the twin towers. I'd not seen him for months and his appearance shocked me and sent a stab of tenderness and pain through me. As he sat cross-legged on his bed in a darkened room, his satisfyingly rounded head was as beautiful as ever, but his cheeks were gaunt and his kurta hung loose over his thinning frame. His countenance showed a life lived wisely, his eyes were moist and alert, and his face was kindly and unperturbed by the rapid demise of the body it was attached to. He seemed so removed from this world that I could have mistaken him for a Vrindavan ascetic who spent his days and nights absorbed in beatific meditations instead of the founder of an international confederation of Krishna conscious centers, the scholarly author of a library of scriptural books, and the fearless promoter of bhakti-yoga.

But Prabhupada was still Prabhupada. Just as, by nature, sugar is sweet and water is wet, similarly Prabhupada was Krishna's servant. Weakness had slightly slurred his speech, yet being in his presence was being in the presence of something beyond him that was immeasurably great; being in his presence was electrifying. His words revealed a memory and intellect as sharp and quick as ever, as he asked Yadubara and me how we were, what we were doing, and of the activities in the Los Angeles ashram where we'd been. From Prabhupada's vibrant interest in others' wellbeing—a concern so deep in him that it seemed more enduring than his very life—by osmosis, in his presence I felt more concern for others. He pulled me out of my habitually myopic orbit. How much I needed Prabhupada in my life! He evoked my selfless desire to give to others. He led me on the best of all adventures: the discovery of the wealth of my own heart. I trusted him implicitly. Seeing him in his current decrepit condition, my whole being ached for him and went out to him. He was transparent: he hid nothing and had nothing to hide. He was, as always, in Krishna's hands and completely pleased to be there. How gladly I would have traded my youth and health for his age and infirmity.

Prabhupada's condition steadily worsened, and in October he returned to his sacred Krishna-Balaram Temple in Vrindavan. Standing with a small group at the side gate of the Krishna-Balaram Temple, I watched as Prabhupada's car inched down the narrow, rutted road. Upon arriving he was transferred to a wooden palanquin and I photographed him sitting high above me, the gray sky forming a vast backdrop to his somber, regal, and frighteningly feeble form—his head bobbing to the rhythm of his bearers' stride. Since I'd seen him in Juhu, minimal eating had scooped caverns in his cheeks, eroded his limbs to sticks, and drained his energy. Yet devotion still dignified his demeanor and deepened his eyes.

Once Prabhupada was in his quarters, I ran to my guesthouse room, overcome by his new look; but weeping could not begin to address the irremediable parting and looming loss, the terrible weeks of anxiety, uncertainty, helplessness, and emptiness that confronted us.

Prabhupada lay on his bed in his large front room; devotees came from throughout the world to chant and read; to face the unfaceable. Now our loyalty to Prabhupada must encounter his passing, must accept it, must try to grow from it, and must continue in spite of it. Only in continuing to follow despite his passing could our loyalty learn the true extent of its commitment, of the spiritual attachment that transcends mortality. Death cannot part the sincere student from the spiritual teacher: simply by continuing to follow, the student triumphs over death—or rather, in the face of the student's determination, death shrinks to insignificance. Prabhupada dedicated his Srimad-Bhagavatam, first published in India in 1962, to his spiritual preceptor, "He lives forever by his divine instructions and the follower lives with him."

Daily, Prabhupada's young disciples put his frail body on a palanquin and, bearing it on their shoulders and accompanied by a kirtan procession, circumambulated the Krishna-Balaram Temple and then entered the temple room, where they placed Prabhupada, still seated in his palanquin, before each of the three deity altars. Prabhupada gazed at his Lords and we gazed at him; he offered his homage to them; we offered ours to him.

A heavy, churning, unrelievable anguish pressed us. One morning, Yadubara and I went to the workplace of a young Spanish-speaking devotee who made brass, nine-inch-high deities of Sri Chaitanya and Nityananda Prabhu. Both had a well-proportioned form, a happy expression and a dancing stance, and we purchased them. I sewed a sequined outfit for them, white cloth for Nityananda and yellow for Sri Chaitanya, and began walking to the Yamuna for their daily bath water. As the river was far from the temple, this solo venture took a few hours and offered relief from the trauma and the daily mini-dramas that surrounded Prabhupada's condition.

Many of Prabhupada's godbrothers came to visit him, and as they sat together on a bench at the head of his bed, with great endeavor Prabhupada honored them by folding his hands and asking their forgiveness for offenses he'd committed to them in the course of his preaching. His parting words to his spiritual brothers were unconditionally loving. Without exception, his godbrothers told him that he should rest assured that no offense was taken. On the contrary, they said, Prabhupada's astounding devotional service must have given their spiritual master, Bhaktisiddhanta Saraswati Thakur, exceptional pleasure.

Although Prabhupada's voice was a whisper and his supine body, covered with a white sheet, was, in his own words, "a bag of bones," Pradyumna knelt by the side of his bed, read the Sanskrit texts of the Srimad-Bhagavatam, and Prabhupada continued to translate and comment. Other disciples huddled around the bed, in a scene reminiscent of one in the Bhagavatam, where grandfather Bhisma, lying on his deathbed and surrounded by his well-wishers, relatives, and heirs to the kingdom, used his final breaths to offer invaluable knowledge.

Yadubara repeatedly asked permission to film Prabhupada translating, but Tamal Krishna Goswami (TKG), Prabhupada's secretary, was hesitant.

He remembered how the bright lights had disturbed Prabhupada in Denver and thought that, especially in Prabhupada's present condition, the lights and our presence would again be taxing. On October 21st Prabhupada, lying motionless, conversed with TKG:

> TKG: Yadubara wants to film you translating. Is that all right? You don't mind? We can have a little light here while he films for about half a minute? It wouldn't disturb you.
> Prabhupada: Yadubara is a good devotee.
> TKG: Yadubara is a good devotee. Very dedicated devotee. You remember he cooked *bati chachuri* very nice also for you. He was cooking for you in Hrishikesh, massaging. Very intelligent.
> Prabhupada: Yes.
> TKG: His wife is also intelligent, Visakha.
> Prabhupada: Yadubara has become a devotee first.
> TKG: Has become first, Prabhupada?
> Prabhupada: First devotee, before his wife.
> TKG: First devotee before his wife, yes. You convinced him. He did not come here thinking to become a devotee. Remember, he came for photography work.
> Prabhupada: Yes.
> TKG: But his good fortune was that he chose to photograph you, Prabhupada, and the devotees.
> Prabhupada: Yadubara has freedom …
> TKG: What, Prabhupada?
> Prabhupada: Yadubara has freedom to do anything.
> TKG: Yadubara? Has freedom to do anything.
> Prabhupada: Hm.
> TKG: I think that will make his service very enhanced to know that.

Yadubara and I sat at the foot of Prabhupada's large bed, becoming part of the cheerless scene, filming, recording, and photographing as Prabhupada used his last bit of energy to continue his lifelong devotional service: translating and commenting on the verses of Srimad-Bhagavatam, at this point the purport to the Tenth Canto, chapter 13, "The Stealing of the Boys and Calves by Brahma," text 53. His words were slightly slurred and followed one another slowly, yet the content was cogent and pristine—knowledge that reached out to us longingly and hauntingly, enveloping and transporting us to another world of awareness:

> One should understand that no one is independent, for everything is part and parcel of Krishna and is acting and moving by the supreme desire of Krishna. This understanding, this consciousness, is Krishna consciousness.

Such simple words expressing the deepest wisdom, spoken in such dire circumstances, went directly from Prabhupada's mouth into my headphones and vibrated in my ears. They at once transcended time and place and yet were utterly applicable to time and place—but I was unable to relate to them or to relate them to the situation. I could not understand that Prabhupada's heartbreakingly dwindled condition was the supreme desire of Krishna, that our recording one of his final purports was also the supreme desire of Krishna, and that his passing from this world would be also the supreme desire of Krishna. Yet death—like life—was Krishna; Prabhupada was in Krishna's grip. Even now theirs was a relationship of love; I was an onlooker who failed to grasp the intimacy and sweetness of that relationship.

Nearing the end of his long and active life, Prabhupada entered a period of reflection and judged his students' conduct differently—words of appreciation and encouragement replaced reprimands—and Prabhupada also made unforgettable statements, as when he said to a senior student, "Don't think that this won't happen to you."

When Jayadvaita commented on the astonishing number of books Prabhupada had translated while he was traveling, opening centers, instructing, initiating, writing thousands of letters, managing, meeting people, and so on, Prabhupada said, "A little water wears the stone." To write daily was to eventually write volumes.

On November 11th, the day of the great festival of Govardhan Puja, Prabhupada asked to be taken by bullock cart on the fourteen-mile path around Govardhan Hill. His Ayurvedic doctor said the bumpy ride would be bad for him. Devotees were divided: Some said if Prabhupada wanted to go, he should go. Others said such a trip would preclude any chance of recovery, and worse, that Prabhupada would die from it. Prabhupada didn't go.

On the 14th of November 1977, my godsisters and I were having lunch when we heard the doctor's prognosis: Prabhupada had five hours left. We went to Prabhupada's room, surrounded his bed, and joined the kirtan—now one of distraught, raw emotion. Prabhupada's face was simply skin wrapped around bone and cartilage; gone were his sobering and penetrating looks; gone were his myriad expressions of love, devotion, patience, disapproval, humor, compassion, and liveliness; gone were his expressive, aristocratic gestures. As he awaited the final moment, his eyes were closed, his breathing unnoticeable; he was suspended in time, beyond everything in time, meditative, indrawn and calm.

In contrast, passions swelled and reeled around him.

Stationed at the head of the bed, a Bengali disciple, Bhakti Charu Swami, who had been too distracted to shave for several days, periodically poured a few drops of Yamuna water from a tiny silver pitcher into Prabhupada's slightly opened mouth. Prabhupada's sister Pishima, grave and downcast, sat on the floor near Bhakti Charu Swami. Our ever well-wisher, our source of knowledge and guidance, of comfort and security and protection, of balance and maturity and enthusiasm—that person who was the focal point of our affection—was departing. What could be said? What was left to say? Prabhupada, withdrawing deep within himself, was leaving his body, us, the Krishna-Balaram Temple, the earth planet and the mundane world altogether.

At first hourly, and then minute by minute, the intensity of the devotees' agony increased, filling every crevice of the room. Where there was great love, there were also miracles: the devotees' crying, wailing, bewilderment, moroseness, devastation, and above all, chanting of God's names, expressed the extraordinary devotion that Prabhupada had aroused in them, young and old, men and women of every nationality and denomination.

Standing on chairs next to each other at the foot of Prabhupada's bed, Yadubara filmed and I photographed and recorded. Since the time I'd frozen when Prabhupada had danced at the Delhi pandal, I had learned to immunize myself emotionally from any situation so that I could continue my service, and somehow that immunization remained strong—I shelved my feelings. Yadubara did the same.

Devotees massaged Prabhupada's feet and stroked his arms, long-faced sannyasis looked at him fixedly. Occasionally, the doctor checked Prabhupada's pulse. The air thickened with despair.

At 7:24 p.m., the tumultuous emotion and chanting reached a climax, like the genuine crying of children for their father, and Prabhupada passed away. We were all asked to leave Prabhupada's room so his body could be bathed and dressed.

When we had entered Prabhupada's quarters it had been bright outside, when we left, night had settled in.

We filed into the temple room, and soon devotees put Prabhupada's body on his raised seat. Until his body was interred, which would be twelve hours later, it was ceremoniously honored, as it had housed a holy person of the highest caliber.

With a voice of divine yearning, Prabhupada's godbrother Krishna das Babaji sang a traditional song of separation in which the songwriter, Narottam das Thakur, laments for the exalted persons who have passed on, "he who brought the treasure of divine love and who was filled with compassion and mercy—where has such a personality gone? I will smash my head against the rock and enter into the fire. Where will I find that person who is the reservoir of all wonderful qualities? Being unable to obtain the association of such a devotee, Narottam das simply weeps."

Although I continued to record and photograph, part of me was in shock. It was irrational, but I never actually believed that Prabhupada would—or could—leave us. His limp form, sitting before me, was present yet inconceivable. I saw it, yet didn't see it. For me, by dint of his staunch conviction, Prabhupada had always been ageless—or rather, he was forever seventy-five, the same age as when I'd met him. A world without precious and relishable moments with him; without his endless, ever-fresh talk of Krishna; without his majestic radiance that evoked love and reverence; without his singing, his instructions, his awesome encouragement, his resounding devotional service, his all-around awareness, his brisk morning walks along beaches and through parks—this would be a world of impossible, intrusive darkness.

Grief swallowed me with an emptiness I'd never before even imagined. My thoughts became so fogged they were practically gone.

Throughout the night, devotees sang to Prabhupada's slumped form, and the next morning, with Prabhupada's body on a palanquin carried by his strong disciples, we went in a kirtan procession to the seven major temples of Vrindavan. Local residents lined the streets to offer their last respects, along with garlands, food, and money, to the great, departed soul. Many gently touched Prabhupada's transcendental form and then touched their foreheads to procure his blessings.

On our return to the Krishna-Balaram Temple, we placed Prabhupada's limp form into a ten-foot pit that had been dug where Prabhupada had specified. The devotees sat him cross-legged on a marble slab and then packed salt around his body. A stick pointing straight up from the top of his head kept track of his position. We offered flowers into the pit and then filled it with earth. As Prabhupada had requested, his disciples cooked a splendid feast and sponsored similar feasts in Vrindavan's seven major temples. We ate and rested and the next day took a small brass deity of Prabhupada to Govardhan Hill, bathed him in the sanctified water of Radha-kund, and circumambulated the hill with him in honor of one of his last wishes.

I was unfamiliar with the various rites and confused about the future. And I had a hazy, cataclysmic feeling of foreboding. But mostly I was numb.

In the summer of 1971, Vrindavan's devoted residents had captivated me when, following Prabhupada's suggestion, we'd made our first visit; during our second Vrindavan trip Prabhupada had introduced me to Krishna's sweetness and initiated me; on my third trip, in October-November of 1972, I had sat at Prabhupada's feet before the tomb of the exalted Vaishnav teacher Rupa Goswami and heard Prabhupada tirelessly explain the philosophy of Krishna consciousness. I regularly returned to Vrindavan for pilgrimages and, in 1975, for the grand opening of the Krishna-Balaram Temple. This time, however, in that same Vrindavan where my spiritual life had set sail, that same Vrindavan where I had accepted Prabhupada as my captain and delighted in his presence and direction, I felt adrift in a violent, strange sea. All I wanted was a world with Prabhupada somewhere in it, making things clear, setting things right, propounding Krishna's words, and that was something I would not have again.

I'd been his initiated disciple for five years, eleven months, sixteen days, and ten hours. In that time he had offered me everything: culture, friendships, family, lifelong service, the possibility of profound, personal, divine realization and love. Now I needed to make sense of his offering—I needed to accept it, to live it, to let it become my own, to grow with it, to so awaken to its reality that I breathed it.

And to so awaken to its reality I let it breathe.

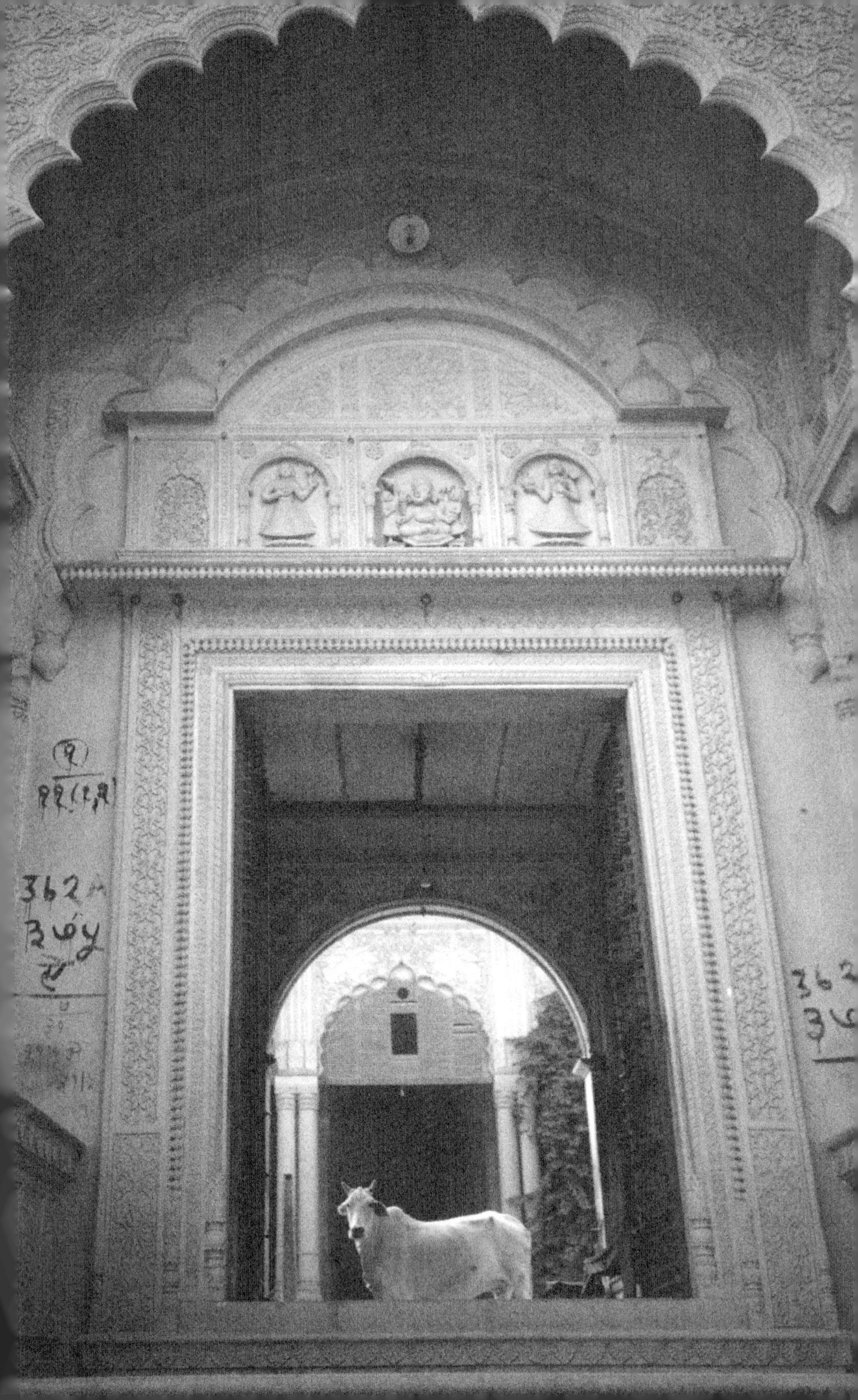

Epilogue

One night after he'd just returned to Bombay from Nairobi, Prabhupada was seated comfortably in his airy, seventh-floor Akash Ganga room overlooking the Arabian Sea. Warm breezes billowed his window curtains. Occasional car horns and the distant drone of heavy traffic melded with the murmurs of lapping waves. Silver reflections from the half moon glittered and gamboled along a sliver of sea. The seagulls had fallen silent.

As Prabhupada exchanged pleasantries with several of his students in the gentle ambiance of that room, a surge of joy washed over me. I felt, as I always did when reunited with him, the sleeping, dark places within me aroused and brightened. I felt his vigorous, multi-dimensional aura of devotion and service lift me into the surprising, delicious air of discovery and freedom. Once again just hearing the sound of his voice aroused happiness in my heart.

Prabhupada turned to me, "And so, Visakha, how are you feeling?"

"In your presence I feel wonderful," I said.

Prabhupada relaxed back against his large white bolster and closed his eyes. After a pause he hummed slightly and said, "I am also feeling the presence of my spiritual master."

This occurred in February 1972, thirty-five years after Prabhupada's spiritual master, Bhaktisiddhanta Saraswati Thakur, had passed away.

By the time Prabhupada passed away five and a half years later, he had completely and enduringly captured me. I loved him. I wanted to be with him always. I wanted to feel his presence in my heart. I wanted his words and spirit to breathe through me. But as Prabhupada had prophetically said one morning as he walked along a pristine beach, "Everywhere the followers make the whole thing bungled." After his passing, for disordered decades Prabhupada's other followers and I sometimes choked on and sometimes were suffocated by our own and each others' bungling. Many of Prabhupada's leading followers became so affected by power and prestige that they broke their vows, fell from their positions, and shattered the faith of thousands. In the midst of this turmoil, I became confused, deeply disturbed, and depressed. Feeling helpless, I clung to my initiation vows and attempted to focus on the basics: that I am not my body but a spiritual being who is part of Krishna, the Supreme Person; that I have an eternal, loving relationship with Krishna; and that there is no material impediment to the process of bhakti—devotional service to Krishna—and that process will eventually enable me to connect with Krishna once and for all.

I yearned to be like Prabhupada: personally unaffected by any and all types of disturbances. And I knew that whatever happened, no one and nothing could ever take from me the precious moments I'd spent in Prabhupada's company and the precious spiritual understandings he'd given me. Those were mine to treasure forever.

Somehow, Yadubara and I continued to produce Krishna conscious documentary films, I continued to write and photograph, and we had two daughters who are beautiful in every way.

Yet for me, the years froze into place after Prabhupada's passing. My mirror, which today reflects a serious-looking old woman, betrays nothing of the bright flame that burns within her—the same flame that had long ago burned within a photographer in the prime of her life, camera in hand, noting the lighting, poised to capture Prabhupada's activities and expressions, poised to go anywhere with him. Over everything, that burning flame casts an expansive glow of unexpected love.

The Photographs

Title page Vrindavan resident, 1971
Dedication Manhattan Hare Krishna temple rooftop, 1976
Contents Vrindavan resident, 1971
Prologue Scene from Indian train, 1971
6 Great Neck, New York, 1965
8 Reuben Papert in his Manhattan office, 1967
12 Macrophotograph of an artichoke heart, 1969
15 New York City, 1970
26 Bombay, 1971
32 Bombay, 1971
39 John Griesser and the author, Nepal, 1971
40 Indian train station, 1971
45 Nepal, 1971
47 Upstate New York, 1968
48 Vrindavan residents, 1971
57 Vrindavan residents, 1971
70 Prabhupada, Calcutta, 1972
76 Pishima, Calcutta, 1972
84 Bus to Vrindavan, 1971
93 Calcutta, 1972
94 Mayapur, 1985
113 Prabhupada, Jaipur, 1972
116 Prabhupada with the author, Mayapur, 1972
118 Ananta Sesa deity, Mayapur, 1972
120 Calcutta, 1972
123 Bombay, 1972
130 Prabhupada in his Vrindavan room, 1972
148 Prabhupada with Sridhar Swami, Mayapur, 1972
168 Morning walk, Visakhapatam, 1972
171 Prabhupada, Juhu, 1974
174 Scene from train, India, 1973
184 Mayapur prasada distribution, 1974
187 Rath-yatra, San Francisco, 1974
194 Reuben Papert, Moscow Fur Auction, 1953
198 Mayapur morning walk, 1975 (the author is on the far left)
208 Vrindavan, 1972
214 The author's parents, Reuben and Louise Papert, Great Neck, 1968
242 Vrindavan residents, 1971
253 Milk and milk products, 1977
254 Yamuna Devi and George Harrison, London, 1969
260 Vrindavan residents, 1977
263 Prabhupada, Vrindavan, 1977
270 Vrindavan, 1977

Glossary

Arati—a traditional ceremony of greeting the deity in the temple.

Bhagavad-gita—a record of a conversation between Sri Krishna and his disciple, Arjuna. In its 700 verses the Gita summarizes all knowledge about the soul, God, dharma, sacrifice, austerity, charity, yoga, karma, reincarnation, time, material nature, and bhakti.

Bhakti—selfless devotional service to the Supreme Person, Krishna.

Bhakti-yoga—the system of cultivation of bhakti, or pure devotional service to the Supreme Person, Krishna.

Bhaktisiddhanta Saraswati Thakur—(1874-1936) the spiritual master of Bhaktivedanta Swami Prabhupada and a powerful preacher who founded sixty-four missions in India.

Bhaktivedanta Swami Prabhupada—(1896-1977) His Divine Grace A.C. Bhaktivedanta Swami Prabhupada, a disciple of Bhaktisiddhanta Saraswati Thakur. He is the tenth generation from Sri Chaitanya and the founder-acharya of the International Society for Krishna Consciousness (ISKCON). Bhaktivedanta Swami Prabhupada was a widely-acclaimed author of more than seventy books on the science of bhakti-yoga and the world's most distinguished teacher of Vedic religion and thought. He worked incessantly to spread Krishna consciousness all over the world. Under his guidance his society grew into a worldwide confederation of hundreds of ashrams, schools, temples, institutes, and farm communities.

Bhaktivinode Thakur—(1838-1914) a great spiritual teacher who was the father of Bhaktisiddhanta Saraswati Thakur and the grand-spiritual master of Bhaktivedanta Swami Prabhupada.

B.R. Sridhar Swami—(1895-1988) a prominent disciple of Bhaktisiddhanta Saraswati Thakur.

Chaitanya Charitamrita—the authorized biography of Sri Chaitanya, written by Krishna das Kaviraj Goswami.

Chaitanya Mahaprabhu, Sri Chaitanya—(1486-1534) the Supreme Person, Krishna, in the mood of his own devotee. Sri Chaitanya taught that one can attain love of God by chanting of the holy names (kirtana).
Demigods—universal controllers and residents of the higher planets who assist God in the management of the universe.
Dharma—the eternal occupational duty of the living entity, inseparable from the living entity itself.
False ego—the soul's wrong identification with matter.
Gaudiya Vaishnav—devotees of Krishna who are followers of Sri Chaitanya.
Gaudiya Math—an organization founded by Prabhupada's spiritual master, Bhaktisiddhanta Saraswati Thakur.
Halavah—a traditional sweet preparation made from toasted semolina or farina, sugar, ghee, and water.
Hare Krishna mantra—a sixteen-word prayer composed of the names Hare, Krishna, and Rama: Hare Krishna, Hare Krishna, Krishna Krishna, Hare Hare, Hare Rama, Hare Rama, Rama Rama, Hare Hare. The chanting of this mantra is the most recommended means for spiritual progress in this age, as it enables one to transcend the temporary designations of race, religion, and nationality and to understand one's true identity as an eternal living entity, a spiritual being.
Hinduism—a word derived from Sindhu, the name of a river in present-day Pakistan. Beginning around 1000 AD, invading armies from the Middle East called the place beyond the Sindhu river Hindustan and the people who lived there the Hindus. (Due to the invaders' language, the 's' sound changed to 'h'.) In the centuries that followed, the term Hindu became accepted even by the Indians themselves as a general name for their religious traditions. The word "Hindu," however, is not found in the Vedic scriptures upon which these traditions are based.
Impersonalist—one who considers that the highest manifestation of God has no form or personality but is a formless energy.
Japa—the quiet recitation of Krishna's holy names: Hare Krishna Hare Krishna, Krishna Krishna Hare Hare/ Hare Rama Hare Rama, Rama Rama Hare Hare.
Kali-yuga—the present age, which is characterized by irreligious practices, quarrel, and stringent material miseries.

Karma—any material action that brings a reaction that binds one to the material world. According to the law of karma, if we cause pain and suffering to other living beings, we must endure pain and suffering in return.

Karma-yoga—the path of God realization through dedicating one's actions and the fruits of one's work to God.

Kirtan—the devotional process of narrating the glories of the Supreme Person or singing his holy names, especially the mahamantra: Hare Krishna Hare Krishna, Krishna Krishna Hare Hare/ Hare Rama Hare Rama, Rama Rama Hare Hare.

Krishna—God, the all-attractive Supreme Person who is the cause of all causes, the supreme controller, and the supreme proprietor. No one is equal to or greater than him. He is full in all opulences.

Krishna das Kaviraj Goswami—(1520-1616?) the author of *Chaitanya Charitamrita*, the biography of Sri Chaitanya.

Mantra—(*man*=mind; *tra*=deliverance) a spiritual sound vibration that delivers the mind from its material inclinations and illusions.

Maya—an energy of Krishna's which deludes the living entity into forgetfulness of him.

Narottam das Thakur—a renowned spiritual master and author of many devotional songs. He lived in the 16th century in West Bengal and was devoted to Sri Chaitanya from birth.

Personalism—the philosophical position that accepts that in his highest manifestation God has form and personality. His formless energy is subordinate to this manifestation.

Prasad (or prasadam)—literally means "mercy," and usually refers to food prepared for the pleasure of Krishna and offered to him with love and devotion. Because Krishna tastes such an offering, the food is said to become spiritualized and will purify anyone who eats it.

Puris—whole wheat flat breads that are deep fried and puff into balls.

Rama—the Absolute Truth who is the source of unlimited pleasure.

Sankirtan—the sacrifice prescribed for this age, namely the congregational chanting of the Supreme Person's names.

Sannyasi—a renounced, celibate mendicant.

Siva—the superintendent of the mode of ignorance who takes charge of destroying the universe at the time of annihilation.

Smarta Brahmins—members of the brahminical social caste who feel themselves entitled to privileges simply by their birth, regardless of their qualifications and activities.
Soul—the eternal living entity who is part of the Supreme Person and is known in Sanskrit as *jiva, jivatma,* or atman. The symptom of the soul is consciousness and it is inherently happy and full of knowledge.
Sri Chaitanya—see Chaitanya Mahaprabhu.
Srimad-Bhagavatam—ancient Sanskrit texts compiled by Srila Vyasadeva that establish the complete science of God.
Supersoul (*Paramatma* in Sanskrit)—God who resides next to the soul in the heart of each embodied living entity. He is the living entity's witness, permitter, and friend and from him come the living entity's knowledge, remembrance, and forgetfulness.
Swami—one fully in control of his senses and mind; the title of one in the renounced, or sannyas, order.
Vedas—literally, knowledge; the most ancient scriptures of the Indian sub-continent, written in early Sanskrit and containing hymns, philosophy, and guidance on rituals for the priests of Vedic religion. Believed to have been directly revealed to seers and preserved by oral tradition.
Vedic—pertaining to a culture in which all aspects of human life are under the guidance of the Vedas.
Vrindavan—Krishna's eternal abode where he fully manifests his quality of sweetness (also a town 90 miles south of present-day Delhi).
Vyasasan—a raised seat for the representative of Vyasadeva.
Yoga—literally, connection; the discipline of self-realization meant for linking one's consciousness with God. According to the Bhagavad-gita, the most sublime form of yoga is bhakti-yoga, the yoga of pure devotion to God.

Acknowledgments

To my family, Yadubara, Shyam, Rasamrita, Haripriya and Kunja for their great company.

To Victoria Taylor who, over twenty years ago, asked me, "What was it *really* like to be with Srila Prabhupada?" a question that eventually became the seed of this book.

Writing is difficult, at least for me, and I'm deeply indebted to the many readers who kindly gave valuable comments for improving the manuscript: Josh Wagner, Susan Wieland Smith, Keli Lalita Reddy, Rambhoru Brinkmann, Chitra Gunderson, Sitala Devi, Nanda Glick, Giriraj Swami, Catherine Ghosh, Dr. Graham M. Schweig, Hari-Kirtana das, Rebecca Gray, Liz Russell, Govardhan Lal, Sara Richardson, Sara Sheikh, Aarti Chopra, Ananga Gopi, Dr. Tanmay Lele, Samir Kagalwala, Vrinda Sheth, Pranada Comtois, Kosa Ely, Danielle Beauvais, Sandra Elsey, Helen Kirklin, Visakha Priya Devi Dasi, Michelle Ross, Stella Herzig, Yadubara Das, and Carl E. Woodham. Nancy Coffin patiently read through two versions of the manuscript, both times offering valuable suggestions. Helen Simpson went beyond the call of duty in proofreading, and Raghu Consbruck and Govinda Cordua somehow carved time out of their full schedules to help with the graphic design. My thanks also to Nandini Kishori (fiveyearseleven@gmail.com), who offers enthusiastic assistance in distributing this book. And most special gratitude to Kaisori Bellach, who helped this book more than even she knows.

About the Author

Visakha (VishAkhA) received an Associate of Applied Science degree with honors from Rochester Institute of Technology and shortly afterwards published her first book, *Photomacrography: Art and Techniques*. In 1971 she traveled to India, where she met Bhaktivedanta Swami Prabhupada, read his *Bhagavad-gita As It Is* and eventually became his student. As a photographer, she traveled with and photographed Bhaktivedanta Swami and his students in India, Europe, and the United States. As a writer, she has written numerous magazine articles, as well as books: *Our Most Dear Friend, Bhagavad-gita for Children; Bhagavad-gita: A Photographic Essay* (recipient of the 2011 Independent Publisher Book Award); and *Harmony and the Bhagavad-gita, Lessons from a Life-Changing Move to the Wilderness* (five-star Readers' Favorite). Visakha also assists her husband, John Griesser, in making documentary films, most recently a 90-minute biography on Bhaktivedanta Swami. They have two daughters.

For the story of Visakha's life after *Five Years, Eleven Months and a Lifetime of Unexpected Love*, please read *Harmony and the Bhagavad-gita, Lessons from a Life-Changing Move to the Wilderness*.

https://our-spiritual-journey.com

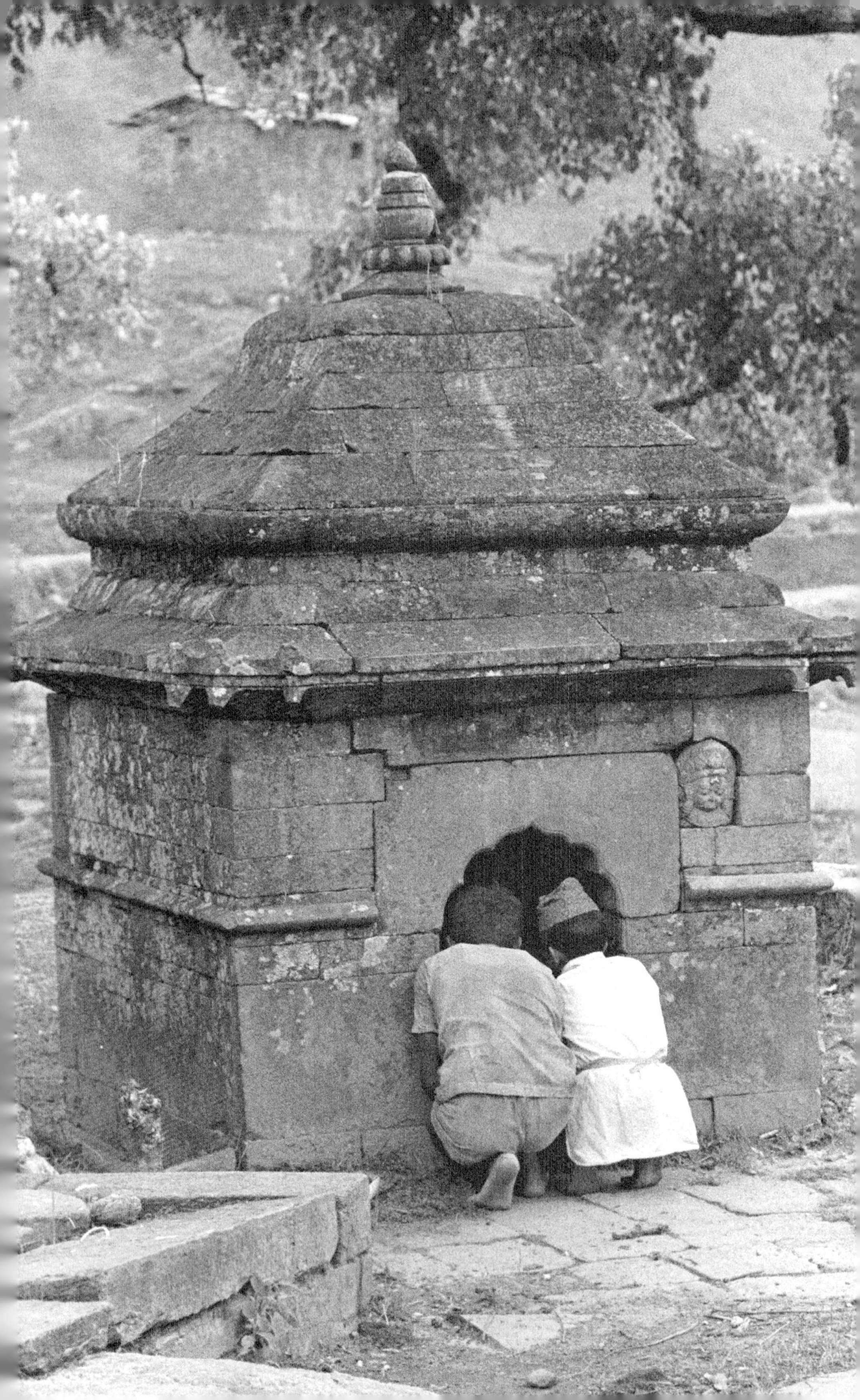

Printed in Great Britain
by Amazon